POETRY OF THE GREAT WAR

An Anthology

POETRY OF THE GREAT WAR

An Anthology

Edited by

Dominic Hibberd and John Onions

*with an Introduction, Notes
and Biographical Outlines*

St. Martin's Press   New York

All rights reserved. For information, write:
Scholarly & Reference Division,
St. Martin's Press, Inc., 175 Fifth Avenue, New York, NY 10010

First published in the United States of America in 1986

Printed in Hong Kong

ISBN 0-312-61926-X

Library of Congress Cataloging-in-Publication Data
Main entry under title:
Poetry of the Great War.
Bibliography: p.
Includes index.
1. World War, 1914–1918–Poetry.   2. English poetry–
20th century.   I. Hibberd, Dominic.   II. Onions, John.
PR1195.W65P64   1986   821'.912'080358   85-27868
ISBN 0-312-61926-X

Contents

Foreword

Each poem in the selection has a serial number. These numbers are used for reference in the Introduction (in *italic* form) and in the Notes (in **bold** form for their primary reference).

A date-indication is placed at the foot of each poem, giving (where possible) the date of composition (e.g. *'written May 1915'*) or of first publication (e.g. *'1st published 1917'*). A date with no prefix is derived from that given in the original printing or a reliable edition. These dates are as accurate as we can get them but some may need revision. For sources, see 'Notes on the Poems' and 'Biographical Notes' at the end of the book.

Formal recognition of the editors' and publisher's obligation to those who have given permission for the reproduction of material still in copyright is made in the Acknowledgements section at the end of the book. Here as editors we wish to express our personal sense of gratitude to the many people who have so kindly answered our enquiries and provided us with help and information. These include: Mr Theo van Beek (son of the poet), Mrs Claire Blunden, Mr Edward Bradby, Mr R. C. G. Dartford, Mr Stanley Ellis, Mr I. S. Hallows, Sir Rupert Hart-Davis, Mrs Joan Heath, Lord Henderson of Brompton, Mr David Jennings, Mrs Sala Leftwich, Mr P. H. B. Lyon, Dr Robyn Marsack, Mr Derick Mirfin, Mr Reginald Pound, Brigadier B. B. Rackham, Sir William Richardson, the late Edgell Rickword, Mr Peter du Sautoy, Professor Jon Stallworthy, Dr F. H. Stubbings, Mr Peter Tudor, Dr Gordon Williams, Mr John Wilson and Mr Alan Wykes.

We also wish to thank the Revd John Watson and the Parochial Church Council of St Mary's, Alsager, the Revd D. M. Lawson of All Saints, Keighley, and Mr John Killham, who helped us in recording *The Great Sacrifice*; and archivists and librarians at George Allen & Unwin Ltd, the Birmingham Reference Library, the Bodley Head, the British Library and

its Newspaper Library, the Pensions Board and the General
Synod of the Church of England, the Co-operative Union,
C. W. Daniel Co. Ltd, Messrs L. E. England & Co.,
Haileybury College, the University of Hull, the Imperial War
Museum, the University of Keele, Lincoln College, the
Ministry of Defence, John Murray Ltd, the Plymouth Local
History Library, Rugby School and the Old Rugbeian Society.

Dominic Hibberd acknowledges a research grant from the
British Academy.

Our account of the poems and poets selected is inevitably
incomplete. We shall be pleased to hear from readers who can
make good any errors or omissions, or who can put us on the
track of the few poets we have been unable to trace.

D.H. J.O.

Introduction

In June 1915, the *Daily Mail* humorously protested at 'A Serious Outbreak of Poets' on the home front, suggesting that more poetry had 'found its way into print in the last eleven months than in the eleven preceding years'.[1]* Things were soon much the same in the army, according to *The Wipers Times*:

> We regret to announce an insidious disease is affecting the Division, and the result is a hurricane of poetry. Subalterns have been seen with a notebook in one hand, and bombs in the other, absently walking near the wire in deep communion with the muse.[2]

Catherine Reilly's invaluable *English Poetry of the First World War: A Bibliography* (1978) lists 2225 poets, showing that the 'First' or 'Great' War did indeed generate an immense quantity of poetry at the time.[3] The war has remained a subject of profound interest to writers, and the modern British imagination has come to see it as an archetype: 'One image haunts us who have read of death / In Auschwitz in our time', Peter Porter has written – not concentration camps or air raids, but the trenches:

> it is just light,
> Shivering men breathing rum crouch beneath
> The sandbag parapet – left to right
>
> The line goes up and over the top . . .[4]

However, although the Great War still 'haunts' the modern mind, most of its poets have been forgotten. Only a handful, of whom Siegfried Sassoon and Wilfred Owen are probably the most familiar, have come to be valued as, in Donald Davie's

---

* Notes to the Introduction will be found on pp. 33–6.

words, 'first-hand and faithful witnesses to a moment in the national destiny'.[5] That some poets are accepted as 'witnesses' while hundreds more are no longer read is a result of a long selection process in which anthologies have played some part. Ever since 1914, anthologists have influenced, and been influenced by, contemporary attitudes to the war. Their choice of material has often not been made solely on the grounds of excellence or imaginative power, as is evident from some of their introductions in 1914–18 or the way in which some modern collections have arranged poems in sequences which imply comments on history and politics ('Visions of Glory', 'Puzzled Questioning', 'The Bitter Truth', 'Bitter Satire'). Such anthologies may have contributed to contemporary debate but they have tended to obscure the original extent and nature of First World War poetry.

It is possible only in a limited sense to regard poets as witnesses to history. They can convey their own experiences more vividly than any historian, but they are individualists and they create as well as perceive. The best poetry of the Great War is necessarily not typical; the most useful historical evidence is often to be found in mere 'verse', even though the dead weight of conventional forms and diction no doubt prevented many versifiers from expressing their full thoughts. For instance, Wilfred Owen wrote in his famous 1918 preface that 'All a poet can do today is warn', but a more representative statement might be Sergeant Walter Olley's, who prefaced *his* 1918 poems with the hope that they would 'convince all my readers that we never once doubted our chance in the field'.[6] Modern readers tend to assume that Owen and Sassoon can be treated as norms by which to read other poets of the war, or as typical of ordinary soldiers. However, A. J. P. Taylor has said that war poets such as these two 'spoke only for a minority'.[7] John Terraine is harsher: 'If even a substantial number, let alone a majority, of these men had been permanently in the condition of nerves expressed by, say, the poems of Owen or Sassoon, it is quite clear that the daily round *could not* have gone on.'[8] This is unfair to Owen and Sassoon, both of whom returned to the fighting, knowing that their poetry would be dismissed if they were not seen to be honourable soldiers, but the unfairness is understandable. The representative status of a small group of poets, and the corresponding notion that the war was a journey from innocence to protest, have become widely established, partly as a result of the success of modern anthologies.

Most Great War anthologies have been designed to reinforce one view or another of the war; few, if any, have been based exclusively on aesthetic criteria. In 1914, a public already addicted to anthologies was soon able to buy *Poems of the Great War* and *Songs and Sonnets for England in War Time*, the first of many patriotic collections. Such books have themselves had a lasting effect on assumptions about First War poetry, since few readers have been aware that some poets questioned the conflict from the start. The 1915–17 vogue for work by 'the fighting men' was reflected in Galloway Kyle's *Soldier Poets* (1916, second series 1917) and E. B. Osborn's *The Muse in Arms* (1917). The tone here was of heroic resistance in a just cause; some mention of horrors was allowed (Osborn included Sassoon) but only to increase respect for soldierly courage. There were many other collections, but not until July 1918 was there one which suggested that some writers had not shared the general commitment: Bertram Lloyd's *Poems Written During the Great War*. This contained contributions by Sassoon, Osbert Sitwell, J. C. Squire, W. N. Ewer, W. W. Gibson and others. His immediately post-war *The Paths of Glory* (1919) was more specific, stating in its preface that 'war must be regarded as an execrable blot upon civilisation'. Even then, that was a very unusual thesis for an anthology. The title and theme of Jacqueline Trotter's *Valour and Vision* (1920) were more typical; the enlarged 1923 edition included some Sassoon and Owen, but it was arranged to tell a tale of heroic events, leading up to 'that great October which brought the long-sought Victory'.

Since the early 1920s, there have been two major revivals of interest in First World War literature, each in a period of political idealism. The first came at the end of that decade, with the publication of numerous war novels and memoirs; these 'war books', as they were called, provoked heated debate at the time. The second came in the 1960s and centred on poetry rather than prose. Both revivals told a story of idealism turning to realism, satire, protest and pity. The pattern for the 1960s view was set by Theatre Workshop's play, *Oh What a Lovely War* (1963), in which ruthless profiteers and generals pursue a game for their own ends while the common soldier suffers helplessly as exploited victim. The war was denounced in this sort of way in 1914 in explicitly socialist terms, but the modern version is not tied to a specific political creed. Some historians support it, some do not, but it does not depend on history for its validity. It has provided a myth for our time, as *The Muse in Arms* or *Valour and Vision* provided myths for theirs. Most modern anthologies have made use of it, particularly Brian Gardner's *Up the Line to Death* (1964), Ian Parsons's *Men Who March Away* (1965), Maurice Hussey's *Poetry of the First World War* (1967) and E. L. Black's *1914–18 in Poetry* (1970). Although none of these compilers makes any serious attempt to date poems or to supply information which might illuminate poets' intentions, they organise their material to fit an assumed progression from idealism to bitterness. Much misrepresentation results. Readers of these anthologies could be forgiven for supposing that satirists such as G. K. Chesterton, A. P. Herbert and Rudyard Kipling turned against the war, or that soldier–poets after 1916 all believed the war to be pointless. Dates and meanings are implied which sometimes prove to be inaccurate when poems are traced back to their sources; early poems by civilians are mistaken for late ones by soldiers, fervent seriousness is presented as irony, flippancy as satire, even militarism as pity. Important areas are neglected. For example, women poets are almost entirely overlooked, although Catherine Reilly's collection of women's poetry, *Scars Upon My Heart* (1981), has since shown that there were plenty; and the story's climax is the stalemate and apparent futility of Passchendaele rather than the events of 1918, when even Owen and Sassoon accepted that only fighting could end the war. Jon Silkin's *Penguin Book of First World War Poetry* (1979) is a more thoughtful development of the 1960s approach. He selects poems not only on the basis of excellence but also as expressions of 'a developing consciousness, in relation to the war and the "good" of society as a whole' – a consciousness which in his view finds its fullest expression in the work of Isaac Rosenberg. Silkin's case is a personal one, based on – and appealing to – a radical political commitment.

It is not really possible to make the war's poetry follow a single inclusive argument. Clearly, there are major differences between the 1914 work of Rupert Brooke and the 1917–18 work of Owen and Sassoon. But there is no one story to tell. In particular, Sassoon is unique. He is a key figure in the present anthology, as in others, since his writing records his changing views with a sincerity and continuity that no other poet's work can match. From 'Absolution' [32]* to 'Everyone Sang' [170], there is a complete development, so that his poems run like a thread through the chronological and thematic patterns of war poetry as a whole. No one else in uniform seems to have protested publicly as he did; no one else gave up protest and went back into the trenches with his strange resignation. If he is used as a lens through which to see other poets, their work is seriously distorted. Rudyard Kipling's epitaph, 'Common Form' [87], is a case in point:

> If any question why we died,
> Tell them, because our fathers lied.

This is now likely to be read as a Sassoonish condemnation of wartime militarists. But Kipling was a consistent 'hawk' himself, and the actual target of 'Common Form' must be the 'doves' who had, in his opinion, failed to warn and arm the country before August 1914.

Biographical information often helps to clarify the meaning of a war poem, and our Notes have been compiled with this in mind. Any account of the poetry of 1917–18 needs to pay very careful attention to chronology. Few poems can be dated precisely, but it is not adequate to ascribe all idealistic verse to 1914 or all realistic work to the post-Somme period. We have appended a date to each poem in this book, although it may only be a rough guide to the time of composition. A date given in the original printing is retained without comment if we have no reason to doubt it. Occasionally we can say with some certainty when a poem was written; in other cases, we can only give what we believe to be the date of first publication. Many poems published in books appeared first in periodicals, but finding them there is often a matter of chance; we may well have missed some. Even periodical dates are not certain proof of when a

* As noted in the Foreword, in this Introduction italicised numbers within square brackets relate to the serial numbers of poems in the selection below.

poem was written. For example, Herbert Asquith's 'The Volunteer', often anthologised as a 1914 poem, was apparently composed in 1912. He sent it to the *Spectator* in 1913 but it was shelved; the war made it suddenly topical, so it appeared in the first wartime issue on 8 August.[9] Or there is the interesting case of W. W. Gibson's 'Breakfast' [*10*], usually treated as a product of trench experience after the Somme; in fact it came out in the *Nation* in October 1914, and its author never saw action. So 'Breakfast' can be recognised as a pioneering effort in imaginative realism – by a civilian, a Georgian and a close friend of Brooke. We have provided this kind of information, and other relevant material, in the notes on both the poems and the poets.

Our choice of poems is based on our general aim, which has been to provide a readable and reliable picture of poetry by British writers composed during or soon after the Great War, showing how poets and poetry responded to the crisis and how some dominant themes were explored. We have chosen some verse that would not have merited inclusion on solely literary grounds and omitted one or two familiar pieces which have perhaps received enough attention. Not everything could be included. There were many poems from sailors, airmen, prisoners, and men at the war's 'sideshows', but they are almost invariably of secondary interest; in order to keep the book to a reasonable size, we have not attempted to represent them, nor work from countries other than Great Britain, nor poetry written well after the war. However, there are a few exceptions: Joseph Leftwich was technically Dutch, though living in London; the last section contains poems from the 1920s; and all Edgell Rickword's war poems, as well as the best of those by Ivor Gurney and Edmund Blunden, were written after the Armistice. If excellence had been our overriding criterion, fewer poets would have been represented and several would have made a stronger showing, but our aim required a wide spread of poets and of comment on immediate experience. Hence the comparatively few poems by Blunden, who wrote in retrospect, and by Edward Thomas, who seldom wrote directly about the war although all his poetry was affected by it. On the other hand, it seemed appropriate to include several early poems by Gurney and Robert Graves, not all of which will be familiar to readers wno know their work only from modern collections. We have not included three long poems rooted in the war, David Jones's *In Parenthesis* (1937), Herbert Read's *The End of a War* (1933) and, less often mentioned in this context, T. S. Eliot's *The Waste Land* (1922); but we have included Read's 'The Scene of War' [59] in its original form (1919), in which the numbered sections, Modernist style, literary allusions and images of fragmentation clearly prefigure Eliot's poem.[10]

We have arranged the book by theme, and to some extent by date, in eight Parts, most of which are subdivided, and we conclude with a Postscript. The parts are not intended as a rigid framework but simply as indications of certain subjects and attitudes which attracted a great deal of writing in 1914–18. Other areas could be defined and many poems could be thought of under several different headings; for instance, 'Strange Meeting' [155] seems to us particularly interesting as a statement about poetry (Part VII), but it could also be read in terms of comradeship (Part VI: 4), spring 1918 (Part VIII: 1), Christ imagery (Part IV: 1) or some further topic, such as hopes for the post-war world. Some of the eight parts relate to the whole war, some to a period in it. The pattern cannot be strictly chronological, since many poems are impossible to date accurately, but two sections (Part III: 1; Part VIII: 1) follow a close historical sequence. The subdivisions allow us to show how, for example, some poets in 1914 took a positive attitude to the war (Part I: 1) while others were sceptical (I: 2). The volume and diversity of First World War poetry are such that an anthology without divisions would be merely confusing, but the parts and sections used here are meant to be helpful rather than definitive.

Part I: 1914

Despite the later belief that the war came as a surprise, a European catastrophe had been dreaded for years before 1914. The literature of late Victorian Decadence is full of imagery of last sunsets, mass slaughter and apocalypse. A number of

Edwardian novels had given warning descriptions of a German invasion, as had two long poems by Charles Doughty, *The Cliffs* (1909) and *The Clouds* (1912). Alfred Noyes's *The Wine Press* (1913) had described a Somme-like battlefield on which young men are mown down by machine guns. The South African War had generated many poems, some prefiguring the poetry of the Great War.[11] Lord Roberts had campaigned for rearmament and conscription; his many supporters had included Rudyard Kipling and George Meredith, both of whom had written verse sympathising with the common soldier. In the first half of 1914, as in our own time, political opinion was divided between those who believed that strong defences would deter aggression and those who saw the arms race as a danger to peace. But almost everyone agreed that war would be terrible; verse in the national press between late July and 4 August 1914 expressed fear and horror at the growing threat.[12]

When war came, however, the general mood changed at once from apprehension to determination, the earlier emphasis on horrors giving way to arguments that the fighting was not only unavoidable but also potentially beneficial (I: 1). Publishers and editors were faced with a crisis of their own as their market suddenly altered and increased its demands. In an age before Modernism had set the poet apart from the public, writers were still close to their readership and were expected to write straightforwardly about matters of current importance; poetry often appeared in newspapers as well as in a great variety of periodicals, and it was widely read. Thus, existing patriotic verse was hurriedly reprinted, while new work was composed in extraordinary quantities.[13] Most well-known authors (except W. B. Yeats) contributed recruiting verses to the press. Provincial papers carried any number of amateur poems about the wicked Kaiser or how our boys were meeting the challenge. Surviving broadsheets show that the ancient tradition of folk verse was still active, with professional reciters selling ballads and performing them at meetings.

The popular response was spontaneous, but that of established authors was subject to a little discreet orchestration. In September, a new government propaganda department held a secret conference for at least twenty-five 'well-known men of letters', including Laurence Binyon, G. K. Chesterton, Conan

Doyle, Thomas Hardy, John Masefield and Owen Seaman.[14] One result was Hardy's 'Song of the Soldiers' [*4 n*]. Newspaper editors gave regular space to professional versifiers such as Jessie Pope and 'Touchstone' in the Northcliffe press or Harold Begbie in the *Daily Chronicle*. These public verses were expressions of the popular spirit rather than of inner feelings; Hardy and Begbie [*14*], for instance, were privately well aware of war's evils. The crudity of much patriotic verse was soon laughed at by reviewers in the more independent-minded journals.[15] A pseudonymous 'Odd Man' (actually C. W. Daniel, the publisher) concluded:

> The farther you get with this dam' nonsense the more difficult it
> becomes,
> And instead of trying to write intelligently you find yourself
> talking of 'drums'
> For no other reason than because 'drums' and 'becomes' rhymes,
> Which seems to be the main idea of all the war poetry I have read
> in *The Times*.[16]

In December, William Watson, perhaps stung by jeers at his pun about the naval action at Heligoland ('bit them in the bight'),[17] said that poets were doing the little they could to help recruiting, in spite of 'so-called critics'. This earned him a further rebuke, from someone who thought he had undervalued the power of poetry: 'Poetry is almost as fashionable as khaki. The literary appeal, and nothing else, has saved this country from conscription.'[18] Faced with such nonsense, discriminating readers began to turn to the work of the younger generation.

Many young men who wrote poetry and took it seriously in the war years were either Georgians or were aware of the Georgians.[19] After the doldrums of Edwardian verse, the publication of the first volume of *Georgian Poetry* in 1912 had aroused lively interest. In place of the grand, vague diction of the late Victorians, the new poetry offered plain language, simplicity, sharpness of detail, and a commitment to realism that did not duck the unpleasant. The anthology, edited by Edward Marsh with the close assistance of Rupert Brooke, was published by Harold Monro from the Poetry Bookshop. The Bookshop itself was a sign of poetry's revival; open from 1913

and throughout the war, it was a magnet for many of the
younger poets, ensuring that they were aware of one another's
work. Post-war changes in taste led to a persistent critical habit
of undervaluing the Georgians or forgetting who they were, so
that one of the neglected aspects of First World War poetry is
that much of the best of it was either Georgian or Georgian-
influenced. Brooke was the pre-war leader, with his cool, witty,
irreverent style; John Masefield had been the pioneer. They,
with W. W. Gibson, Monro and others, were founder–
contributors to *Georgian Poetry*. Siegfried Sassoon, Robert
Graves and Robert Nichols were well represented in the 1917
and 1919 volumes, and Blunden came in after the war. The
1917 collection even included a lyric by Isaac Rosenberg, who,
though hardly a typical Georgian, much admired Gibson's early
war poems. Wilfred Owen regarded himself as a Georgian in
1917. Edward Thomas was friendly with the group. Ivor
Gurney delighted in Gibson's work, and both he and Charles
Sorley thought highly of Masefield.

The Georgian response to the outbreak of war went largely
unnoticed until 1915, but it was more thoughtful than that of
the older generation. Masefield's 'August 1914' [5], apparently
written before he became involved in propaganda, was perhaps
the first of many war poems celebrating 'England' as a rural
ideal, a 'picture of the mind' inherited from a long tradition of
pastoral elegy. Similar visions were to sustain many soldiers,
including Sassoon and Gurney. Urban Britain, by contrast,
seemed 'a world grown old and cold and weary', an exhausted
civilisation that might be rejuvenated by war. In their different
ways, Brooke [6], Rosenberg [8] and Owen [9] expected in 1914
that destruction would bring renewal, a view long preached by
some nineteenth-century writers. But even before Brooke
wrote his sonnets, his friend Gibson had begun a series of
typically Georgian poems which portrayed in simple language
the absurdity of war and the sufferings of ordinary soldiers. Not
that Gibson was the first poet to doubt the war; journalist–poets
in left-wing newspapers, such as T. W. Mercer in the *Labour
Leader* and W. N. Ewer in the *Herald*, wrote protests from
August onwards (I: 2).[20] Ewer's 'Five Souls', which became
well known, was in the *Nation* a fortnight before the first of
Gibson's poems. (Socialist poets like these, writing from a firm

ideological standpoint, can be described, in a much-used epithet, as 'anti-war', in the sense that they consistently opposed the war in its entirety. Used to describe other poets, however, the term can be misleading, in that many protests, such as Kipling's, were against aspects of the war rather than against the undertaking as a whole.) The Georgian imagination resisted political, religious or even literary doctrines, as can be seen from Gibson's work and from Monro's 'Youth in Arms' [15]; Monro, like Gibson, was a civilian in 1914 and was never to serve abroad, but between them these two poets anticipated some of the principal elements in the best war poetry that was to come: simplicity of diction, realistic detail, the role of the poet as observer and pleader, the pity of war, the ruthlessness of 'old men', the beauty and innocence of youth that dies.

Part II: Heroes

The many thousands who joined up before conscription was introduced in 1916 were bound to include men with a literary turn of mind who would write about their experiences.[21] Of the poets represented in this anthology, over forty seem to have been volunteers[22] and of these only a few, such as Edward Thomas or R. E. Vernède, were professional writers. Many were fresh from public schools. They embarked on what was called 'the Great Adventure', 'the Last Crusade', or, in *Punch*'s phrase, 'the Greater Game', comparing themselves – often rather nervously – to classical heroes, medieval knights[23] or sportsmen, playing as gentlemen amateurs against barbarian professionals. Similar comparisons were made more boldly by civilians, for the nation took a deep pride in its new soldiers. Sporting imagery was especially popular and elaborate; occasionally, it was even acted out on the battlefield [27], but after the Somme it faded away as the need for professionalism became obvious. Its relics provided material for post-war literature about 'disenchantment' and the 'lost generation'. Experience taught that the Western Front was not comparable to a football match; nevertheless, the belief in heroism remained.

Early soldier-poetry was strongly affected by the public-school tradition, which had educated the new subalterns in an austere discipline of classical studies and team games, where 'hard knocks'[24] were to be expected and pain was a 'friend'[25] in the battle of life. The writings of these young recruits show many of them to have been conventional and naïve, but the public schools also produced such highly intelligent men as Robert Graves (Charterhouse), Siegfried Sassoon and Charles Sorley (Marlborough), Godfrey Elton and Rupert Brooke (Rugby), and Julian Grenfell and Patrick Shaw-Stewart (Eton), all of whom were critical of accepted attitudes before and during the war.[26] At its best, the ideal of heroism was an ideal of service, self-denial and comradeship, calling up loyalty from all who had been trained in it, traditionalists and sceptics [29] alike. The embodiment of the ideal in the public imagination was Rupert Brooke, whose death on St George's Day, 1915, coinciding with the sudden fame of his *1914* sonnets, provided an image of poetic gallantry and sacrifice which remained a reference point for both soldiers and civilians. His *1914 and Other Poems* ran through twenty-five impressions between May 1915 and October 1918; its author was rivalled only by Kitchener as a subject for commemorative verses. The image bore little more relation to the real Brooke than the modern view of him as a representative of gilded privilege and public-school orthodoxy (he was in fact a socialist), but, like its modern counterpart, it satisfied a contemporary need. A month later, *The Times* announced the death of another young hero, Julian Grenfell, and published his 'Into Battle'.[27] The so-called 'soldier–poets' became symbols for the bravery, culture and sacrifice of the country's youth.

In time, however, soldiers became disgusted by the rhetoric of civilian patriots and wary of describing themselves or their comrades as heroes. The ideal persisted – whether it was for the sake of the regiment, as with Graves [20], or of the troops, as with Sassoon, or of the nation, as with many soldier–poets still – but it was more cautiously expressed than in the early stages of the war. In 1918, Wilfred Owen said firmly that his poems were 'not about heroes' because English poetry was 'not yet fit to speak of them', although for him, as for many other officers, one of the war's few enduring certainties was that the troops really were heroes [22]. It was one of the truths that could not be directly told at home. The soldier–poet, himself acclaimed as a hero, became possessed of secret knowledge; he began to see himself as isolated from society, not unlike his principal masters, the Romantic poets.

As early as Brooke, the enlisted poet had turned away scornfully from middle-class insensitivity, becoming preoccupied with his own imaginative processes and self-sacrifice.[28] Devotional language was common ('absolution', 'consecration', 'sacrifice'), and there were many poems of self-dedication, with titles like 'Before Action' (II: 3).[29] This ready acceptance of pain and death owed much not only to religious and caste ideals but also to late Romanticism. The early work of Brooke, Owen, Sassoon, Rosenberg and others shows their familiarity with Decadent poets such as Swinburne and Wilde, who had portrayed the artist as alienated from a doomed society and exclusively concerned with the refinement of his own feelings, including pain, in the fatal pursuit of beauty. The supreme sensation would be at the moment when death and beauty met in exquisite agony. Thus, even the realities of trench warfare were material for art when they came.

Among living writers, Thomas Hardy and A. E. Housman were particularly influential. Innumerable echoes of Housman's *A Shropshire Lad* (1896), even in the work of Owen, Sassoon and Gibson, show that his melancholy lyrics were standard models for war poems [cp. *18 n*], but Sassoon thought Hardy the greatest living poet. Hardy's verse drama of the Napoleonic wars, *The Dynasts* (1903–8),[30] had explored the heroism, pity and irony of war well before 1914; Gurney, Sorley and Sassoon admired it, and Owen is likely to have had it in mind when he defined his subject in 1918 as 'War, and the pity of War'. Hardy's sense of fate and his half-rebellion against conventions appealed to the mood of the more literary recruits, many of whom were rebels yet felt themselves to be a doomed generation with only one road to follow.

The personal challenge of volunteering was at first all-absorbing. It seemed to offer a new liberty, as one shed one's routine responsibilities and went forward as a 'new Titan' [21], 'grim-lipped, clear-eyed and resolute-hearted' [33 n], like a swimmer 'into cleanness leaping' [6], thinking of one's own death but only very rarely, apparently, of the deaths that one might inflict. H. G. Wells's belief was widely shared that this was 'the war that will end war', even that it was being led by 'a militant God' in the interests of a new world.[31] Some recruits were devout Christians. Some were aware of Nietzsche, who had declared that God was dead and that man had to complete his destiny alone. Whatever one's creed, the destruction of militarism seemed a cause worth dying for.

Part III: The Western Front

Trench warfare has been written about too often to need describing here. It is broadly true that the best poetry of the war was written after 1915 by men who had fought in France and Flanders, and that satire and protest are more common in soldiers' verse after mid-1916 than before. However, the assumption now often made that the horrors of the Somme in 1916 brought about a fundamental change of attitudes in war poetry is misleading; there was a continuous development throughout the war, though the work of individuals developed at different times and in different ways or in some cases scarcely changed at all. Arthur Graeme West began to lose his faith in the cause well before the Somme fighting started on 1 July 1916, whereas Gilbert Frankau still fervently believed in it in 1918; both poets had been in the trenches. Sassoon's first 'outspoken' poem, 'In the Pink', was written in February 1916; Rosenberg's 'Break of Day in the Trenches', regarded by Paul Fussell as the finest poem of the war, was written in June of that year.

Section III: 1 gives a chronological selection of poems relating to the first Somme offensive, the 'Big Push' long awaited and discussed by both troops and civilians. The opening of the campaign took neither the enemy nor the home front by surprise. Newspapers welcomed it with exultant hopes that it would prove decisive [40], while some soldier-poets went into action in the mood of self-sacrifice established by Brooke more than a year earlier [39]. The outcome was grievously disappointing to both survivors and civilians, the latter only slowly realising that by November the casualties were far worse than in any previous battle. Yet the soldier–poets' response was not unanimous. Leslie Coulson questioned the divine purpose [*44*]; R. E. Vernède expressed grim determination [*45*]; A. P. Herbert saluted the courage he had seen [*46*]. The emphasis in Herbert's poem on the exclusiveness of front-line achievement and suffering is one theme in soldier–poetry that did become more common after the Somme than before. Men who had fought developed a strong sense of comradeship and of separation from the world at home (and from soldiers who had not been in action); when they went on leave, they missed the fellowship of the trenches [*49*] and chafed silently at civilian ignorance. That ignorance was not altogether the civilians' fault, for the general public had to rely on press reports which were highly selective and often written in the language of adventure stories. There were exhibition trenches in Kensington and a widely shown film of the Somme; according to Owen in January 1917, they were 'the laughing stock of the army',[32] but home audiences were thrilled by the film's scenes of the front (mostly faked) and of columns of smiling Tommies marching up to the line [*47*]. Nevertheless, civilians were thoughtless or worse in their fulsome praise of the troops; it invited cynicism and resentment from those who knew what the front was really like.

It is often said that once poets had been in the trenches their work became more realistic, with the added implication that such realism was 'modern' and a sign of opposition to the war. Such statements are much too simple. Those poets who wanted to represent the actuality of trench experience (some, like Vernède, did not, on the grounds that such poetry would weaken morale or cause pointless distress) had many techniques at their disposal, only one of which was 'realism'. In its proper literary sense, 'realism' is a nineteenth-century term referring to the close, detailed and unbiassed reporting of daily life, including, where necessary, the sordid and brutal. This method of writing was as much available to authors who supported the war [cp. *154*] as to those who opposed it. The poems in III: 2 make only limited use of realism, although all of them are based on vividly recalled experience. They draw on a range of literary traditions, conventional forms and technical devices, from blank-verse narrative to Owen's famous pararhyme, and they frequently allude to the literature of earlier periods. Edgell Rickword's controlled, Donne-like urbanity contrasts with Sassoon's Georgian directness, Owen's Keatsian diction and Frederic Manning's aesthetic mysteriousness. Rosenberg moves from the awkward Victorian sentimentality of 'A Dying Soldier' [56] to the extraordinary, rugged grandeur of 'Dead Man's Dump' [57], perhaps the most intensely realised of all front-line poems but one which owes more to the Romantics than to Modernism or realism.

Few soldier–poets were in touch with *avant-garde* movements in the arts. Herbert Read was an exception. His 'The Scene of War' [59] observes the rules of Imagism as defined by Ezra Pound just before the war and developed by Read himself. Some, if not all, of the six constituent sections were composed in 1918 with two motives: one, to capture beauty ('the cold grace of immaculate cameos' [59 n]), which was still the poet's goal; the other, to protest against war and the rhetoric of glory which some civilians, and some soldiers, continued to use long after the Somme. It was possible still to strive for a poetry that would achieve both beauty and truth without sacrificing either one to the other.

Part IV: Christ and Nature

Throughout the war, as in other periods, religion (IV: 1) and nature (IV: 2) were major sources of poetic imagery and subject-matter. Both topics had to do with death and renewal, and both could be made to support almost any view of the war.

In 1914 and later, verse and cartoons in left-wing periodicals contrasted Christ the pacifist with man's new violence. Supporters of the war altered this a little by insisting that the violence was the work of the Devil and his friend, the Kaiser; the nation had joined in what was 'manifestly a war between Christ and the Devil', as the Poet Laureate, Robert Bridges, explained in a letter to *The Times*. It followed that 'Britain's call was God's' [1]. Soon, there were many pictures and poems on the theme of Christ appearing to a dying soldier.[33] The earliest was possibly 'The Great Sacrifice', a colour print which the *Graphic* gave away with its Christmas 1914 number. There was frequently a strong verbal or visual suggestion that the soldier could actually be identified with Christ as hero, sacrificial victim and redeemer. Newbolt was not untypical in reacting to the Somme film as though to a Communion service [*47*]. The image was valuable to civilians and soldiers alike because it made sense of passive suffering and drew attention away from the fact that fighting involved killing as well as being killed. If death in this war was a martyrdom, its hideousness could be accepted; as Chesterton said, arguing as late as 1918 against 'realism' in war poetry, to 'allow the horror of the martyrdom to eclipse the halo of the martyr is simply a very stupid confusion of thought'.[34]

Although at least one Evangelical journal[35] protested that thinking of soldiers as Christs made nonsense of the uniqueness of Christ's sacrifice, the image became so well known that it was eventually proposed as the subject for a national war memorial.[36] Christ's saying before the crucifixion, 'Greater love hath no man than this, that a man lay down his life for his friends' (John 15: 13), was frequently quoted and used as a title or epigraph for poems.[37] Many parallels were possible. The soldier waiting behind the lines was like Christ in Gethsemane [*70*]. As he carried burdens up the communication trenches, he was Christ carrying the cross [*64*]. He was 'crucified' in a place of skulls, where, like Christ, he might feel that even God had abandoned him. Laying down his life for his friends (either the nation or his comrades), he saved humanity and earned eternal life – or so he was often assured.

The jingoist editor of *John Bull*, Horatio Bottomley, had no doubts:

> Every hero of this war who has fallen on the field of battle has performed an act of Greatest Love, so penetrating and intense in its purifying character that I do not hesitate to express my belief that any and every present sin is automatically wiped out from the record of his life.[38]

Bottomley is one of several writers who had an enormous readership among troops and civilians during the war and are now disregarded. Another is John Oxenham [63], whose little khaki-covered books, designed to fit into a tunic pocket, sold in hundreds of thousands. Oxenham was undoubtedly the most popular war poet of all at the time. Writing without any literary pretensions, he adapted the Victorian tradition of simple devotional verse to wartime purposes. One of his poems was based on the widely believed propaganda story that the Germans had crucified a Canadian soldier, and many others used the soldier–Christ metaphor to reassure and encourage the troops: 'Ye are all christs in this your self-surrender.'[39]

A very different version of the soldier–Christ story was told by poets who believed that the war was no part of any divine plan: the modern Christ, betrayed by priests and politicians, suffered a slow agony which militarists neither understood nor cared about; his death was a challenge to the world's false values [69]. Owen, who in 1914 had talked about 'the thousand redeemers by whose blood my life is being redeemed', decided in 1917 that the redeemer idea was 'a distorted view to hold in a general way' and condemned Oxenham for holding 'the Moslem doctrine – preached by Horatio Bottomley but not by the Nazarene – of salvation by *death in war*'.[40] Even so, he went on to write 'Greater Love' [137], a Decadent variation on the theme.

The most talented poets of the war, Romantics by inheritance, often had more success with nature than with religion as a source of imagery. A section on nature in an anthology of 1914–18 verse could include a large proportion of the period's most imaginative poems, from Gibson's early pieces about farmworkers turned soldiers to Rosenberg's 'Break of Day in the Trenches' [110] and Owen's 'Futility' [106]. We have limited ourselves to a selection which illustrates some of the ways in which soldiers wrote about nature. Sometimes death was accepted, even welcomed, as part of the natural process [71, 72]. The dead were often said to live on in the landscape [73], a notion which did not convince every writer [77]. Edward Thomas's poems, all written before he went out to France, reveal how extensively his response to the English countryside was influenced by his awareness of the war [74], while the post-war work of Gurney [76] or Blunden shows a comparable awareness of nature's omnipresence in the battle zone. Nature might console, threaten, punish, be indifferent; like man, it seemed at times to share the general suffering and at others to be an arbitrary killer. As a reminder of home, it might bring comfort or mockery. Always it was there as a setting and contrast, a fact which allowed for much sub-Wordsworthian moralising and facile comparison as well as excellent writing. In reflecting on the antithesis between war and nature, Blunden is outstanding; for him, war sometimes becomes a nightmare version of nature, providing its own suns and growths. Nevertheless, it is noticeable that even at his best he tends to circle back rather than break new ground, exploring literary tradition with an unrivalled precision of language but not going further. Writing his finest poems ten years or so after the events they describe, he was already trapped in the past. His poetry never achieves the fiery originality of Rosenberg's 'Dead Man's Dump' (1917 [57]) or Owen's 'Spring Offensive' (1918 [165]), where the earth teems violence and gathers in soldiers like an outraged lover.

Part V: Civilians

Part V consists of poems by non-combatants written after 1914 and, in most if not all cases, before the Armistice. Readers of Sassoon and Owen might suppose that home-front verse in that period was invariably bellicose, but in fact some civilian poets were sharper in their criticisms of the war and less tight-lipped about grief than many soldiers were. Nevertheless, British 'prussianism' had many voices.

Prussia was regarded as the source of Germany's aggression, its undemocratic national life allegedly dominated by materialism, bureaucracy and a callous ruling class dedicated to war. It was the object of a torrent of official and unofficial British propaganda in the first year, so that everyone knew about Lissauer's 'Hymn of Hate', *Gott strafe England!*, 'Might is Right', 'Kultur', 'frightfulness' and other unattractive features of what was supposed to be Germany's self-image. However, the attitudes of some British writers seemed little better; as early as 1914, Norman Angell was warning of the

'Prussian Within Our Midst'.[41] When Owen spoke of 'whiskied prussianists' in 1917, he was referring to Britons rather than Germans.[42] Two marks of a prussianist were an insistence on total military victory and the ruthlessness described in the last stanza of Owen's 'Insensibility' [152] – for those who believed that German power had to be crushed were logically obliged to resist arguments based on pity. After the hard battles of early 1915, the general mood changed from euphoria to a grim resolve to carry on at any cost. Since the cost was men, even the most patriotic soldiers were not likely to appreciate statements of the theme by high-minded poets writing comfortably at home. It is true that there were some soldier–poets, such as Streets, who wrote sacrificial verse specifically intended to encourage civilians in such thinking, but even Streets might have been repelled by Jessie Pope's jaunty heroics [82] or a similar flight of fancy by a famous judge:

> Lend you a hand, my Lady? There;
> How I wish I could give you two –
> But the Boche decided I'd one to spare,
> And left me but this for you.[43]

Katherine Tynan was even less sensitive:

> They shot Flynn's eyes out. That was good.
> Eyes that saw God are better blind.[44]

Even among the non-prussianist majority, the civilian imagination never fully grasped the scale and nature of trench warfare. When the casualties at Passchendaele ('Third Ypres') were running into hundreds of thousands in 1917, the home front cheered itself by commemorating the first battle of Ypres in 1914, when the original British Expeditionary Force had stopped the German advance. There were poems in newspapers and a solemn concert at the Albert Hall; in a war sadly lacking in inspiring victories, it was reassuring to remember how a little 'army of mercenaries' [86] had 'fought the rushing legions to a stand' [85] and shown a professional courage worthy to be compared with that of the Spartans at Thermopylae.

Idealistic civilian poets who supported the war tended to assume a unity between themselves, the troops and the nation;

but where they saw unity, sceptics saw division – between those who benefited from the fighting and those who did it, between profiteers and exploited, old men and young, women and soldiers, rhetoric and reality. A young pacifist like Joseph Leftwich could regard the war as divisive and self-perpetuating even in 1915 [*88*]. Civilians who worked openly for peaceful reconciliation had to endure many insults, although they earned respect from a few soldier–poets. The Union of Democratic Control, founded as soon as hostilities began, sought to end the fighting by democratic, non-violent means; one of its leading members, Margaret Sackville, condemned civilian warmongering in her poems, blaming women in particular [*93*]. Pacifists and socialists could get verse into print in a few periodicals, and in book form through at least two pacifist publishers, Stanley Unwin (of Allen & Unwin) and C. W. Daniel. In 1916, Unwin published J. C. Squire's little book of cutting epigrams about clergymen–patriots and other public figures. But the case of Squire is cautionary, since he was actually a defender of the war and later suppressed his satires; scorn for prussianism is not proof that a poet disbelieved in the Allied cause.

For most civilians, political and moral views about the war took second place to concern for the people they knew. There was much genuine hardship at home, but the worst deprivation was bereavement. Innumerable men and women at every social level tried to put their sorrows into poetry. Feeling was often too strong for language, so that the pain of bereaved parents or young wives touches the reader through the very shortcomings of the verse. There were comforts in religion, patriotism and the hope that the world was being made a better place, but not everyone was convinced:

> They made a man of you this year, the sort
> That England's rich and proud to own, they say . . .
> And then they went and killed you. That's their way.[45]

Part VI: Soldiers

Part VI contains work by soldiers, almost all of whom served in the trenches. Most of the poems were published in 1916–18; they express some of the imaginative responses, personal motives, attitudes and inner feelings of soldier–poets in those years.

To committed poets, interpreting and commenting on the war's fearsome power represented an artistic challenge, demanding not only honest description and integrity of language but also the resources of myth and metaphor (VI: 1). There seemed to be a new chaos, as though some cosmic will were driving the world back into formlessness. Several poets made use of reversed creation myths or Bible stories. Imagery was borrowed from Dante and ancient legend. Graves described his war experiences in a characteristic blend of mythology and plain, soldierly language [*104, 108, 20*]; he was still in his early Georgian phase, working closely with Sassoon, admiring Sorley and, in 1917, encouraging Owen. Although his war poems show his unique talent already emerging, he was later to withdraw them as inferior work. They certainly lack the political decisiveness of Sassoon's 1916–17 verse; Graves was not to express a consistent view of the war until he came to write his memoirs a decade later. Rosenberg, on the other hand, found that the war made a continuity with his earlier poetic thinking, so that by 1917 he had come closer than any poet, until David Jones in the thirties, to shaping a myth of his own that would embody his perception of the fighting.

Rosenberg had enlisted in 1915 with no patriotic illusions but with hopes for his artistic future. 'One might succumb, be destroyed – but one might also (and the chances are the greater for it) be renewed, be made larger, healthier.'[46] In the event, he never finished his major work on the war, a verse play called *The Unicorn*, and he regarded most of his 'trench poems' as digressions from his central creative effort; but he did say that his best poem was 'Daughters of War' [*111*]. The biblical-sounding title (cp. 'daughters of Zion') is a reminder of his Jewish inheritance and the ancient Hebrew fondness for myth and personification. He was a painter as well as a poet, with a profound admiration for Blake and, to a lesser extent, Rossetti;

the visionary females in the poem have something of the massive strength and mystery of figures in Blake's drawings and prophecies, as well as the dreamy voluptuousness of Rossetti's *femmes fatales*. He had been developing similar imagery before 1914, having always been interested in the destructive and creative energy which he had perceived first in God and then, as he lost his faith, in female sexuality. The daughters of war are superhuman but sexual, embracing the souls of men with a desire that turns bodies to ash (cp. the cancelled stanza of 'Dead Man's Dump' [*57 n*]). Immediately before the war, lecturing on contemporary upheavals in the arts, he had said that a dead culture was being uprooted by 'hands, feverish and consuming . . . and . . . we watch the corroding doom'.[47] Within weeks, he was describing the war in similar language ([*8*]: 'Corrode, consume'). In 'Daughters of War', men are again consumed, their faces 'corroding' as they are swept from the 'doomed' earth. The implication remains that a new society and a new art might be born out of this terrible process. Rosenberg's strenuously original imagination would not allow him to be negative, even about war, and it was never overcome by the torments he saw and suffered at the front.

The pursuit of art was a motive that could keep a dedicated poet going. There were many other motives, for talented and untalented writers alike (VI: 2). Brooke, and perhaps Thomas, had welcomed the war as a release from private difficulties. Frederic Manning found it a supreme test of moral self-sufficiency [*123*], a theme explored in his fine post-war novel, *The Middle Parts of Fortune*. For some, the public sentiments of Brooke became absurd [*112*], as one either struggled to keep alive or hoped for death; for others, the war could still be idealised in noble Victorian language [*116*], although poems of this kind that had any force were usually about soldiers rather than patriotism. Soldiers produced devoutly patriotic poems in 1917–18, but we could find none that was not very feebly written. Our one example [*119*] is typically laboured and sentimental, interesting only for its superficiality and the fact that it was published as late as 1919 (in a book called *The Greater Love*) by a subaltern who had fought in the trenches.

It is in the soldier–poetry of 1917–18 that the modern reader expects to find protest against the war. 'What's it all about?' certainly became a common question among the troops. There was any amount of 'grousing', in verse as in conversation, some of it humorous, against such favourite targets as lice or plum-and-apple jam, and some of it serious, against profiteering, the lack of reinforcements, or the inefficiency of the General Staff. There were many ferocious attacks on civilians, including shirkers ('Me brother wot stayed at 'ome'), pacifists ('Lapping the spilt blood of the crucified'), and strikers ('You lepers in a paradise of health').[48] But all three of the soldier–poets just quoted were fervently committed to winning the war. Even in July 1918, a survey of the troops' letters suggested that most men believed in their commanders and found civilian defeatism unappealing.[49] Commentators often say that 'Tommy' developed respect, even affection, for 'Fritz', but it has to be added that Fritz was likely to be killed without compunction if he came within sight or reach [*113, 126*]. The majority of soldiers seem to have remained determined on victory, however much they loathed the means of achieving it.

Very few soldier–poets spoke out against the war before it ended, although numbers of them did so afterwards. The poems in section VI: 3 are protests by soldiers at civilian attitudes, but it should be noticed that one of them [*128*] combines such protest with praise of war. Sassoon's 1917 protest may have been without parallel. He declared in a public statement that politicians had secretly changed their war aims from 'defence and liberation' to 'aggression and conquest'. He claimed to be speaking on behalf of the troops, pointedly adding that he had 'seen and endured' their sufferings. His statement can be regarded as the rationale for the savage poems he was already writing for his next book, *Counter-Attack* (1918). Although he was never a pacifist, his protest was one event in a great civilian debate about war aims in 1917, when liberal opinion believed that peace might be achieved by negotiation if the hostile powers could be persuaded to say what they were fighting for. He was personally influenced by the already well-known pacifist, Bertrand Russell. Russell's arguments affected at least one other soldier–poet, A. G. West, who had almost nerved himself to take a public stand in 1916. Sassoon himself passed his own and Russell's ideas on to his friends, Wilfred Owen and Osbert Sitwell. Herbert Read reached a comparable position independently.

There seem to be few other recorded examples,[50] although private letters and diaries often show soldiers drifting away from crusading enthusiasm in 1914–15 towards resentment against civilians in 1917–18. Gurney, for instance, believed in the war against evil in 1915, although he admitted that he never felt Brooke's 'splendid readiness for death'; in 1917, aware of Sassoon's protest and disgusted by the speeches of politicians, he came to think that the war was being prolonged by British rigidity and a 'wrong materialistic system', and he wrote a poem against the 'Prussians of England' [131]. Nevertheless, the subject he most wanted to write about was the courage and comradeship of the troops.[51] He does not seem to have thought that the war was futile, nor that he should have spoken openly against it. The less well-documented case of Edgell Rickword may also be noted; whatever his political views about the war may have been, neither they nor the fact that he was a committed Marxist after, and perhaps before, 1918 are evident from his few war poems, all of which were written after hostilities ended.

Sassoon was applauded by civilians opposed to the fighting and patiently tolerated even by prussianists, who, noting his fine military record, concluded that he was under severe strain. The painful honesty of his verse was admired by Winston Churchill and Henry Newbolt. Soldiers were more sceptical. Bernard Freyberg, the celebrated VC and friend of Brooke, objected that in refusing to lead men any more Sassoon was claiming a monopoly of virtue and implying that other officers *liked* doing their duty.[52] Sassoon's fellow-officers wrote to him from the front that the war had to go on. Graves was appalled by the protest, saying that such acts only served to weaken morale (every officer knew from training and experience that a drop in morale meant a rise in casualties).[53] Army discipline may have prevented some protests; loyalty to comrades may have prevented many more.

The comradeship which developed at the front (VI: 4) became so strong that by 1917–18 it was for many the principal motive for staying in the line. Men sometimes refused Staff postings or came back early from sick leave in order to share the lot of their friends. Officers felt a particular devotion to the troops for whom they were responsible:

> Oh, never will I forget you,
> My men that trusted me,
> More my sons than your fathers',
>
> . . .
>
> They could not see you dying,
> And hold you while you died.
>
> . . .
>
> For they were only your fathers
> But I was your officer.[54]

It was love for his men that drove Sassoon both to make his statement and to return to the fighting [138]. Such love was part of the incommunicable knowledge which trench experience gave. The nearest language for expressing it belonged to religious or erotic poetry, so that some poems of comradeship are startling in their portrayal of dying men as lovers or Christs [137]. A few poets, including Owen, Sassoon, Sitwell and (until 1917) Graves, were actually homosexual in tendency, and others recognised a specifically sexual element in their own feelings. However, close relationships between men had been esteemed by the Victorians and were still largely free from the implication of sexuality which has since become attached to them. It was a love 'passing the love of women', and for many soldiers it was the most intense bond in their lives.

Part VII: Poets and Poetry in Wartime

Poets and critics in 1914–18 often discussed the nature and function of 'war poetry'. In 1914, thoughtful readers were ready to look for new writing, aware that the arts had been in turmoil for several years. But even Harold Monro [143] failed to foresee the sudden triumph of the soldier–poet, although, as a Georgian looking for reform, he suspected that neither the Modernist *avant garde* nor the literary establishment would be generally successful at writing about what was to come. However, more conventional authors like William Watson [*144*] or Henry Newbolt, both of whom were soon to be knighted for their public-spirited verse, were in no doubt that the war poet's duty was the ancient one of calling men to the colours, celebrating the character of the Happy Warrior, and commending the national cause.

The public demand for verse in 1914–18 was probably higher than at any time in this century. Despite a perceptible falling-off after 1915, most newspapers and periodicals carried poems regularly and often. The *Nation*, under the discriminating editorship of Harold Massingham, perhaps had the best record for printing honest, questioning work of good quality; its many verse contributions included Wilfrid Gibson's *Battle* poems in 1914–15, early poems of protest or pity by Margaret Sackville, W. N. Ewer and Edward Shillito, some Sassoon, Graves and Sitwell in 1917, and three pieces by Owen in 1918. However, most editors and publishers chose verse that would contribute to the nation's morale. The editor of the *Poetry Review*, Galloway Kyle, was particularly active in promoting the fashion for poetry by soldiers, putting many young aspirants into print for the first (and often the last) time and receiving warm acclaim for doing so. (The publisher 'Erskine Macdonald' was an alias for Kyle himself, who traded on the gullibility of new authors and made them pay for publication). Most publishers advertised war poetry prominently in their lists. Memorial volumes brought fame to Charles Sorley, Leslie Coulson, W. N. Hodgson and other 'fallen heroes'.

Early soldier–poetry was heavily influenced by Brooke, although Sorley condemned his attitude as 'sentimental'. Sorley himself preferred an unemotional, Homeric stance [*146 n*], but that too was conventional and he was venerated as a soldier–poet along with the rest. There were bound to be reactions; one of the first and angriest was A. G. West's 'War Poets' (October 1916), later rewritten as 'God! How I Hate You, You Young Cheerful Men' [*149*]. A year or so later, Gilbert Frankau still found it necessary to satirise soldiers who persisted in writing about the war as 'a kind of Military Tournament' [*154*]. Such writing continued [*158*], but by

1917–18 most soldier-verse was tougher than it had been and more concerned with actuality than ideals.

The later soldier–poets differed widely in their political views. Their common ground was not that they all believed the war was futile, for some were deeply convinced of its justice; nor that they wanted it stopped by negotiation, for some were intent on military victory; nor that they rejected soldierly values, for most proudly accepted them. They shared one aim for their poetry: 'we are poets / And shall tell the truth' [151]. What distinguished them from Brooke was not that they dismissed notions of heroism and sacrifice but that they were determined to report actual front-line conditions to the Nation at Home. The 1917–18 soldier–poet thus becomes an important figure in modern literature: the writer who shares and articulates suffering, thereby earning the right to act as the conscience of his times.[55] But an insistence on the value of honest description and plain words was not new, since it had been a feature of first-generation Georgian poetry, particularly in the pre-war work of Gibson and Brooke himself. As second-generation Georgians, Graves and Sassoon developed it further, Graves saying early in 1916 that Brooke's was 'exactly the language I'm floundering to catch, musical, restrained, refined and not crabbed or conventionally antique, reading almost like ordinary speech'.[56] By the end of that year, Sassoon was convinced that poetry must be based on experience. He taught the lesson to other writers who came under his influence, notably Owen, who began 1917 by writing archaic sonnets about such subjects as 'Golden Hair' and ended it by declaring that 'Nothing great was said of anything but a definite experience'.[57] In 1918, Sassoon met Vivian de Sola Pinto, whose poems were then an uneasy combination of Georgian bluntness and Edwardian rhetoric [56]. Pinto recalled the fervent advice he received:

> Poetry must grow out of the realities of the human condition. Plain, direct language must be used and all inversions and archaisms must be avoided like the plague. Only everyday speech was fit for the bare truthfulness and sincerity of poetry. We must write with our 'eye on the object' and eschew literary themes.[58]

No one thought more deeply or wrote more fully about the task of the soldier–poet than Owen, who by early 1918 was dedicating himself to his 'job' ('I confess I *bring on* what few war dreams I now have, entirely by *willingly* considering war of an evening. I do so because I have my duty to perform towards War').[59] His 'Insensibility' [*152*] is a unique study of poetic duty and imagination in wartime. Its deliberate similarities to Wordsworth's 'Immortality' ode, one of the great Romantic poems about imagination and its loss, demonstrate Owen's strong sense of being an inheritor and developer of literary tradition. Like Keats and Shelley, the poet is made 'wise' by suffering, but the 'spontaneous overflow of powerful feelings' which the Romantics had sought would now merely drown the mind in blood. The extreme conditions of modern warfare require the poet to exercise an extreme self-discipline; fully participating in the imaginative experience of the troops, he becomes entitled to report on it and to pronounce a powerful Shelleyan curse against those at home who have chosen to feel no pity. There is optimism as well as anger in this position, for the poet has a positive, reforming purpose. 'Insensibility', and other poems like it, belong to the winter of 1917–18, when Owen ceased to be simply a follower of Sassoon and hammered out a poetry of his own. It was still possible then to hope for peace talks, but the events of March 1918 (cp. VIII: 1) were to turn hope into despair.

Owen's most pessimistic poems, including 'Futility' [*106*], 'The Send-Off' [*161*] and 'Strange Meeting' [*155*], were probably written in March–May 1918. 'Strange Meeting' is one of the few Great War poems that faces up to the fact of killing; the meeting is between two soldier–poets in hell, one of whom has killed the other. The dead man reveals how they alone would have had the power and secret knowledge to speak of 'the pity of war', the one truth worth salvaging because it grew from the triumph of beauty over horror, love over death. In a passage probably deriving from Russell, he foretells the chaos of post-war Europe, with its totalitarianism and revolutions. Had he lived, his role would have been like that of an Old Testament prophet, a Romantic poet or even Christ (hence his biblical and Shelleyan diction), warning, teaching and healing. The last line shows that the first poet's escape 'out of battle' was death, not just a vision; war has overcome his imaginative power, too, and he must join his victim, nightmare-ridden, in an inferno which war has shaped in all ages for the men and hopes it has destroyed.

In a sense, Owen was unduly pessimistic. War did silence him, as in another way it silenced Sassoon, but the two friends were to exercise a far-reaching influence on modern attitudes to war. Critics observe the failings of their verse, historians point out that few soldiers shared their views, but no other poets of the Great War have surpassed them as its spokesmen. This success has had the side-effect of obscuring their uniqueness and the differences between them. For example, commentators rarely notice that Sassoon largely gave up writing against the war in the spring of 1918. His farewell to protest was recorded in 'Testament', a little poem published here from his own manuscript for the first time [156]. As he said, he had 'played his part'; for the few months that were left, Owen took it over.

Part VIII: 1918 and After

The dramatic changes at the front in the first half of 1918 provoked a strong poetic response at the time (VIII: 1), but the modern literary imagination tends to notice little alteration in the war after Passchendaele. The year actually began with a 'deceitful calm' [157], 'the longest quiet spell we had known for two years' (Lloyd George). At the beginning of March, Russia dropped out of the war; on the 21st, the massed German armies launched a huge offensive westwards, driving the Allies into headlong retreat. It seemed obvious that the German government was no longer interested in a negotiated peace. Every available man was caught up in the disaster. Among the poets who were not already casualties, Rosenberg was killed, Read was in the thick of the retreat, Sassoon was brought back from Palestine on a crowded troopship, Owen was sent for final training. There was a general stiffening of morale. Established poets were heard in the press once more, calling on the nation to prove its worth [159]. Despite a few protests from civilian pacifists [160], the spirit of 1914 revived. Civilians and soldiers came closer together in attitude than they had been for some time. It is a measure of how far 1918 has been forgotten that readers are likely to be surprised that F. W. D. Bendall's 'À Outrance' [*158*], with its imagery of war as a 'Military Tournament', was written by a professional soldier in the last year of the war, or that Robert Nichols's salute to 'morning heroes' [*162*] was not only written by a soldier who had (briefly) seen action but was also dedicated to Sassoon.

Nichols's exalted style reflects the beginning of the Allied recovery. As the British line began to advance again in the summer, 'prussianism' rejoiced that the intellectuals' campaign for peace moves had been swept aside and that moral scruples could no longer obstruct military action [*164*]. Sassoon and Owen sadly accepted their duty as officers and poets to fight and die with their men. Owen's last poem developed his theme that soldiers were both heroic and damned [*165*]. Despite his earlier disclaimer, his final poetry is 'about heroes'; to that extent, it is characteristic of the general mood in 1918. By October, the end was in sight. Kipling made one more appeal that 'justice' should be done to Germany [*166*]; and Frankau, a soldier–poet though now invalided out, echoed him in terms which show how far Owen and Sassoon were from being typical:

> . . . Free Peoples,
> By the God of your Fathers, slay!
> Let the sword decide what the sword began:
> 'No truce with the Beasts in Gray!'[60]

The Armistice was greeted with excitement in the streets but not in poetry (VIII: 2). There seemed little left to say. The 'men of letters' who had dominated 1914 again came to the fore, with verses by the Poet Laureate and others in *The Times*. Binyon's 'For the Fallen', originally published in 1914, provided lines for many war memorials, and Kipling was commissioned to compose epitaphs for the great cemeteries overseas. Soldier–poets were weary, and doubtful of the future. Men in the armed forces were released only slowly, many remaining in uniform until well into 1919. Most were sure that the war had been won by military victory and that it had been fought, as Elton later said, 'to prevent Prussian militarism and materialism from dominating Europe. And this tremendous object it had very palpably achieved.'[61] Some people, including Sassoon [170 n], hoped that the dreams of a new world which recruits had entertained in 1914–15 would come true through socialism. However, the country seemed to be uncomprehending, ungrateful and trivial-minded. Remembering dead friends, some veterans wondered whether they would have died with 'laughter won from war and hope from pain' if they could have foreseen

> No sunlit vision manifest as prize
> Of our youth's Calvary, but a world of stress,
>   With little men making their little moans
>   Like sparrows bickering on the market stones;
> And ever hate, and greed, and faithlessness . . .[62]

Rupert Brooke was long dead. Neither the style nor the ideas made sense any more.

War poetry went out of fashion in the early twenties; even the flood of war books at the end of the decade included only one poetry anthology. Most of the verse that had been published in 1917–18 was never to be looked at again, except by a few scholars and collectors. It remains as a unique and still largely unresearched chapter in British social and literary history. For the most part, it is only verse; but the best of it is poetry, to be valued not as highly finished art nor as factual history but as a true record of imaginative experience, each poet speaking with an individual voice in a world of stock rhetoric and silent suffering.

Postscript

Ivor Gurney has the last word. His view of the fighting had been that of the private soldier, aware of war's ironies, unimpressed by pointless daring, quietly amused at the 'finicking' accents of his officers [52], but convinced that the men who sang 'I don't want to die' before the Somme were braver than anyone at home could guess [19 n]. After the war, he shared the general bitterness that the nation seemed to take the troops' 'vast endurance' for granted [*176*], and from an asylum in the early 1920s he wrote his impressively sane response to the critics' disdain for war poetry [*184*]:

What did they expect of our toil and extreme
Hunger – the perfect drawing of a heart's dream?
Did they look for a book of wrought art's perfection . . .?
Out of the heart's sickness the spirit wrote . . .

Notes

1. Twells Brex, 'A Serious Outbreak of Poets', *Daily Mail*, 23 June 1915.
2. F. J. Roberts, in *The Wipers Times* (Spring 1916); reprint, ed. Patrick Beaver (1973), p. 45.
3. Like Catherine Reilly, we use the words 'poetry' and 'poet' to include 'verse' and 'versifier'. Her list of poets would have been considerably longer if she had included those whose work appeared only in periodicals. She records 131 anthologies, including revised editions. The phrase 'Great War' had been current since the 1890s to describe a frequently prophesied war between Britain and either France or Germany: see I. F. Clarke, *Voices Prophesying War 1763–1984* (1966). It was immediately accepted in 1914, as is evident, for example, from the anthology title, *Poems of the Great War* (1914).
4. Peter Porter, 'Somme and Flanders', *Once Bitten Twice Bitten* (1961).
5. Donald Davie, 'In the Pity', *New Statesman*, 28 Aug. 1964, pp. 282–3.
6. Walter Olley, *Tommy's Own Poems* (Dundee, n.d.). Olley records that all his poems were written during the great retreat in 1918. His book is not listed in Reilly.
7. A. J. P. Taylor, *English History 1914–1945* (1965), p. 61. As recently as 1973, an elderly General said in a radio interview that the reason some young men had protested against the war at the time was simply that they were 'damn bad soldiers'.
8. John Terraine, Introduction to Graham Greenwell, *An Infant in Arms* (1972), XIII. For similar objections to prose 'war books' such as Sassoon's and Graves's memoirs, see Douglas Jerrold, *The Lie about the War* (1930) and Correlli Barnett, 'A Military Historian's View of the Great War', *Essays by Divers Hands*, XXXVI (1970), pp. 1–18. Both essays argue that the literature which suggested that the war was futile only served to make subsequent war more likely.
9. *Spectator*, 1 Jan. 1916, p. 22; Cynthia Asquith, *Diaries 1915–1918* (1968), p. 485.
10. Eliot reviewed Read's book as 'the best war poetry I can remember

having seen', *Egoist*, July 1919, p. 39. Parts of *The Waste Land* were drafted during the war.

11. For South African War poetry, see Malvern van Wyk Smith, *Drummer Hodge* (1978).

12. The 5 August issue of *Punch* was still strongly opposed to war, having gone to press before Britain ceased to be neutral.

13. Books and broadsheets often announced that all profits would be given to war charities.

14. D. G. Wright, 'The Great War, Government Propaganda and English "Men of Letters" 1914–16', *Literature and History*, VII (Spring 1978), pp. 70–100.

15. For example, anonymous reviews in the *Nation* of the prolific Canon Rawnsley (31 July 1915), who wrote 148 war poems between August 1914 and May 1915, and of other war poets (14 Aug. 1915); and reviews or verse by J. G. Fletcher in the *Egoist* (2 and 16 Nov. 1914), 'Solomon Eagle' (J. C. Squire) in the *New Statesman* (14 Nov. 1914), Edward Moore in the *New Age* (8 Oct. 1914), Theodore Maynard in the *New Age* (12 Nov. 1914).

16. Undated cutting, *Poems Relating to the European War* (36 volumes of newspaper cuttings, Birmingham Reference Library), VI, p. 42.

17. William Watson, 'The Battle of the Bight', in *Songs and Sonnets for England in War Time* (1914) and other anthologies. Watson later rewrote the passage, several reviewers having seized on it gleefully.

18. 'Can Poets Help?', *Evening News*, 11 Dec. 1914, and a further article (17 Dec.). Inevitably, 'C. E. B.' (Burton) joined in with 'The Poet and the Soldier', saying that poets could help if they remembered that Tommy was 'a simple sort of chap' (12 Dec.).

19. 'Georgians' here simply means poets who contributed to *Georgian Poetry*.

20. The *Daily Herald* came out as the weekly *Herald* during the war.

21. Hence the slightly misleading notion that this was a peculiarly 'literary war': see Paul Fussell, *The Great War and Modern Memory* (1975), ch. V.

22. Grenfell, Bendall, W. S. S. Lyon and – much out of character – Sitwell were already in the army when war broke out.

23. For examples of the persistence of Victorian chivalric imagery into 1914–18, see Mark Girouard, *The Return to Camelot* (1981), ch. XVIII, and, for example, the poems and pictures in J. S. Arkwright, *The Supreme Sacrifice* (1919).

24. A phrase from *Tom Brown's Schooldays* (1857), the classic account of public-school life as an heroic battle against evil.

25. Henry Newbolt, 'Clifton Chapel'. Like Drake, Newbolt was playing bowls when he heard that war had been declared. He coolly announced the news, then said 'Your turn' to the next player (A. P. Herbert, *A. P. H.*, 1970, p. 35).

26. For a thoughtful contemporary comment on the public-school type, see the review of Charles Sayle, *Archibald Don: A Memoir*, in the *Nation*, 27 July 1918. Alec Waugh's *The Loom of Youth* (1917) gives some insight into public-school life in this period.

27. *The Times*, 28 May 1916. Similar marks of respect were paid to Rex

Freston (3 Feb. 1916), E. W. Tennant (29 Sept. 1916) and R. E. Vernède (5 May 1917).

28. Similar attitudes were still being expressed in 1918, for example by Robert Nichols [*142*], but they were more common in 1914–16.

29. Geoffrey Dearmer even wrote on 'Keats, Before Action' dedicating himself to beauty and truth in the smoke of battle (*Poems*, 1918).

30. Selected scenes from *The Dynasts*, such as the death of Nelson, were dramatised in London in autumn 1914 by Harley Granville Barker (*Westminster Gazette*, 26 Nov. 1914).

31. H. G. Wells, *The War That Will End War* (1914) and *God the Invisible King* (1917).

32. Wilfred Owen, *Collected Letters* (1967), p. 429.

33. There were also many descriptions of Christ appearing alone in the 'Golgotha' of the trenches [66] or even dying there [67]. In one remarkable instance, he was made to pick up a dead man's rifle and join with 'strong and righteous hand' in the sorrowful task of shooting the enemy (A. St J. Adcock, 'Christ in the Trenches', *Songs of the World-War*, 1916).

34. G. K. Chesterton, 'The Case for the War Song', *New Witness*, XII (17 May 1918), pp. 48–9.

35. *The Christian* (3 Sept. 1914), p. 7.

36. *The Times* (12 Nov. 1921) refers to a drawing by Louis Raemaekers of this proposed memorial, published on the first Poppy Day. A 1925 Poppy Day leaflet in our possession bears what is presumably the same picture, showing a haloed soldier in a posture strongly suggesting crucifixion and resurrection.

37. The text was used often for memorials of the Great War and sometimes for those of the Boer War but we have found no earlier examples. The idea of the soldier as Christ is set out in G. M. Hopkins's sonnet, 'The Soldier' (1885); being closer to Roman Catholic than to Protestant thinking, the image may have become attractive in England during the Victorian shift towards Rome.

38. *Great Thoughts of Horatio Bottomley: A Book for Pessimists* (n.d.), p. 8. In 'God and the War', one of his regular articles in the *Sunday Pictorial*, Bottomley said that the whole nation was suffering Christ's agony as a preliminary to entering 'the Land Beyond'; the paper claimed that this was 'the greatest message ever penned since the war began' (24 Oct. 1915).

39. John Oxenham, 'Christs All!', *All's Well* (1915). See also 'The Ballad of Jim Baxter', *The Vision Splendid* (1917).

40. Owen, *Collected Letters*, pp. 304, 468.

41. Norman Angell, *Prussianism and its Destruction* (1914).

42. Owen, *Collected Letters*, p. 498.

43. Charles Darling, 'The Empty Sleeve', *On the Oxford Circuit* (3rd edn, 1924).

44. Katherine Tynan, 'The Vision', *New Witness* (27 Jan. 1916). Tynan also wrote that 'the little Knights of Paradise of eighteen and nineteen' were singing on their way to heaven, washed clean by the blood of their sacrifice ('The Short Road to Heaven', *Herb o' Grace*, 1918).

45. Margaret Postgate, 'Recruited – Poplar. March 1917', *Poems* (1918).
46. Isaac Rosenberg, *Collected Works* (1979), p. 294.
47. Ibid., pp. 221–2.
48. Tom Skeyhill, 'Me Brother Wot Stayed at 'Ome', *Soldier Songs from Anzac* (1916); Geoffrey Fyson, 'To a Pacifist', *The Survivors* (1919); Ivan Firth, 'To Strikers in Wartime', *Bellicosities* (1915).
49. John Terraine, *Impacts of War: 1914 and 1918* (1970), pp. 171–6. Soldier-verse against the strategy, and not just the sensitivity, of generals was almost unknown during the war; Sassoon's 'The March-Past' [50] and 'The General' are two very rare examples.
50. For sources, see biographical notes on the poets named. Read's 'Kneeshaw Goes to War' was published in June 1918 (in *Art and Letters*). See also the note on Theo van Beek.
51. Ivor Gurney, *War Letters* (1983): p. 95 ('Against a huge evil there has risen up a huger force of good', 1915); p. 178 (on Grenfell, Brooke, Nichols, art and materialism, 1917); p. 231 (Sassoon's protest, 1917); pp. 235–6 (soldiers' courage); p. 236 ('The real Prussian attitude!'); p. 130 (his sonnets written as 'a sort of counterblast' against Brooke); etc.
52. Cynthia Asquith, *Diaries 1915–1918* (1968), pp. 380–1.
53. Graves's attitude to the protest is recorded in several of his published and unpublished 1917 letters, including one to Edmund Gosse of 24 Oct. (Brotherton Collection, Leeds).
54. E. A. Mackintosh, 'In Memoriam', *A Highland Regiment* (1918).
55. Cp. Samuel Hynes, *The Auden Generation* (1976), pp. 250–1. Hynes's first chapter discusses 'the Myth of the War', pp. 17–26.
56. Letter to Edward Marsh (9 Feb. 1916), Berg Collection, New York.
57. A hitherto unpublished phrase from a letter of 9 Dec. 1917.
58. Vivian de Sola Pinto, *The City that Shone* (1969), pp. 221–2.
59. Owen, *Collected Letters*, pp. 533–4.
60. Gilbert Frankau, 'The Beasts in Gray', *Daily Mail* (1 Nov. 1918), one of several similar poems by this poet.
61. Lord Elton (Godfrey Elton), *Among Others* (1938), p. 259.
62. Geoffrey Fyson, 'Desertion', *The Survivors* (1919).

Part I: 1914

1. Sowings for new spring

(1) *Fall In*

What will you lack, sonny, what will you lack
 When the girls line up the street,
Shouting their love to the lads come back
 From the foe they rushed to beat?
Will you send a strangled cheer to the sky
 And grin till your cheeks are red?
But what will you lack when your mate goes by
 With a girl who cuts you dead?

Where will you look, sonny, where will you look
 When your children yet to be
Clamour to learn of the part you took
 In the War that kept men free?
Will you say it was naught to you if France
 Stood up to her foe or bunked?
But where will you look when they give the glance
 That tells you they know you funked?

How will you fare, sonny, how will you fare
 In the far-off winter night,
When you sit by the fire in an old man's chair
 And your neighbours talk of the fight?
Will you slink away, as it were from a blow,
 Your old head shamed and bent?
Or say – I was not with the first to go,
 But I went, thank God, I went?

Why do they call, sonny, why do they call
 For men who are brave and strong?

Is it naught to you if your country fall,
　　And Right is smashed by Wrong?
Is it football still and the picture show,
　　The pub and the betting odds,
When your brothers stand to the tyrant's blow
　　And Britain's call is God's?

written August 1914   HAROLD BEGBIE

(2)　*From Whitechapel*

A white and wolfish face, with fangs
　　Half-snarling out of flaccid lips;
An unkempt head that loosely hangs;
　　Shoulders that cower from gaolers' grips;

Eyes furtive in their greedy glance;
　　Slim fingers not untaught to thieve; –
He shambles forward to the chance
　　His whole life's squalor to retrieve.

1st published October 1914   J. A. NICKLIN

(3)　*The Two Mothers*

'Poor woman, weeping as they pass,
　　Yon brave recruits, the nation's pride,
You mourn some gallant boy, alas!
　　Like mine who lately fought and died?'

'Kind stranger, not for soldier son,
  Of shame, not grief, my heart will break,
Three stalwarts have I, but not one
  Doth risk his life for England's sake!'

1st published December 1914   MATILDA BETHAM-EDWARDS

(4)   Men Who March Away

(Song of the Soldiers)

What of the faith and fire within us
    Men who march away
    Ere the barn-cocks say
    Night is growing gray,
Leaving all that here can win us;
What of the faith and fire within us
    Men who march away?

Is it a purblind prank, O think you,
    Friend with the musing eye,
    Who watch us stepping by
    With doubt and dolorous sigh?
Can much pondering so hoodwink you!
Is it a purblind prank, O think you,
    Friend with the musing eye?

Nay. We well see what we are doing,
    Though some may not see –
    Dalliers as they be –
    England's need are we;
Her distress would leave us rueing:
Nay. We well see what we are doing,
    Though some may not see!

In our heart of hearts believing
    Victory crowns the just,
    And that braggarts must
    Surely bite the dust,

Press we to the field ungrieving,
In our heart of hearts believing
    Victory crowns the just.

Hence the faith and fire within us
    Men who march away
    Ere the barn-cocks say
    Night is growing gray,
Leaving all that here can win us;
Hence the faith and fire within us
    Men who march away.

written 5 September 1914   THOMAS HARDY

(5) *August, 1914*

How still this quiet cornfield is to-night!
By an intenser glow the evening falls,
Bringing, not darkness, but a deeper light;
Among the stooks a partridge covey calls.

The windows glitter on the distant hill;
Beyond the hedge the sheep-bells in the fold
Stumble on sudden music and are still;
The forlorn pinewoods droop above the wold.

An endless quiet valley reaches out
Past the blue hills into the evening sky;
Over the stubble, cawing, goes a rout
Of rooks from harvest, flagging as they fly.

So beautiful it is, I never saw
So great a beauty on these English fields,
Touched by the twilight's coming into awe,
Ripe to the soul and rich with summer's yields.

*   *   *

These homes, this valley spread below me here,
The rooks, the tilted stacks, the beasts in pen,
Have been the heartfelt things, past-speaking dear
To unknown generations of dead men,

Who, century after century, held these farms,
And, looking out to watch the changing sky,
Heard, as we hear, the rumours and alarms
Of war at hand and danger pressing nigh.

And knew, as we know, that the message meant
The breaking off of ties, the loss of friends,
Death, like a miser getting in his rent,
And no new stones laid where the trackway ends.

The harvest not yet won, the empty bin,
The friendly horses taken from the stalls,
The fallow on the hill not yet brought in,
The cracks unplastered in the leaking walls.

Yet heard the news, and went discouraged home,
And brooded by the fire with heavy mind,
With such dumb loving of the Berkshire loam
As breaks the dumb hearts of the English kind,

Then sadly rose and left the well-loved Downs,
And so by ship to sea, and knew no more
The fields of home, the byres, the market towns,
Nor the dear outline of the English shore,

But knew the misery of the soaking trench,
The freezing in the rigging, the despair
In the revolting second of the wrench
When the blind soul is flung upon the air,

And died (uncouthly, most) in foreign lands
For some idea but dimly understood
Of an English city never built by hands
Which love of England prompted and made good.

★   ★   ★

If there be any life beyond the grave,
It must be near the men and things we love,
Some power of quick suggestion how to save,
Touching the living soul as from above.

An influence from the Earth from those dead hearts
So passionate once, so deep, so truly kind,
That in the living child the spirit starts,
Feeling companioned still, not left behind.

Surely above these fields a spirit broods
A sense of many watchers muttering near
Of the lone Downland with the forlorn woods
Loved to the death, inestimably dear.

A muttering from beyond the veils of Death
From long-dead men, to whom this quiet scene
Came among blinding tears with the last breath,
The dying soldier's vision of his queen.

All the unspoken worship of those lives
Spent in forgotten wars at other calls
Glimmers upon these fields where evening drives
Beauty like breath, so gently darkness falls.

Darkness that makes the meadows holier still,
The elm-trees sadden in the hedge, a sigh
Moves in the beech-clump on the haunted hill,
The rising planets deepen in the sky,

And silence broods like spirit on the brae,
A glimmering moon begins, the moonlight runs
Over the grasses of the ancient way
Rutted this morning by the passing guns.

1st published September 1914   JOHN MASEFIELD

(6) *Peace*

Now, God be thanked Who has matched us with His hour,
    And caught our youth, and wakened us from sleeping,
With hand made sure, clear eye, and sharpened power,
    To turn, as swimmers into cleanness leaping,
Glad from a world grown old and cold and weary,
    Leave the sick hearts that honour could not move,
And half-men, and their dirty songs and dreary,
    And all the little emptiness of love!

Oh! we, who have known shame, we have found release there,
    Where there's no ill, no grief, but sleep has mending,
        Naught broken save this body, lost but breath;
Nothing to shake the laughing heart's long peace there
    But only agony, and that has ending;
        And the worst friend and enemy is but Death.

written November 1914   RUPERT BROOKE

(7) *To-day*

No longer art, but artifice,
    No unrefracted ray:
No streamings from the infinite,
    No rough, inspired way:
No motive self-less, free from taint.
    But 'will it pay?'

The charlatan ascends the rock
    Where prophets stood of yore:
The shallow cynic dons the garb
    That Trust and Honour wore
And viperous Scorn stands sentinel
    Beside Truth's half-shut door.

Say, Spirit, what this England needs,
　Is it a common foe?
Must we through tears be led to smiles,
　To happiness through woe?
Shall blood of slaughtered sons buy grace?
　Then, England, let it flow.

1st published 1917　　　　　　　　　　　WILFRID J. HALLIDAY

(8)　*On Receiving News of the War*

Snow is a strange white word;
No ice or frost
Have asked of bud or bird
For Winter's cost.

Yet ice and frost and snow
From earth to sky
This Summer land doth know,
No man knows why.

In all men's hearts it is.
Some spirit old
Hath turned with malign kiss
Our lives to mould.

Red fangs have torn His face.
God's blood is shed.
He mourns from His lone place
His children dead.

O! ancient crimson curse!
Corrode, consume.
Give back this universe
Its pristine bloom.

Cape Town, 1914　　　　　　　　　　　ISAAC ROSENBERG

(9)   1914

War broke: and now the Winter of the world
With perishing great darkness closes in.
The foul tornado, centred at Berlin,
Is over all the width of Europe whirled,
Rending the sails of progress. Rent or furled
Are all Art's ensigns. Verse wails. Now begin
Famines of thought and feeling. Love's wine's thin.
The grain of human Autumn rots, down-hurled.

For after Spring had bloomed in early Greece,
And Summer blazed her glory out with Rome,
An Autumn softly fell, a harvest home,
A slow grand age, and rich with all increase.
But now, for us, wild Winter, and the need
Of sowings for new Spring, and blood for seed.

written 1914 (?)   WILFRED OWEN

2.   War exalts

(10)   Breakfast

We ate our breakfast lying on our backs,
Because the shells were screeching overhead.
I bet a rasher to a loaf of bread
That Hull United would beat Halifax
When Jimmy Stainthorp played full-back instead
Of Billy Bradford. Ginger raised his head
And cursed, and took the bet; and dropt back dead.
We ate our breakfast lying on our backs,
Because the shells were screeching overhead.

1st published October 1914   W. W. GIBSON

(11)   The Messages

'I cannot quite remember . . . There were five
Dropt dead beside me in the trench – and three
Whispered their dying messages to me. . .'

Back from the trenches, more dead than alive,
Stone-deaf and dazed, and with a broken knee,
He hobbled slowly, muttering vacantly:

'I cannot quite remember . . . There were five
Dropt dead beside me in the trench, and three
Whispered their dying messages to me. . .

'Their friends are waiting, wondering how they thrive –
Waiting a word in silence patiently. . .
But what they said, or who their friends may be

'I cannot quite remember . . . There were five
Dropt dead beside me in the trench – and three
Whispered their dying messages to me. . .'

1st published October 1914   W. W. GIBSON

(12)   The Climax

In this strange world in which we live,
    Great marvels never cease:
But, lo! a wonder passing all, –
    Wells preaches War for peace!

1st published October 1914   T. W. MERCER

(13) 1814–1914

On reading *The Dynasts*

Read here the tale of how England fought for freedom
Under Pitt and Castlereagh;
Gave unstintingly of her blood and treasure
To break a tyrant's sway.

'Europe in danger – her liberties imperilled.'
So the statesmen cried.
Stern, stupid Englishmen, foolishly believing them,
Marched and fought and died.

When the Corsican was broken and the pale suffering peoples
Thought their freedom due;
France got – her Bourbons back; Italy – her Bomba,
England – Peterloo.

A hundred years passed – once again: – 'The liberties
Of Europe are at stake!'
Once again the statesmen bid the silent Englishmen
Die for freedom's sake.

Stern, stupid Englishmen, nowise disbelieving them,
March cheerfully away,
Heedless of the story of their fathers' 'War for Freedom'
Under Pitt and Castlereagh.

November 1914

W. N. EWER

(14) War Exalts

War exalts and cleanses: it lifts man from the mud!
Ask God what He thinks of a bayonet dripping blood.

By War the brave are tested, and cowards are disgraced!
Show God His own image shrapnel'd into paste.

Fight till tyrants perish, slay till brutes are mild!
Then go wash the blood off and try to face your child.

1st published 1914   HAROLD BEGBIE

3.   Youth in arms

(15)   *Youth in Arms*

I

Happy boy, happy boy,
David the immortal willed,
Youth a thousand thousand times
Slain, but not once killed,
Swaggering again to-day
In the old contemptuous way;

Leaning backward from your thigh
Up against the tinselled bar –
Dust and ashes! is it you?
Laughing, boasting, there you are!
First we hardly recognised you
In your modern avatar.

Soldier, rifle, brown khaki –
Is your blood as happy so?
Where's your sling, or painted shield,
Helmet, pike, or bow?
Well, you're going to the wars –
That is all you need to know.
Greybeards plotted. They were sad.
Death was in their wrinkled eyes.
At their tables, with their maps
Plans and calculations, wise
They all seemed; for well they knew
How ungrudgingly Youth dies.

At their green official baize
They debated all the night
Plans for your adventurous days
Which you followed with delight,
Youth in all your wanderings,
David of a thousand slings.

II   SOLDIER

Are you going? To-night we must all hear your laughter;
We shall need to remember it in the quiet days after.
Lift your rough hands, grained like unpolished oak.
Drink, call, lean forward, tell us some happy joke.
Let us know every whim of your brain and innocent soul.
Your speech is let loose; your great loafing words roll
Like hill-waters. But every syllable said
Brings you nearer the time you'll be found lying dead
In a ditch, or rolled stiff on the stones of a plain.
(Thought! Thought go back into your kennel again:
Hound, back!) Drink your glass, happy soldier, to-night.
Death is quick; you will laugh as you march to the fight.
We are wrong. Dreaming ever, we falter and pause:
You go forward unharmed without Why or Because.
Spring does not question. The war is like rain;
You will fall in the field like a flower without pain;
And who shall have noticed one sweet flower that dies?
The rain comes; the leaves open, and other flowers rise.
The old clock tolls. Now all our words are said.
We drift apart and wander away to bed.
We dream of War. *Your* closing eyelids keep
Quiet watch upon your heavy dreamless sleep.
You do not wonder if you shall, nor why,
If you must, by whom, for whom, you will die.
You are snoring. (The hound of thought by every breath
Brings you nearer for us to your foreign death.)

Are you going? Good-bye, then, to that last word you spoke
We must try to remember you best by some happy joke.

III RETREAT

That is not war – oh it hurts! I am lame.
A thorn is burning me.
We are going back to the place from which we came.
I remember the old song now:

> *Soldier, soldier, going to war,*
> *When will you come back?*

Mind that rut. It is very deep.
All these ways are parched and raw.
Where are we going? How we creep!
Are you there? I never saw –

Damn this jingle in my brain.
I'm full of old songs – Have you ever heard this?

> *All the roads to victory*
> *Are flooded as we go.*
> *There's so much blood to paddle through,*
> *That's why we're marching slow.*

Yes sir; I'm here. Are you an officer?
I can't see. Are we running away?
How long have we done it? One whole year,
A month, a week, or since yesterday?

Damn the jingle. My brain
Is scragged and banged –

> *Fellows, these are happy times;*
> *Tramp and tramp with open eyes.*
> *Yet, try however much you will,*
> *You cannot see a tree, a hill,*
> *Moon, stars, or even skies.*

I won't be quiet. Sing too, you fool.
I had a dog I used to beat.
Don't try it on me. Say that again.
Who said it? *Halt!* Why? Who can halt?
We're marching now. Who fired? Well. Well.
I'll lie down too. I'm tired enough.

IV   CARRION

It is plain now what you are. Your head has dropped
Into a furrow. And the lovely curve
Of your strong leg has wasted and is propped
Against a ridge of the ploughed land's watery swerve.

You are swayed on waves of the silent ground;
You clutch and claim with passionate grasp of your fingers
The dip of earth in which your body lingers;
If you are not found,
In a little while your limbs will fall apart;
The birds will take some, but the earth will take most of your
        heart.

You are fuel for a coming spring if they leave you here;
The crop that will rise from your bones is healthy bread.
You died – we know you – without a word of fear,
And as they loved you living I love you dead.

No girl would kiss you. But then
No girls would ever kiss the earth
In the manner they hug the lips of men:
You are not known to them in this, your second birth.

No coffin-cover now will cram
Your body in a shell of lead;
Earth will not fall on you from the spade with a slam,
But will fold and enclose you slowly, you living dead.

Hush, I hear the guns. Are you still asleep?
Surely I saw you a little heave to reply.
I can hardly think you will not turn over and creep
Along the furrows trenchward as if to die.

1st published December 1914   HAROLD MONRO

Part II: Heroes

1. Soldier twentieth-century

(16)   Gheluvelt

Epitaph on the Worcesters. October 31, 1914

Askest thou of these graves? They'll tell thee, O stranger, in
    England
How we Worcesters lie where we redeem'd the battle.

1st published 1920

ROBERT BRIDGES

(17)   Epitaph: Neuve Chapelle

Tell them at home, there's nothing here to hide:
We took our orders, asked no questions, died.

1st published 1919

H. W. GARROD

(18) 'I saw a man this morning'

I saw a man this morning
   Who did not wish to die:
I ask, and cannot answer,
   If otherwise wish I.

Fair broke the day this morning
   Against the Dardanelles;
The breeze blew soft, the morn's cheeks
   Were cold as cold sea-shells.

But other shells are waiting
   Across the Aegean Sea,
Shrapnel and high explosive,
   Shells and hells for me.

O hell of ships and cities,
   Hell of men like me,
Fatal second Helen,
   Why must I follow thee?

Achilles came to Troyland
   And I to Chersonese:
He turned from wrath to battle,
   And I from three days' peace.

Was it so hard, Achilles,
   So very hard to die?
Thou knowest and I know not –
   So much the happier I.

I will go back this morning
   From Imbros over the sea;
Stand in the trench, Achilles,
   Flame-capped, and shout for me.

written 1915   PATRICK SHAW-STEWART

(19)　To England – A Note

I watched the boys of England where they went
Through mud and water to do appointed things.
See one a stake, and one wire-netting brings,
And one comes slowly under a burden bent
Of ammunition. Though the strength be spent
They 'carry on' under the shadowing wings
Of Death the ever-present. And hark, one sings
Although no joy from the grey skies be lent.

Are these the heroes – these? have kept from
　　you
The power of primal savagery so long?
Shall break the devil's legions? These they are
Who do in silence what they might boast to do;
In the height of battle tell the world in song
How they do hate and fear the face of War.

written June 1916　　　　　　　　　　　　IVOR GURNEY

(20)　The Legion

'Is that the Three-and-Twentieth, Strabo mine,
Marching below, and we still gulping wine?'
From the sad magic of his fragrant cup
The red-faced old centurion started up,
Cursed, battered on the table. 'No,' he said,
'Not that! The Three-and-Twentieth Legion's dead,
Dead in the first year of this damned campaign –
The Legion's dead, dead, and won't rise again.
Pity? Rome pities her brave lads that die,
But we need pity also, you and I,
Whom Gallic spear and Belgian arrow miss,
Who live to see the Legion come to this,
Unsoldierlike, slovenly, bent on loot,
Grumblers, diseased, unskilled to thrust or shoot.

O brown cheek, muscled shoulder, sturdy thigh!
Where are they now? God! watch it struggle by,
The sullen pack of ragged ugly swine.
Is that the Legion, Gracchus? Quick, the wine!'
'Strabo,' said Gracchus, 'you are strange to-night.
The Legion is the Legion; it's all right.
If these new men are slovenly, in your thinking,
God damn it! you'll not better them by drinking.
They all try, Strabo; trust their hearts and hands.
The Legion is the Legion while Rome stands,
And these same men before the autumn's fall
Shall bang old Vercingetorix out of Gaul.'

late 1916   ROBERT GRAVES

(21)   Soldier: Twentieth Century

I love you, great new Titan!
Am I not you?
Napoleon and Caesar
Out of you grew.

Out of unthinkable torture,
Eyes kissed by death,
Won back to the world again,
Lost and won in a breath,

Cruel men are made immortal,
Out of your pain born.
They have stolen the sun's power
With their feet on your shoulders worn.

Let them shrink from your girth,
That has outgrown the pallid days,
When you slept like Circe's swine,
Or a word in the brain's ways.

written late 1917   ISAAC ROSENBERG

(22) *Schoolmistress*

Having, with bold Horatius, stamped her feet
And waved a final swashing arabesque
O'er the brave days of old, she ceased to bleat,
Slapped her Macaulay back upon the desk,
Resumed her calm gaze and her lofty seat.

There, while she heard the classic lines repeat,
Once more the teacher's face clenched stern;
For through the window, looking on the street,
Three soldiers hailed her. She made no return.
One was called 'Orace whom she would not greet.

written January–March 1918   WILFRED OWEN

2. Playing the game

(23) from *Lord's Leave*

(1915)

No Lord's this year: no silken lawn on which
    A dignified and dainty throng meanders.
The Schools take guard upon a fierier pitch
    Somewhere in Flanders.

Bigger the cricket here; yet some who tried
    In vain to earn a Colour while at Eton
Have found a place upon an England side
    That can't be beaten!

. . .

Cricket? 'Tis Sanscrit to the super-Hun –
    Cheap cross between Caligula and Cassius,
To whom speech, prayer, and warfare are all one –
    Equally gaseous!

Playing a game's beyond him and his hordes;
   Theirs but to play the snake or wolf or vulture:
Better one sporting lesson learnt at Lord's
      Than all their Kultur. . . .

. . .

Now for their flares . . . and now at last the stars . . .
   Only the stars now, in their heavenly million,
Glisten and blink for pity on our scars
      From the Pavilion.

1st published 1919   E. W. HORNUNG

(24) Cricket – 1915

The cricket pitch is lush and rank,
Meek daisies lift their heads, and swank,
And golden dandelion clumps
Annex the place reserved for stumps.
The wandering zephyrs pause and pass
Like silver waves across the grass,
And rustics nod their heads and say,
''Twill be a proper crop o' hay.'

The white pavilion's stripped and bare,
No thumping sticks or clapping there,
No heart-wrung gasp, no frenzied shout
Of 'Chuck her up!' or 'Run it out!'
No sporting urchins risk a fall
To yell their plaudits from the wall.
The skylark, lilting to his mate,
This season, constitutes the 'gate'.

Where are those hefty sporting lads
Who donned the flannels, gloves and pads?
They play a new and deadly game
Where thunder bursts in crash and flame.

Our cricketers have gone 'on tour',
To make their country's triumph sure.
They'll take the Kaiser's middle wicket
And smash it by clean British Cricket.

1st published May 1915   JESSIE POPE

(25) *Ginger*

'Strong as a little 'orse,' the sergeant said,
    ''E never got no dysentery,' and now
The sniper's got him, see him lying dead,
    Down in the trench, and blood upon his brow.

Dumb-souled, dull-witted, heavy as the sod,
    An ignorant farm-labourer; for shame!
Off with your hats, you worldlings, to this clod:
    He played the game.

Suvla Bay, 1915   V. DE SOLA PINTO

(26) *The Field of Honour*

Mud-stained and rain-sodden, a sport for flies and lice,
Out of this vilest life into vile death he goes;
His grave will soon be ready, where the grey rat knows
There is fresh meat slain for her; – our mortal bodies rise,
In those foul scampering bellies, quick – and yet, those eyes
That stare on life still out of death, and will not close,
Seeing in a flash the Crown of Honour, and the Rose
Of Glory wreathed about the Cross of Sacrifice,

Died radiant. May some English traveller to-day
Leaving his city cares behind him, journeying west
To the brief solace of a sporting holiday,
Quicken again with boyish ardour, as he sees,
For a moment, Windsor Castle towering on the crest
And Eton still enshrined among remembering trees.

1st published December 1915   CHARLES SCOTT MONCRIEFF

(27) *The Game*

A company of the East Surrey Regiment is reported to have dribbled footballs, the gift of their captain who fell in the fight, for a mile and a quarter into the enemy trenches.

On through the hail of slaughter
    Where gallant comrades fall,
Where blood is poured like water,
    They drive the trickling ball.
The fear of death before them
    Is but an empty name;
True to the land that bore them
    The Surreys play the game!

On without check or falter,
    They press towards the goal;
Who falls on freedom's altar
    The Lord shall rest his soul.
But still they charge, the living,
    Into that hell of flame;
Ungrudging in the giving,
    Our soldiers play the game!

And now at last is ended
    The task so well begun.
Though savagely defended
    The lines of death are won.

In this, their hour of glory,
     A deathless place they claim
In England's splendid story,
     The men who played the game!

written July 1916   TOUCHSTONE*

(28) *Sportsmen in Paradise*

They left the fury of the fight,
And they were very tired.
The gates of Heaven were open, quite
Unguarded, and unwired.
There was no sound of any gun;
The land was still and green:
Wide hills lay silent in the sun,
Blue valleys slept between.

They saw far off a little wood
Stand up against the sky.
Knee-deep in grass a great tree stood . . .
Some lazy cows went by . . .
There were some rooks sailed overhead –
And once a church-bell pealed.
'God! but it's England,' someone said,
'And there's a cricket field!'

1st published June 1917   T. P. CAMERON WILSON

* Pseudonym of C. E. C. H. Burton.

(29) Machine-Guns

Gold flashes in the dark,
And on the road
Each side, behind, in front of us,
Gold sparks
Where the fierce bullets strike the stones.

In a near shell-hole lies a wounded man,
The stretcher-bearers bending over him;
And at our feet
Cower shrinkingly against the ground
Dark shadowy forms of men.

Only we two stand upright;
All differences of life and character smoothed out
And nothing left
Save that one foolish tie of caste
That will not let us shrink.

1st published 1919   RICHARD ALDINGTON

3. We are the happy legion

(30) The Soldier

If I should die, think only this of me:
    That there's some corner of a foreign field
That is for ever England. There shall be
    In that rich earth a richer dust concealed;
A dust whom England bore, shaped, made aware,
    Gave, once, her flowers to love, her ways to roam,
A body of England's, breathing English air,
    Washed by the rivers, blest by suns of home.

And think, this heart, all evil shed away,
A pulse in the eternal mind, no less
    Gives somewhere back the thoughts by England given;
Her sights and sounds; dreams happy as her day;
    And laughter, learnt of friends; and gentleness,
    In hearts at peace, under an English heaven.

written November–December 1914   RUPERT BROOKE

(31)   *Fragment*

I strayed about the deck, an hour, to-night
Under a cloudy moonless sky; and peeped
In at the windows, watched my friends at table,
Or playing cards, or standing in the doorway,
Or coming out into the darkness. Still
No one could see me.

              I would have thought of them
– Heedless, within a week of battle – in pity,
Pride in their strength and in the weight and firmness
And link'd beauty of bodies, and pity that
This gay machine of splendour 'ld soon be broken,
Thought little of, pashed, scattered. . . .

                      Only, always,
I could but see them – against the lamplight – pass
Like coloured shadows, thinner than filmy glass,
Slight bubbles, fainter than the wave's faint light,
That broke to phosphorus out in the night,
Perishing things and strange ghosts – soon to die
To other ghosts – this one, or that, or I.

written April 1915   RUPERT BROOKE

(32) *Absolution*

The anguish of the earth absolves our eyes
Till beauty shines in all that we can see.
War is our scourge; yet war has made us wise,
And, fighting for our freedom, we are free.

Horror of wounds and anger at the foe,
And loss of things desired; all these must pass.
We are the happy legion, for we know
Time's but a golden wind that shakes the grass.

There was an hour when we were loth to part
From life we longed to share no less than others.
Now, having claimed this heritage of heart,
What need we more, my comrades and my brothers?

written April–September 1915 SIEGFRIED SASSOON

(33) *Youth's Consecration*

Lovers of Life! Dreamers with lifted eyes!
O Liberty, at thy command we challenge Death!
The monuments that show our fathers' faith
Shall be the altars of our sacrifice.
Dauntless, we fling our lives into the van,
Laughing at Death because within Youth's breast
Flame lambent fires of Freedom. Man for man
We yield to thee our heritage, our best.
Life's highest product, Youth, exults in life;
We are Olympian Gods in consciousness;
Mortality to us is sweet; yet less
We value Ease when Honour sounds the strife.
Lovers of Life, we pledge thee Liberty
And go to death, calmly, triumphantly.

1st published Spring 1916 J. W. STREETS

(34)   Before Action

By all the glories of the day
   And the cool evening's benison,
By that last sunset touch that lay
   Upon the hills when day was done,
By beauty lavishly outpoured
   And blessings carelessly received,
By all the days that I have lived
   Make me a soldier, Lord.

By all of all man's hopes and fears,
   And all the wonders poets sing,
The laughter of unclouded years,
   And every sad and lovely thing;
By the romantic ages stored
   With high endeavour that was his,
By all his mad catastrophes
   Make me a man, O Lord.

I, that on my familiar hill
   Saw with uncomprehending eyes
A hundred of Thy sunsets spill
   Their fresh and sanguine sacrifice,
Ere the sun swings his noonday sword
   Must say good-bye to all of this; –
By all delights that I shall miss,
   Help me to die, O Lord.

1st published June 1916   WILLIAM NOEL HODGSON

(35)   A Petition

All that a man might ask, thou hast given me, England,
   Birth-right and happy childhood's long heart's-ease,
And love whose range is deep beyond all sounding
   And wider than all seas.

A heart to front the world and find God in it,
  Eyes blind enow, but not too blind to see
The lovely things behind the dross and darkness,
  And lovelier things to be.

And friends whose loyalty time nor death shall weaken,
  And quenchless hope and laughter's golden store;
All that a man might ask thou hast given me, England,
  Yet grant thou one thing more:

That now when envious foes would spoil thy splendour,
  Unversed in arms, a dreamer such as I
May in thy ranks be deemed not all unworthy,
  England, for thee to die.

written Summer 1916   R. E. VERNÈDE

(36)   The Zenith

To-day I reach the zenith of my life,
No time more noble in my span of years
Than this, the glorious hour of splendid strife,
Of War, of cataclysmal woe, and tears.
All petty are the greatest things of yore,
All mean and sordid is my dearest lay;
I have done nothing more worth while before . . .
My hour, my chance, my crisis, are to-day!

Albert (en route for the Somme), 9 October 1916   HAMISH MANN

(37)   *No One Cares Less than I*

'No one cares less than I,
Nobody knows but God,
Whether I am destined to lie
Under a foreign clod,'
Were the words I made to the bugle call in the
    morning.

But laughing, storming, scorning,
Only the bugles know
What the bugles say in the morning,
And they do not care, when they blow
The call that I heard and made words to early this
    morning.

written May 1916   EDWARD THOMAS

(38)   *Lights Out*

I have come to the borders of sleep,
The unfathomable deep
Forest where all must lose
Their way, however straight,
Or winding, soon or late;
They cannot choose.

Many a road and track
That, since the dawn's first crack,
Up to the forest brink,
Deceived the travellers,
Suddenly now blurs,
And in they sink.

Here love ends –
Despair, ambition ends;
All pleasure and all trouble,

Although most sweet or bitter,
Here ends in sleep that is sweeter
Than tasks most noble.

There is not any book
Or face of dearest look
That I would not turn from now
To go into the unknown
I must enter, and leave, alone,
I know not how.

The tall forest towers;
Its cloudy foliage lowers
Ahead, shelf above shelf;
Its silence I hear and obey
That I may lose my way
And myself.

written November 1916   EDWARD THOMAS

Part III: The Western Front

1.   The Somme

(39)   *Before Action*

Over the down the road goes winding,
   A ribbon of white in the corn –
The green, young corn. O, the joy of binding
   The sheaves some harvest morn!

But we are called to another reaping,
   A harvest that will not wait.
The sheaves will be green. O, the world of weeping
   Of those without the gate!

For the road we go they may not travel,
   Nor share our harvesting;
But watch and weep. O, to unravel
   The riddle of this thing!

Yet over the down the white road leading
   Calls; and who lags behind?
Stout are our hearts; but O, the bleeding
   Of hearts we may not bind!

Somme, July 1916   J. E. STEWART

(40)   from *The Golden Dawn*

('At dawn on July 1st, 1916, the great forward movement commenced on the Western battle front' – *Vide Press*)

. . .

The Golden Dawn! O, blessed glorious day!
  When frightfulness of Hunnish might is slain;
Then righteousness and love shall have the sway,
  And freedom's flag float proudly once again.
    The Prince of Peace shall bless us from above,
    With peace embracing Liberty and Love!

1st published 1916   ALFRED J. GILMORE

(41)   from *July 1, 1916*

We were unprepared,
We were most unwise;
We have been like that
For centuries –
But we've taught ourselves a thing or two,
And we're muddling through.

. . .

Shells and soldiers,
Piles and files; –
The roar goes up
On seventy miles:
We know now what we always knew –
We shall muddle through!

. . .

1st published October 1916   T. W. H. CROSLAND

(42) At Carnoy

Down in the hollow there's the whole Brigade
Camped in four groups: through twilight falling slow
I hear a sound of mouth-organs, ill-played,
And murmur of voices, gruff, confused, and low.
Crouched among thistle-tufts I've watched the glow
Of a blurred orange sunset flare and fade;
And I'm content. To-morrow we must go
To take some cursèd Wood . . . O world God made!

3 July 1916   SIEGFRIED SASSOON

(43) A Dead Boche

To you who'd read my songs of War
    And only hear of blood and fame,
I'll say (you've heard it said before)
    'War's Hell!' and if you doubt the same,
To-day I found in Mametz Wood
A certain cure for lust of blood:

Where, propped against a shattered trunk,
    In a great mess of things unclean,
Sat a dead Boche; he scowled and stunk
    With clothes and face a sodden green,
Big-bellied, spectacled, crop-haired,
Dribbling black blood from nose and beard.

written July 1916   ROBERT GRAVES

(44) *Who Made the Law?*

Who made the Law that men should die in meadows?
Who spake the word that blood should splash in lanes?
Who gave it forth that gardens should be bone-yards?
Who spread the hills with flesh, and blood, and brains?
        Who made the Law?

Who made the Law that Death should stalk the village?
Who spake the word to kill among the sheaves,
Who gave it forth that death should lurk in hedgerows,
Who flung the dead among the fallen leaves?
        Who made the Law?

Those who return shall find that peace endures,
Find old things old, and know the things they knew,
Walk in the garden, slumber by the fireside,
Share the peace of dawn, and dream amid the dew –
        Those who return.

Those who return shall till the ancient pastures,
Clean-hearted men shall guide the plough-horse reins,
Some shall grow apples and flowers in the valleys,
Some shall go courting in summer down the lanes –
        THOSE WHO RETURN.

But who made the Law? the Trees shall whisper to him:
'See, see the blood – the splashes on our bark!'
Walking the meadows, he shall hear bones crackle,
And fleshless mouths shall gibber in silent lanes at dark.
        Who made the Law?

Who made the Law? At noon upon the hillside
His ears shall hear a moan, his cheeks shall feel a breath,
And all along the valleys, past gardens, croft, and homesteads,
He who made the Law,
HE who made the Law,
HE who made the Law shall walk alone with Death.
        WHO made the Law?

October 1916   LESLIE COULSON

(45) *Before the Assault*

If thro' this roar o' the guns one prayer may reach Thee,
  Lord of all Life, whose mercies never sleep,
Not in our time, not now, Lord, we beseech thee
  To grant us peace. The sword has bit too deep.

We may not rest. We hear the wail of mothers
  Mourning the sons who fill some nameless grave:
Past us, in dreams, the ghosts march of our brothers
  Who were most valiant . . . whom we could not save.

We may not rest. What though our eyes be holden,
  In sleep we see dear eyes yet wet with tears,
And locks that once were, oh, so fair and golden,
  Grown grey in hours more pitiless than years.

We see all fair things fouled – homes love's hands builded
  Shattered to dust beside their withered vines,
Shattered the towers that once Thy sunsets gilded,
  And Christ struck yet again within His shrines.

Over them hangs the dust of death, beside them
  The dead lie countless – and the foe laughs still;
We may not rest, while those cruel mouths deride them,
  We, who were proud, yet could not work Thy will.

We have failed – we have been more weak than these betrayers –
  In strength or in faith we have failed; our pride was vain.
How can we rest, who have not slain the slayers?
  What peace for us, who have seen Thy children slain?

Hark, the roar grows . . . the thunders reawaken –
  We ask one thing, Lord, only one thing now:
Hearts high as theirs, who went to death unshaken,
  Courage like theirs to make and keep their vow.

To stay not till these hosts whom mercies harden,
  Who know no glory save of sword and fire,
Find in our fire the splendour of Thy pardon,
  Meet from our steel the mercy they desire. . . .

Then to our children there shall be no handing
  Of fates so vain – of passions so abhorr'd . . .
But Peace . . . the Peace which passeth understanding . . .
  Not in our time . . . but in their time, O Lord.

written February–November 1916   R. E. VERNÈDE

(46) *Beaucourt Revisited*

I wandered up to Beaucourt; I took the river track,
And saw the lines we lived in before the Boche went back;
But Peace was now in Pottage, the front was far ahead,
The front had journeyed Eastward, and only left the dead.

And I thought, How long we lay there, and watched across the
    wire,
While the guns roared round the valley, and set the skies afire!
But now there are homes in HAMEL and tents in the Vale of
    Hell,
And a camp at Suicide Corner, where half a regiment fell.

The new troops follow after, and tread the land we won,
To them 'tis so much hill-side re-wrested from the Hun;
We only walk with reverence this sullen mile of mud;
The shell-holes hold our history, and half of them our blood.

Here, at the head of Peche Street, 'twas death to show your
    face;
To me it seemed like magic to linger in the place;
For me how many spirits hung round the Kentish Caves,
But the new men see no spirits – they only see the graves.

I found the half-dug ditches we fashioned for the fight,
We lost a score of men there – young James was killed that
    night;
I saw the star shells staring, I heard the bullets hail,
But the new troops pass unheeding – they never heard the tale.

I crossed the blood-red ribbon, that once was No-Man's Land.
I saw a misty daybreak and a creeping minute-hand;
And here the lads went over, and there was Harmsworth shot,
And here was William lying – but the new men know them
    not.

And I said, 'There is still the river, and still the stiff, stark
    trees,
To treasure here our story, but there are only these;'
But under the white wood crosses the dead men answered low,
'The new men know not BEAUCOURT, but we are here – we
    know.'

1st published September 1917   A. P. HERBERT

(47) *The War Films*

O living pictures of the dead,
    O songs without a sound,
O fellowship whose phantom tread
    Hallows a phantom ground –
How in a gleam have these revealed
    The faith we had not found.

We have sought God in a cloudy Heaven,
    We have passed by God on earth:
His seven sins and his sorrows seven,
    His wayworn mood and mirth,
Like a ragged cloak have hid from us
    The secret of his birth.

Brother of men, when now I see
    The lads go forth in line,
Thou knowest my heart is hungry in me
    As for thy bread and wine:
Thou knowest my heart is bowed in me
    To take their death for mine.

written September–October 1916   HENRY NEWBOLT

(48) Somme Film 1916

There is no cause, sweet wanderers in the dark,
For you to cry aloud from cypress trees
To a forgetful world; since you are seen
Of all twice nightly at the cinema,
While the munition makers clap their hands.

1st published 1919   C. H. B. KITCHIN

(49) Home Service

'At least it wasn't your fault' I hear them console
When they come back, the few that will come back.
I feel those handshakes now. 'Well, on the whole
You didn't miss much. I wish I had your knack
Of stopping out. You still can call your soul
Your own, at any rate. What a priceless slack
You've had, old chap. It must have been top-hole.
How's poetry? I bet you've written a stack.'

What shall I say? That it's been damnable?
That all the time my soul was never my own?
That we've slaved hard at endless make-believe?
It isn't only actual war that's hell,
I'll say. It's spending youth and hope alone
Among pretences that have ceased to deceive.

Sutton Veny, September 1916   GEOFFREY FABER

2.   Nothing but chance of death

(50)   The March-Past

In red and gold the Corps-Commander stood,
With ribboned breast puffed out for all to see:
He'd sworn to beat the Germans, if he could;
For God had taught him strength and strategy.
He was our leader, and a judge of Port –
Rode well to hounds, and was a damned good sort.

'Eyes right!' We passed him with a jaunty stare.
'Eyes front!' He'd watched his trusted legions go.
I wonder if he guessed how many there
Would get knocked out of time in next week's show.
'Eyes right!' The corpse-commander was a Mute;
And Death leered round him, taking our salute.

25 December 1916   SIEGFRIED SASSOON

(51)   The Night Patrol

Over the top! The wire's thin here, unbarbed
Plain rusty coils, not staked, and low enough:
Full of old tins, though – 'When you're through, all three,
Aim quarter left for fifty yards or so,
Then straight for that new piece of German wire;
See if it's thick, and listen for a while
For sounds of working; don't run any risks;
About an hour; now, over!'
                              And we placed
Our hands on the topmost sand-bags, leapt, and stood
A second with curved backs, then crept to the wire,
Wormed ourselves tinkling through, glanced back, and
     dropped.
The sodden ground was splashed with shallow pools,

And tufts of crackling cornstalks, two years old,
No man had reaped, and patches of spring grass,
Half-seen, as rose and sank the flares, were strewn
With the wrecks of our attack: the bandoliers,
Packs, rifles, bayonets, belts, and haversacks,
Shell fragments, and the huge whole forms of shells
Shot fruitlessly – and everywhere the dead.
Only the dead were always present – present
As a vile sickly smell of rottenness;
The rustling stubble and the early grass,
The slimy pools – the dead men stank through all,
Pungent and sharp; as bodies loomed before,
And as we passed, they stank: then dulled away
To that vague fœtor, all encompassing,
Infecting earth and air. They lay, all clothed,
Each in some new and piteous attitude
That we well marked to guide us back: as he,
Outside our wire, that lay on his back and crossed
His legs Crusader-wise; I smiled at that,
And thought on Elia and his Temple Church.
From him, at quarter left, lay a small corpse,
Down in a hollow, huddled as in bed,
That one of us put his hand on unawares.
Next was a bunch of half a dozen men
All blown to bits, an archipelago
Of corrupt fragments, vexing to us three,
Who had no light to see by, save the flares.
On such a trail, so lit, for ninety yards
We crawled on belly and elbows, till we saw,
Instead of lumpish dead before our eyes,
The stakes and crosslines of the German wire.
We lay in shelter of the last dead man,
Ourselves as dead, and heard their shovels ring
Turning the earth, then talk and cough at times.
A sentry fired and a machine-gun spat;
They shot a flare above us; when it fell
And spluttered out in the pools of No Man's Land,
We turned and crawled past the remembered dead:
Past him and him, and them and him, until,
For he lay some way apart, we caught the scent
Of the Crusader and slid past his legs,
And through the wire and home, and got our rum.

France, March 1916   ARTHUR GRAEME WEST

(52)   The Silent One

Who died on the wires, and hung there, one of two –
Who for his hours of life had chattered through
Infinite lovely chatter of Bucks accent:
Yet faced unbroken wires; stepped over, and went
A noble fool, faithful to his stripes – and ended.
But I weak, hungry, and willing only for the chance
Of line – to fight in the line, lay down under unbroken
Wires, and saw the flashes and kept unshaken,
Till the politest voice – a finicking accent, said:
'Do you think you might crawl through there: there's a hole.'
Darkness, shot at: I smiled, as politely replied –
'I'm afraid not, Sir.' There was no hole no way to be seen
Nothing but chance of death, after tearing of clothes.
Kept flat, and watched the darkness, hearing bullets
    whizzing –
And thought of music – and swore deep heart's deep oaths
(Polite to God) and retreated and came on again,
Again retreated – and a second time faced the screen.

written 1919–22   IVOR GURNEY

(53)   Pillbox

Just see what's happening, Worley! – Worley rose
And round the angled doorway thrust his nose
And Serjeant Hoad went too to snuff the air.
Then war brought down his fist, and missed the pair!
Yet Hoad was scratched by a splinter, the blood came,
And out burst terrors that he'd striven to tame,
A good man, Hoad, for weeks. *I'm blown to bits,*
He groans, he screams. *Come, Bluffer, where's your wits?*
Says Worley, *Bluffer, you've a blighty, man!*
All in the pillbox urged him, here began
His freedom: *Think of Eastbourne and your dad.*
The poor man lay at length and brief and mad

Flung out his cry of doom; soon ebbed and dumb
He yielded. Worley with a tot of rum
And shouting in his face could not restore him.
The ship of Charon over channel bore him.
All marvelled even on that most deathly day
To see this life so spirited away.

1st published 1925   EDMUND BLUNDEN

(54)   *Trench Poets*

I knew a man, he was my chum,
But he grew blacker every day,
And would not brush the flies away,
Nor blanch however fierce the hum
Of passing shells; I used to read,
To rouse him, random things from Donne;
Like 'Get with child a mandrake-root,'
But you can tell he was far gone,
For he lay gaping, mackerel-eyed,
And stiff and senseless as a post
Even when that old poet cried
'I long to talk with some old lover's ghost.'

I tried the Elegies one day,
But he, because he heard me say
'What needst thou have more covering than a man?'
Grinned nastily, and so I knew
The worms had got his brains at last.
There was one thing that I might do
To starve the worms; I racked my head
For healthy things and quoted *Maud*.
His grin got worse and I could see
He laughed at passion's purity.
He stank so badly, though we were great chums
I had to leave him; then rats ate his thumbs.

1st published 1921   EDGELL RICKWORD

(55) *Exposure*

Our brains ache, in the merciless iced east winds that knive us . . .
Wearied we keep awake because the night is silent . . .
Low, drooping flares confuse our memory of the salient . . .
Worried by silence, sentries whisper, curious, nervous,
   But nothing happens.

Watching, we hear the mad gusts tugging on the wire,
Like twitching agonies of men among its brambles.
Northward, incessantly, the flickering gunnery rumbles,
Far off, like a dull rumour of some other war.
   What are we doing here?

The poignant misery of dawn begins to grow . . .
We only know war lasts, rain soaks, and clouds sag stormy.
Dawn massing in the east her melancholy army
Attacks once more in ranks on shivering ranks of grey,
   But nothing happens.

Sudden successive flights of bullets streak the silence.
Less deathly than the air that shudders black with snow,
With sidelong flowing flakes that flock, pause, and renew;
We watch them wandering up and down the wind's
  nonchalance,
   But nothing happens.

Pale flakes with fingering stealth come feeling for our faces –
We cringe in holes, back on forgotten dreams, and stare,
  snow-dazed,
Deep into grassier ditches. So we drowse, sun-dozed,
Littered with blossoms trickling where the blackbird fusses,
   – Is it that we are dying?

Slowly our ghosts drag home: glimpsing the sunk fires, glozed
With crusted dark-red jewels; crickets jingle there;
For hours the innocent mice rejoice: the house is theirs;
Shutters and doors, all closed: on us the doors are closed, –
   We turn back to our dying.

Since we believe not otherwise can kind fires burn;
Nor ever suns smile true on child, or field, or fruit.

For God's invincible spring our love is made afraid;
Therefore, not loath, we lie out here; therefore were born,
    For love of God seems dying.

Tonight, this frost will fasten on this mud and us,
Shrivelling many hands, puckering foreheads crisp.
The burying-party, picks and shovels in shaking grasp,
Pause over half-known faces. All their eyes are ice,
    But nothing happens.

written 1918   WILFRED OWEN

(56)   *The Dying Soldier*

'Here are houses', he moaned,
'I could reach but my brain swims.'
Then they thundered and flashed
And shook the earth to its rims.

'They are gunpits', he gasped,
'Our men are at the guns.
Water – water – O water
For one of England's dying sons.'

'We cannot give you water,
Were all England in your breath,'
'Water! – water! – O water!'
He moaned and swooned to death.

1st published 1922   ISAAC ROSENBERG

(57) *Dead Man's Dump*

The plunging limbers over the shattered track
Racketed with their rusty freight,
Stuck out like many crowns of thorns,
And the rusty stakes like sceptres old
To stay the flood of brutish men
Upon our brothers dear.

The wheels lurched over sprawled dead
But pained them not, though their bones crunched,
Their shut mouths made no moan,
They lie there huddled, friend and foeman,
Man born of man, and born of woman,
And shells go crying over them
From night till night and now.

Earth has waited for them
All the time of their growth
Fretting for their decay:
Now she has them at last!
In the strength of their strength
Suspended – stopped and held.

What fierce imaginings their dark souls lit
Earth! have they gone into you?
Somewhere they must have gone,
And flung on your hard back
Is their souls' sack,
Emptied of God-ancestralled essences.
Who hurled them out? Who hurled?

None saw their spirits' shadow shake the grass,
Or stood aside for the half used life to pass
Out of those doomed nostrils and the doomed mouth,
When the swift iron burning bee
Drained the wild honey of their youth.

What of us, who flung on the shrieking pyre,
Walk, our usual thoughts untouched,
Our lucky limbs as on ichor fed,
Immortal seeming ever?

Perhaps when the flames beat loud on us,
A fear may choke in our veins
And the startled blood may stop.

The air is loud with death,
The dark air spurts with fire
The explosions ceaseless are.
Timelessly now, some minutes past,
These dead strode time with vigorous life,
Till the shrapnel called 'an end!'
But not to all. In bleeding pangs
Some borne on stretchers dreamed of home,
Dear things, war-blotted from their hearts.

A man's brains splattered on
A stretcher-bearer's face;
His shook shoulders slipped their load,
But when they bent to look again
The drowning soul was sunk too deep
For human tenderness.

They left this dead with the older dead,
Stretched at the cross roads.
Burnt black by strange decay,
Their sinister faces lie
The lid over each eye,
The grass and coloured clay
More motion have than they,
Joined to the great sunk silences.

Here is one not long dead;
His dark hearing caught our far wheels,
And the choked soul stretched weak hands
To reach the living word the far wheels said,
The blood-dazed intelligence beating for light,
Crying through the suspense of the far torturing wheels
Swift for the end to break,
Or the wheels to break,
Cried as the tide of the world broke over his sight.

Will they come? Will they ever come?
Even as the mixed hoofs of the mules,
The quivering-bellied mules,
And the rushing wheels all mixed

With his tortured upturned sight,
So we crashed round the bend,
We heard his weak scream,
We heard his very last sound,
And our wheels grazed his dead face.

written February–May 1917   ISAAC ROSENBERG

(58)   *Relieved*

We are weary and silent,
There is only the rhythm of marching feet;
Tho' we move tranced, we keep it
As clock-work toys.

But each man is alone in this multitude;
We know not the world in which we move,
Seeing not the dawn, earth pale and shadowy,
Level lands of tenuous grays and greens;
For our eye-balls have been seared with fire.

Only we have our secret thoughts,
Our sense floats out from us, delicately apprehensive,
To the very fringes of our being,
Where light drowns.

1st published 1917   FREDERIC MANNING

3.   The scene of war

(59)   *The Scene of War*

And perhaps some outer horror,
some hideousness to stamp beauty
a mark
on our hearts.   H. D.

I   VILLAGES DÉMOLIS

The villages are strewn
In red and yellow heaps of rubble:

Here and there
Interior walls
Lie upturned and interrogate the skies amazedly

Walls that once held
Within their cubic confines
A soul that now lies strewn
In red and yellow
Heaps of rubble.

II   THE CRUCIFIX

His body is smashed
Through the belly and chest,
And the head hangs lopsided
From one nailed hand.

Emblem of agony,
We have smashed you!

III Fear

Fear is a wave
Beating through the air
And on taut nerves impingeing
Till there it wins
Vibrating chords.

All goes well
So long as you tune the instrument
To simulate composure.

(So you will become
A gallant gentleman.)

But when the strings are broken. . . .
Then you will grovel on the earth
And your rabbit eyes
Will fill with the fragments of your shattered soul.

IV The Happy Warrior

His wild heart beats with painful sobs,
His strained hands clench an ice-cold rifle,
His aching jaws grip a hot parched tongue,
And his wide eyes search unconsciously.

He cannot shriek.

Bloody saliva
Dribbles down his shapeless jacket.

I saw him stab
And stab again
A well-killed Boche.

This is the happy warrior,
This is he. . . .

V   LIEDHOLZ

When I captured Liedholz
I had a blackened face
Like a nigger's,
And my teeth like white mosaics shone.

We met in the night at half-past one,
Between the lines.
Liedholz shot at me
And I at him;
And in the ensuing tumult he surrendered to me.

Before we reached our wire
He told me he had a wife and three children.
In the dug-out we gave him a whiskey.
Going to the Brigade with my prisoner at dawn,
The early sun made the land delightful,
And larks rose singing from the plain.

In broken French we discussed
Beethoven, Nietzsche and the International.

He was a professor
Living at Spandau;
And not too intelligible.

But my black face and nigger's teeth
Amused him.

VI   THE REFUGEES

Mute figures with bowed heads
They travel along the road:
Old women, incredibly old,
And a hand-cart of chattels.

They do not weep:
Their eyes are too dark for tears.

Past them have hastened
Processions of retreating gunteams,
Baggage-wagons and swift horsemen.

Now they struggle along
With the rearguard of a broken army.

We will hold the enemy towards nightfall
And they will move
Mutely into the dark behind us,
Only the creaking cart
Disturbing their sorrowful serenity.

1st published 1919   HERBERT READ

Part IV: Christ and Nature

1.   I say that He was Christ

(60)   Three Hills

There is a hill in England,
  Green fields and a school I know,
Where balls fly fast in summer,
  And the whispering elm trees grow,
    A little hill, a dear hill,
  And the playing fields below.

There is a hill in Flanders,
  Heaped with a thousand slain,
Where the shells fly night and noontide
  And the ghosts that died in vain,
    A little hill, a hard hill
  To the souls that died in pain.

There is a hill in Jewry,
  Three crosses pierce the sky,
On the midmost He is dying
  To save all those who die,
    A little hill, a kind hill
  To souls in jeopardy.

Harrow, December 1915   EVERARD OWEN

(61)   *The War*

Man was arraigned;
For Christ was challenged by another king,
The king of Might, with hatred in his wing,
    And strength arrayed.

Christ called from Heaven
For noble martyrs in His glorious cause,
To justify the Cross, and Christian laws,
    His love for men.

We heard the call;
And England's manhood stood by Christ the King,
Who comes with love and healing in His wing,
    And gives His all.

With changèd eyes,
And faces glowing with a holy ray,
Our boys, transfigured by the conflict, pray
    In Paradise.

1st published 1916   WILLIAM EVANS

(62)   *Solomon in All His Glory*

Still I see them coming, coming
    In their ragged broken line,
Walking wounded in the sunlight,
    Clothed in majesty divine.

For the fairest of the lilies,
    That God's summer ever sees,
Ne'er was clothed in royal beauty
    Such as decks the least of these.

Tattered, torn, and bloody khaki,
    Gleams of white flesh in the sun,
Raiment worthy of their beauty
    And the great things they have done.

Purple robes and snowy linen
    Have for earthly kings sufficed,
But these bloody sweaty tatters
    Were the robes of Jesus Christ.

1st published 1927   G. A. STUDDERT KENNEDY

(63) *The Vision Splendid*

Here – or hereafter – you shall see it ended,
This mighty work to which your souls are set;
If from beyond – then, with the vision splendid,
You shall smile back and never know regret.

Be this your vision! – through you, Life transfigured,
Uplift, redeemed from its forlorn estate,
Purged of the stains which once its soul disfigured,
Healed and restored, and wholly consecrate.

Christ's own rich blood, for healing of the nations,
Poured through his heart the message of reprieve;
God's holy martyrs built on His foundations,
Built with their lives and died that Life might live.

Now, in their train, your blood shall bring like healing;
You, like the Saints, have freely given your all,
And your high deaths, God's purposes revealing,
Sound through the earth His mighty Clarion Call.

O, not in vain has been your great endeavour;
For, by your dyings, Life is born again,
And greater love hath no man tokened ever,
Than with his life to purchase Life's high gain.

1st published March 1917   JOHN OXENHAM

(64)   *The Redeemer*

Darkness: the rain sluiced down; the mire was deep;
It was past twelve on a mid-winter night,
When peaceful folk in beds lay snug asleep;
There, with much work to do before the light,
We lugged our clay-sucked boots as best we might
Along the trench; sometimes a bullet sang,
And droning shells burst with a hollow bang;
We were soaked, chilled and wretched, every one;
Darkness; the distant wink of a huge gun.

I turned in the black ditch, loathing the storm;
A rocket fizzed and burned with blanching flare,
And lit the face of what had been a form
Floundering in mirk. He stood before me there;
I say that He was Christ; stiff in the glare,
And leaning forward from His burdening task,
Both arms supporting it; His eyes on mine
Stared from the woeful head that seemed a mask
Of mortal pain in Hell's unholy shine.

No thorny crown, only a woollen cap
He wore – an English soldier, white and strong,
Who loved his time like any simple chap,
Good days of work and sport and homely song;
Now he has learned that nights are very long,
And dawn a watching of the windowed sky.
But to the end, unjudging, he'll endure
Horror and pain, not uncontent to die
That Lancaster on Lune may stand secure.

He faced me, reeling in his weariness,
Shouldering his load of planks, so hard to bear.
I say that He was Christ, who wrought to bless
All groping things with freedom bright as air,
And with His mercy washed and made them fair.
Then the flame sank, and all grew black as pitch,
While we began to struggle along the ditch;
And someone flung his burden in the muck,
Mumbling: 'O Christ Almighty, now I'm stuck!'

written November 1915–March 1916   SIEGFRIED SASSOON

(65) *Christ and the Soldier*

I

The straggled soldier halted – stared at Him –
Then clumsily dumped down upon his knees,
Gasping, 'O blessed crucifix, I'm beat!'
And Christ, still sentried by the seraphim,
Near the front-line, between two splintered trees,
Spoke him: 'My son, behold these hands and feet.'

The soldier eyed Him upward, limb by limb,
Paused at the Face; then muttered, 'Wounds like these
Would shift a bloke to Blighty just a treat!'
Christ, gazing downward, grieving and ungrim,
Whispered, 'I made for you the mysteries,
Beyond all battles moves the Paraclete.'

II

The soldier chucked his rifle in the dust,
And slipped his pack, and wiped his neck, and said –
'O Christ Almighty, stop this bleeding fight!'
Above that hill the sky was stained like rust
With smoke. In sullen daybreak flaring red
The guns were thundering bombardment's blight.

The soldier cried, 'I was born full of lust,
With hunger, thirst, and wishfulness to wed.
Who cares today if I done wrong or right?'
Christ asked all pitying, 'Can you put no trust
In my known word that shrives each faithful head?
Am I not resurrection, life and light?'

III

Machine-guns rattled from below the hill;
High bullets flicked and whistled through the leaves;
And smoke came drifting from exploding shells.
Christ said, 'Believe; and I can cleanse your ill.
I have not died in vain between two thieves;
Nor made a fruitless gift of miracles.'

The soldier answered, 'Heal me if you will,
Maybe there's comfort when a soul believes
In mercy, and we need it in these hells.
But be you for both sides? I'm paid to kill
And if I shoot a man his mother grieves.
Does that come into what your teaching tells?'

A bird lit on the Christ and twittered gay;
Then a breeze passed and shook the ripening corn.
A Red Cross waggon bumped along the track.
Forsaken Jesus dreamed in the desolate day –
Uplifted Jesus, Prince of Peace forsworn –
An observation post for the attack.

'Lord Jesus, ain't you got no more to say?'
Bowed hung that head below the crown of thorns.
The soldier shifted, and picked up his pack,
And slung his gun, and stumbled on his way.
'O God,' he groaned, 'why ever was I born?' . . .
The battle boomed, and no reply came back.

5 August 1916   SIEGFRIED SASSOON

(66) *Advent, 1916*

I dreamt last night Christ came to earth again
To bless His own. My soul from place to place
On her dream-quest sped, seeking for His face
Through temple and town and lovely land, in vain.
Then came I to a place where death and pain
Had made of God's sweet world a waste forlorn,
With shattered trees and meadows gashed and torn,
Where the grim trenches scarred the shell-seared plain.

And through that Golgotha of blood and clay,
Where watchers cursed the sick dawn, heavy-eyed,
There (in my dream) Christ passed upon His way,
Where His cross marks their nameless graves who died
Slain for the world's salvation, where all day
For others' sake strong men are crucified.

1st published 1919   EVA DOBELL

(67)   'I tracked a dead man down a trench'

I tracked a dead man down a trench,
  I knew not he was dead.
They told me he had gone that way,
  And there his foot-marks led.

The trench was long and close and curved,
  It seemed without an end;
And as I threaded each new bay
  I thought to see my friend.

I went there stooping to the ground.
  For, should I raise my head,
Death watched to spring; and how should then
  A dead man find the dead?

At last I saw his back. He crouched
  As still as still could be,
And when I called his name aloud
  He did not answer me.

The floor-way of the trench was wet
  Where he was crouching dead:
The water of the pool was brown,
  And round him it was red.

I stole up softly where he stayed
  With head hung down all slack,
And on his shoulders laid my hands
  And drew him gently back.

And then, as I had guessed, I saw
  His head, and how the crown –
I saw then why he crouched so still,
  And why his head hung down.

written April 1915   W. S. S. LYON

(68)   *The Conscript*

Indifferent, flippant, earnest, but all bored,
The doctors sit in the glare of electric light
Watching the endless stream of naked white
Bodies of men for whom their hasty award
Means life or death maybe, or the living death
Of mangled limbs, blind eyes, or a darkened brain;
And the chairman, as his monocle falls again,
Pronounces each doom with easy indifferent breath.

Then suddenly I shudder as I see
A young man stand before them wearily,
Cadaverous as one already dead;
But still they stare untroubled as he stands
With arms outstretched and drooping thorn-crowned head,
The nail-marks glowing in his feet and hands.

1st published 1920   W. W. GIBSON

(69)   *'My men go wearily'*

My men go wearily
With their monstrous burdens.

They bear wooden planks
And iron sheeting
Through the area of death.

When a flare curves through the sky
They rest immobile.

Then on again,
Sweating and blaspheming –
'Oh, bloody Christ!'

My men, my modern Christs,
Your bloody agony confronts the world.

1st published 1919   HERBERT READ

(70)   *Gethsemane*

The Garden called Gethsemane
    In Picardy it was,
And there the people came to see
    The English soldiers pass.
We used to pass – we used to pass
    Or halt, as it might be,
And ship our masks in case of gas
    Beyond Gethsemane.

The Garden called Gethsemane,
    It held a pretty lass,
But all the time she talked to me
    I prayed my cup might pass.
The officer sat on the chair,
    The men lay on the grass,
And all the time we halted there
    I prayed my cup might pass –

It didn't pass – it didn't pass –
    It didn't pass from me.
I drank it when we met the gas
    Beyond Gethsemane.

1st published 1919   RUDYARD KIPLING

2.   Unploughed the grown field

(71)   *'All the hills and vales along'*

All the hills and vales along
Earth is bursting into song,
And the singers are the chaps
Who are going to die perhaps.

O sing, marching men,
Till the valleys ring again.
Give your gladness to earth's keeping,
So be glad, when you are sleeping.

Cast away regret and rue,
Think what you are marching to.
Little live, great pass.
Jesus Christ and Barabbas
Were found the same day.
This died, that, went his way.
    So sing with joyful breath.
    For why, you are going to death.
    Teeming earth will surely store
    All the gladness that you pour.

Earth that never doubts nor fears
Earth that knows of death, not tears,
Earth that bore with joyful ease
Hemlock for Socrates,
Earth that blossomed and was glad
'Neath the cross that Christ had,
Shall rejoice and blossom too
When the bullet reaches you.
    Wherefore, men marching
    On the road to death, sing!
    Pour gladness on earth's head,
    So be merry, so be dead.

From the hills and valleys earth
Shouts back the sound of mirth,
Tramp of feet and lilt of song
Ringing all the road along.
All the music of their going,
Ringing swinging glad song-throwing,
Earth will echo still, when foot
Lies numb and voice mute.
    On, marching men, on
    To the gates of death with song.
    Sow your gladness for earth's reaping,
    So you may be glad, though sleeping.
    Strew your gladness on earth's bed,
    So be merry, so be dead.

written August 1914 (?)   CHARLES SORLEY

(72) Into Battle

The naked earth is warm with spring,
   And with green grass and bursting trees
Leans to the sun's gaze glorying,
   And quivers in the sunny breeze;
And life is colour and warmth and light,
   And a striving evermore for these;
And he is dead who will not fight;
   And who dies fighting has increase.

The fighting man shall from the sun
   Take warmth, and life from the glowing earth;
Speed with the light-foot winds to run,
   And with the trees to newer birth;
And find, when fighting shall be done,
   Great rest, and fullness after dearth.

All the bright company of Heaven
   Hold him in their high comradeship,
The Dog-Star, and the Sisters Seven,
   Orion's Belt and sworded hip.

The woodland trees that stand together,
   They stand to him each one a friend;
They gently speak in the windy weather;
   They guide to valley and ridge's end.

The kestrel hovering by day,
   And the little owls that call by night,
Bid him be swift and keen as they,
   As keen of ear, as swift of sight.

The blackbird sings to him, 'Brother, brother,
   If this be the last song you shall sing,
Sing well, for you may not sing another;
   Brother, sing.'

In dreary, doubtful, waiting hours,
   Before the brazen frenzy starts,
The horses show him nobler powers;
   O patient eyes, courageous hearts!

And when the burning moment breaks,
    And all things else are out of mind,
And only joy of battle takes
    Him by the throat, and makes him blind,

Through joy and blindness he shall know,
    Not caring much to know, that still
Nor lead nor steel shall reach him, so
    That it be not the Destined Will.

The thundering line of battle stands,
    And in the air death moans and sings;
But Day shall clasp him with strong hands,
    And Night shall fold him in soft wings.

written 29 April 1915   JULIAN GRENFELL

(73)   *Not Dead*

Walking through trees to cool my heat and pain,
I know that David's with me here again.
All that is simple, happy, strong, he is.
Caressingly I stroke
Rough bark of the friendly oak.
A brook goes bubbling by: the voice is his.
Turf burns with pleasant smoke;
I laugh at chaffinch and at primroses.
All that is simple, happy, strong, he is.
Over the whole wood in a little while
Breaks his slow smile

1st published 1917   ROBERT GRAVES

(74)   As the Team's Head-Brass

As the team's head-brass flashed out on the turn
The lovers disappeared into the wood.
I sat among the boughs of the fallen elm
That strewed the angle of the fallow, and
Watched the plough narrowing a yellow square
Of charlock. Every time the horses turned
Instead of treading me down, the ploughman leaned
Upon the handles to say or ask a word,
About the weather, next about the war.
Scraping the share he faced towards the wood,
And screwed along the furrow till the brass flashed
Once more.
⠀⠀⠀⠀⠀⠀The blizzard felled the elm whose crest
I sat in, by a woodpecker's round hole,
The ploughman said. 'When will they take it away?'
'When the war's over.' So the talk began –
One minute and an interval of ten,
A minute more and the same interval.
'Have you been out?' 'No.' 'And don't want to, perhaps?'
'If I could only come back again, I should.
I could spare an arm. I shouldn't want to lose
A leg. If I should lose my head, why, so,
I should want nothing more. . . . Have many gone
From here?' 'Yes.' 'Many lost?' 'Yes, a good few.
Only two teams work on the farm this year.
One of my mates is dead. The second day
In France they killed him. It was back in March,
The very night of the blizzard, too. Now if
He had stayed here we should have moved the tree.'
'And I should not have sat here. Everything
Would have been different. For it would have been
Another world.' 'Ay, and a better, though
If we could see all all might seem good.' Then
The lovers came out of the wood again:
The horses started and for the last time
I watched the clods crumble and topple over
After the ploughshare and the stumbling team.

written May 1916⠀⠀⠀⠀⠀⠀⠀⠀⠀⠀⠀⠀⠀⠀⠀⠀⠀⠀⠀⠀⠀EDWARD THOMAS

(75) Returning, We Hear the Larks

Sombre the night is.
And though we have our lives, we know
What sinister threat lurks there.

Dragging these anguished limbs, we only know
This poison-blasted track opens on our camp –
On a little safe sleep.

But hark! joy – joy – strange joy.
Lo! heights of night ringing with unseen larks.
Music showering our upturned list'ning faces.

Death could drop from the dark
As easily as song –
But song only dropped,
Like a blind man's dreams on the sand
By dangerous tides,
Like a girl's dark hair for she dreams no ruin lies there,
Or her kisses where a serpent hides.

written Summer 1917   ISAAC ROSENBERG

(76) Riez Bailleul

Riez Bailleul in blue tea-time
Called back the Severn lanes, the roads
Where the small ash leaves lie, and floods
Of hawthorn leaves turned with night's rime.
No Severn though, nor great valley clouds . . .

Now, in the thought, comparisons
Go with those here-and-theres and fancy
Sees on the china firelight dancy,
The wall lit where the sofa runs.
A dear light like Sirius or spring sun's.

But the trench thoughts will not go, tomorrow
Up to the line, and no straw laid
Soft for the body, and long nights' dread,
Lightless, all common human sorrow.
Unploughed the grown field once was furrow.

Meanwhile soft azure, and fall's emerald
Lovely the road makes, a softness clings
Of colour and texture of light; there rings
Metal, as it were, in air; and the called
Of twilight, dim stars of the dome, appear.

There's dusk here; west hedgerows show thin;
In billets there's sound of packs reset,
Tea finished; the dixies dried of the wet.
Some walk, some write, and the cards begin.
Stars gather in heaven and the pools drown in.

written 1919–20   IVOR GURNEY

(77)   A Soldier

He laughed. His blue eyes searched the morning,
Found the unceasing song of the lark
In a brown twinkle of wings, far out.
Great clouds, like galleons, sailed the distance.
The young spring day had slipped the cloak of dark
And stood up straight and naked with a shout.
Through the green wheat, like laughing schoolboys,
Tumbled the yellow mustard flowers, uncheck'd.
The wet earth reeked and smoked in the sun . . .
He thought of the waking farm in England.
The deep thatch of the roof – all shadow-fleck'd –
The clank of pails at the pump . . . the day begun.
'After the war . . .' he thought. His heart beat faster
With a new love for things familiar and plain.

The Spring leaned down and whispered to him low
Of a slim, brown-throated woman he had kissed . . .
He saw, in sons that were himself again,
The only immortality that man may know.

And then a sound grew out of the morning,
And a shell came, moving a destined way,
Thin and swift and lustful, making its moan.
A moment his brave white body knew the Spring,
The next, it lay
In a red ruin of blood and guts and bone.

. . .

Oh! nothing was tortured there! Nothing could know
How death blasphemed all men and their high birth
With his obscenities. Already moved,
Within those shattered tissues, that dim force,
Which is the ancient alchemy of Earth,
Changing him to the very flowers he loved.

. . .

'Nothing was tortured there!' Oh, pretty thought!
When God Himself might well bow down His head
And hide His haunted eyes before the dead.

written 1916   T. P. CAMERON WILSON

(78)   *Moonrise over Battlefield*

After the fallen sun the wind was sad
like violins behind immense old walls.
Trees were musicians swaying round the bed
of a woman in gloomy halls.

In privacy of music she made ready
with comb and silver dust and fard;
under her silken vest her little belly
shone like a bladder of sweet lard.

She drifted with the grand air of a punk
on Heaven's streets soliciting white saints;
then lay in bright communion on a cloud-bank
as one who near extreme of pleasure faints.

Then I thought, standing in the ruined trench,
(all round, dead Boche white-shirted lay like sheep),
'Why does this damned entrancing bitch
seek lovers only among them that sleep?'

1st published 1921   EDGELL RICKWORD

(79) *Come On, My Lucky Lads*

O rosy red, O torrent splendour
    Staining all the Orient gloom,
O celestial work of wonder –
    A million mornings in one bloom!

What, does the artist of creation
    Try some new plethora of flame,
For his eye's fresh fascination?
    Has the old cosmic fire grown tame?

In what subnatural strange awaking
    Is this body, which seems mine?
These feet towards that blood-burst making,
    These ears which thunder, these hands which twine

On grotesque iron? Icy-clear
    The air of a mortal day shocks sense,
My shaking men pant after me here.
    The acid vapours hovering dense,

The fury whizzing in dozens down,
  The clattering rafters, clods calcined,
The blood in the flints and the trackway brown –
  I see I am clothed and in my right mind;

The dawn but hangs behind the goal.
  What is that artist's joy to me?
Here limps poor Jock with a gash in the poll,
  His red blood now is the red I see,

The swooning white of him, and that red!
  These bombs in boxes, the craunch of shells,
The second-hand flitting round; ahead!
  It's plain we were born for this, naught else.

1st published 1925   EDMUND BLUNDEN

(80) Vlamertinghe: Passing the Chateau, July 1917

'And all her silken flanks with garlands drest' –
But we are coming to the sacrifice.
Must those have flowers who are not yet gone West?
May those have flowers who live with death and lice?
This must be the floweriest place
That earth allows; the queenly face
Of the proud mansion borrows grace for grace
Spite of those brute guns lowing at the skies.

Bold great daisies, golden lights,
Bubbling roses' pinks and whites –
Such a gay carpet! poppies by the million;
Such damask! such vermilion!
But if you ask me, mate, the choice of colour
Is scarcely right; this red should have been much duller.

1st published 1928   EDMUND BLUNDEN

(81)   *Premature Rejoicing*

What's that over there?
      Thiepval Wood.
Take a steady look at it; it'll do you good.
Here, these glasses will help you. See any flowers?
There sleeps Titania (correct – the Wood is ours);
There sleeps Titania in a deep dugout,
Waking, she wonders what all the din's about,
And smiles through her tears, and looks ahead ten years,
And sees her Wood again, and her usual Grenadiers,
  All in green,
  Music in the moon;
 The burnt rubbish you've just seen
 Won't beat the Fairy Queen;
  All the same, it's a shade too soon
  For you to scribble rhymes
  In your army book
  About those times;
  Take another look;
That's where the difficulty is, over there.

1st published 1930   EDMUND BLUNDEN

Part V: Civilians

1. And this he gives

(82) *The Beau Ideal*

Since Rose a classic taste possessed,
  It naturally follows
Her girlish fancy was obsessed
  By Belvedere Apollos.
And when she dreamed about a mate,
  If any hoped to suit, he
Must in his person illustrate
  A type of manly beauty.

He must be physically fit,
  A graceful, stalwart figure,
Of iron and elastic knit
  And full of verve and vigour.
Enough! I've made the bias plain
  That warped her heart and thrilled it.
It was a maggot of her brain,
  And Germany has killed it.

To-day, the sound in wind and limb
  Don't flutter Rose one tittle.
Her maiden ardour cleaves to him
  Who's proved that he is brittle,
Whose healing cicatrices show
  The colours of a prism,
Whose back is bent into a bow
  By Flanders rheumatism.

The lad who troth with Rose would plight,
  Nor apprehend rejection
Must be in shabby khaki dight
  To compass her affection.

Who buys her an engagement ring
And finds her kind and kissing,
Must have one member in a sling
Or, preferably, missing.

1st published February 1915   JESSIE POPE

(83)   *The Anvil*

Burned from the ore's rejected dross
The iron whitens in the heat.
With plangent strokes of pain and loss
The hammers on the iron beat.
Searched by the fire, through death and dole
We feel the iron in our soul.

O dreadful Forge! if torn and bruised
The heart, more urgent comes our cry
Not to be spared but to be used,
Brain, sinew, and spirit, before we die.
Beat out the iron, edge it keen,
And shape us to the end we mean!

1st published May 1915   LAURENCE BINYON

(84)   *The Cost*

'Greater love than this hath no man . . .'

The young man home from war,
Clean-limbed and strong,
His face is stern,
His voice is low and even, passionless,
His eyes are calm.

What have you seen?
What tense and solemn musing sets its mark
Upon your brow?

'This, . . .
The dead but die and dying are released,
It is the living body which enchains
Our souls to horror!
So have I given
My soul for you, a spiritual mighty gift!
For I can look
Upon the limbs and broken flesh of men
Which once were beautiful,
And shed no tears!

'And this again!
Men laugh to die,
But God has doomed to life
My body through the whelm and shock of war
And after it!
How shall I know
Peace in the night of dreams until I die?
For lo! the stain of twice ten thousand deaths,
Seems grav'n with steel upon my inmost soul.'

What answer can I give
The full-lipped mighty-limbed
Young hero from the war?

'The dead but die and dying live with God,
It is the living body which enchains
My soul to horror!'

And this he gives
That you and I and England may be free!

1st published 1915   FRANCIS ANDREWS

(85) *To the Vanguard*

Oh, little mighty Force that stood for England!
That, with your bodies for a living shield,
Guarded her slow awaking, that defied
The sudden challenge of tremendous odds
And fought the rushing legions to a stand –
Then stark in grim endurance held the line.
O little Force that in your agony
Stood fast while England girt her armour on,
Held high our honour in your wounded hands,
Carried our honour safe with bleeding feet –
We have no glory great enough for you,
The very soul of Britain keeps your day!
Procession? – Marches forth a Race in Arms;
And, for the thunder of the crowd's applause,
Crash upon crash the voice of monstrous guns,
Fed by the sweat, served by the life of England,
    Shouting your battle-cry across the world.

Oh, little mighty Force, your way is ours,
This land inviolate your monument.

1st published November 1916   BEATRIX BRICE

(86) *Epitaph on an Army of Mercenaries*

These, in the day when heaven was falling,
    The hour when earth's foundations fled,
Followed their mercenary calling
    And took their wages and are dead.

Their shoulders held the sky suspended;
    They stood, and earth's foundations stay;
What God abandoned, these defended,
    And saved the sum of things for pay.

1st published October 1917   A. E. HOUSMAN

(87)   from *Epitaphs*

'EQUALITY OF SACRIFICE'

A. 'I was a "have".' *B.* 'I was a "have-not".'
(*Together*). 'What hast thou given which I gave not?'

A SERVANT

We were together since the War began.
He was my servant – and the better man.

AN ONLY SON

I have slain none except my Mother. She
(Blessing her slayer) died of grief for me.

COMMON FORM

If any question why we died,
Tell them, because our fathers lied.

1st published 1919   RUDYARD KIPLING

2.   We murderers of mankind

(88)   *War*

Over the World
Rages war.
Earth, sea and sky
Wince at his roar.

He tramples down
At every tread,
A million men,
A million dead.

We say that we
Must crush the Hun,
Or else the World
Will be undone.
But Huns are we
As much as they.
All men are Huns,
Who fight and slay.

And if we win,
And crush the Huns,
In twenty years
We must fight their sons,
Who will rise against
Our victory,
Their fathers', their own
Ignominy.

And if their Kaiser
We dethrone,
They will his son restore,
Or some other one.
If we win by war,
War is a force,
And others to war
Will have recourse.

And through the World
Will rage new war.
Earth, sea and sky
Will wince at his roar.
He will trample down
At every tread,
Millions of men,
Millions of dead.

1915   JOSEPH LEFTWICH

(89)   To W. in the Trenches

You live with Death: yet over there
You breathe a somewhat cleaner air.

1st published May 1916   J. C. SQUIRE

(90)   The Dilemma

God heard the embattled nations sing and shout
'Gott strafe England!' and 'God save the King!'
God this, God that, and God the other thing –
'Good God!' said God, 'I've got my work cut out.'

1st published June 1915   J. C. SQUIRE

(91)   The Trinity

Cry 'God for Harry! England and Saint George!' – *Henry V*

Customs die hard in this our native land;
And still in Northern France, I understand,
Our gallant boys, as through the fray they forge,
Cry 'God for Harmsworth! England and Lloyd George!'

1st published May 1916   J. C. SQUIRE

(92) *The Higher Life for Clergymen*

'Conscription is a step towards the Higher Life.' – *A Living Dean*

'. . . he who made the earthquake and the storm,
Perchance made battles too.' – *A Dead Archbishop*

Christ, when you hung upon that tree accurst,
Bleeding, and bruised, and agonized by thirst,
Mocked, tantalized, and spat on and defiled,
On a near rising ground there stood and smiled,
Serene behind those ravening Hebrew beasts,
Annas and Caiaphas, the two high priests.

They felt uplifted, doubtless; for their god
Was Moloch who was always pleased with blood.
Under all names this one red God they love,
And when the evidence appeared to prove
The divine origin of him who died,
They thought 'twas Moloch they had crucified!

Nor will they change; when the last worst war is done,
And all mankind lies rotting in the sun,
High on the highest pile of skulls will kneel,
Thanking his god for that he did reveal
This crowning proof of his great grace to man,
A radiant, pink, well-nourished Anglican.

1st published May 1916   J. C. SQUIRE

(93) *Nostra Culpa*

We knew, this thing at least we knew, – the worth
Of life: this was our secret learned at birth.
We knew that Force the world has deified,
How weak it is. We spoke not, so men died.
Upon a world down-trampled, blood-defiled,
Fearing that men should praise us less, we smiled.

We knew the sword accursed, yet with the strong
Proclaimed the sword triumphant. Yea, this wrong
Unto our children, unto those unborn
We did, blaspheming God. We feared the scorn
Of men; men worshipped pride; so were they led,
We followed. Dare we now lament our dead?

Shadows and echoes, harlots! We betrayed
Our sons; because men laughed we were afraid.
That silent wisdom which was ours we kept
Deep-buried; thousands perished; still we slept.
Children were slaughtered, women raped, the weak
Down-trodden. Very quiet was our sleep.

Ours was the vision, but the vision lay
Too far, too strange; we chose an easier way.
The light, the unknown light, dazzled our eyes. –
Oh! sisters in our choice were we not wise?
When all men hated, could we pity or plead
For love with those who taught the Devil's creed?

Reap we with pride the harvest! it was sown
By our own toil. Rejoice! it is our own.
This is the flesh we might have saved – our hands,
Our hands prepared these blood-drenched, dreadful lands.
What shall we plead? That we were deaf and blind?
We mothers and we murderers of mankind.

1st published 1916   MARGARET SACKVILLE

(94)   *A Christian to a Quaker*

I much regret that I must frown
  Upon your cocoa nibs;
I simply hate to smite you down
  And kick you in the ribs;

But since you will not think as I,
  It's clear you must be barred,
So in you go (and may you die)
  To two years' hard.

We are marching on to freedom and to love;
  We're fighting every shape of tyrant sin;
    We are out to make it worth
    God's while to love the earth,
  And, damn it, you won't join in!

To drive you mad, as I have done,
  Has almost made me sick.
To torture Quakers like a Hun
  Has hurt me to the quick.
But since your logic wars with mine
  You're something I must guard,
So in you go, you dirty swine,
  To two years' hard.

We are marching to destroy the hosts of hate:
  We've taken, every man, a Christian vow;
    We are out to make war cease,
    That men may live at peace,
  And, damme, you're at it now!

1st published November 1917   HAROLD BEGBIE

(95) *Grasshoppers*

A low wind creeps along the fern
And makes a murmur in the furze.
The path at every sunny turn
Is populous with grasshoppers.

I cannot tell the words they say;
Yet sure the burden of their speech
Is just that life is good to-day,
And Heaven within our easy reach.

Far off, no doubt, great men of State,
Diplomatists and Chancellors
Discuss explosives and debate
Of bloodshed in the Common Cause.

But I must think, do what I may,
We're wiser here among the furze;
For if mankind is what you say,
Then God is for the grasshoppers!

1st published December 1917   OLAF BAKER

(96) *Joining-Up*

No, not for you the glamour of emprise,
Poor driven lad with terror in your eyes.

No dream of wounds and medals and renown
Called you like Love from your drab Northern town.

No haunting fife, dizzily shrill and sweet,
Came lilting drunkenly down your dingy street.

You will not change, with a swift catch of pride,
In the cold hut among the leers and oaths,
Out of your suit of frayed civilian clothes,
Into the blaze of khaki they provide.

Like a trapped animal you crouch and choke
In the packed carriage where the veterans smoke
And tell such pitiless tales of Over There,
They stop your heart dead short and freeze your hair.
Your body's like a flower on a snapt stalk,
Your head hangs from your neck as blank as chalk.

What horrors haunt you, head upon your breast!
. . . O but you'll die as bravely as the rest!

1st published 1919   LOUIS GOLDING

3. When dreams are shattered

(97) *My Boy Jack*

'Have you news of my boy Jack?'
  Not this tide.
'When d'you think that he'll come back?'
  Not with this wind blowing, and this tide.

'Has any one else had word of him?'
  Not this tide.
For what is sunk will hardly swim,
  Not with this wind blowing, and this tide.

'Oh, dear, what comfort can I find?'
  None this tide,
  Nor any tide,
Except he did not shame his kind –
  Not even with that wind blowing, and that tide.

Then hold your head up all the more,
  This tide,
  And every tide;
Because he was the son you bore,
  And gave to that wind blowing and that tide!

1st published October 1916   RUDYARD KIPLING

(98) *Hardness of Heart*

In the first watch no death but made us mourn;
Now tearless eyes run down the daily roll,
Whose names are written in the book of death;
For sealed are now the springs of tears, as when
The tropic sun makes dry the torrent's course

"**We will Remember them**"

They
shall grow not old,
as we that are left grow old;
Age shall not weary them,
Nor the years condemn.
At the going down of the sun,
And in the morning
We will
Remember them.

Laurence Binyon, from 'For the Fallen'.

1. Postcard. Famous lines from Laurence Binyon's 'For the Fallen' (September 1914).

To William II.

You who sowed the seas with death and filled the world with weeping,
You whose pride was glutted with an unmeasured pain.
You who fired on drowning lads, threw bombs on children sleeping,
You who wrecked the Rose of Rheims, you who sacked Louvain:
Caitiff, you shall see ere your vile day is ended,
Springing from the blood of these unnumbered slain,
Europe's One Republic rise serene and splendid,
Happy lands and holy seas from Russia into Spain.

R·L·Gales

Reprinted from the Daily News and Leader'

2. A typical verse postcard. A condemnation of the Kaiser, reprinted from the *Daily News* early in the war.

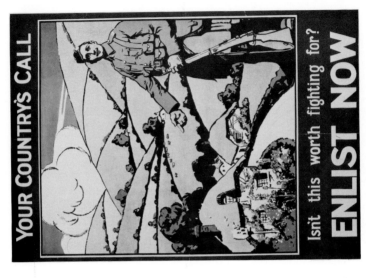

4. Recruiting poster. The appeal to love of countryside.

3. Recruiting poster. The appeal to justice.

Will they never come?

REPRINTED FROM

"THE WEEKLY DISPATCH"
November 22nd, 1914

Printed and Published by The Associated Newspapers, Ltd, Carmelite House, London, E.C.

6. Recruiting poster (November 1914). Another appeal to sportsmanship.

PUNCH, OR THE LONDON CHARIVARI.—October 21, 1914.

THE GREATER GAME.

Mr. Punch (to Professional Association Player). "NO DOUBT YOU CAN MAKE MONEY IN THIS FIELD, MY FRIEND, BUT THERE'S ONLY ONE FIELD TO-DAY WHERE YOU CAN GET HONOUR."

[The Council of the Football Association apparently proposes to carry out the full programme of the Cup Competition, in spite of the country did not need the services of all its athletes for the serious business of War.]

5. Mr Punch urges a civilian footballer to play the 'Greater Game' in France (21 October 1914).

7. James Clark, *The Great Sacrifice* (1914). Large re-
productions of this painting were given away with
the Christmas supplement of the *Graphic* in 1914.

8. *Despised and Rejected.* A cartoon filling the back
page of the *Herald* (8 July 1916), a week after the
Somme offensive started.

9.   Frank Dobson, *In the Trenches* (1916). A Modernist sketch.

10. Louis Raemaekers, *The Crumbling Shield.* A comment on the start of Germany's collapse in 1918.

11. William Nicholson, *The End of the War* (1917). War to end war.

12. Sir George Clausen, *Youth Mourning* (1916). An elderly academician's image of suffering. Compare Nevinson's realism below.

13. C.R.W. Nevinson, *The Paths of Glory* (1917). Nevinson was forbidden to exhibit this painting (see notes).

14. Sir William Orpen, *To the Unknown Soldier in France* (1919-1922), as it was before Orpen altered it in 1928 (see notes).

After the rains. They are too many now
For mortal eyes to weep, and none can see
But God alone the Thing itself and live.
We look to seaward, and behold a cry!
To skyward, and they fall as stricken birds
On autumn fields; and earth cries out its toll,
From the Great River to the world's end – toll
Of dead, and maimed and lost; we dare not stay;
Tears are not endless and we have no more.

1st published 1916   EDWARD SHILLITO

(99) *The Mother*

Written after reading Rupert Brooke's sonnet, 'The Soldier':
               If I should die, think only this of me:
               That there's some corner of a foreign field
               That is for ever England.

If you should die, think only this of me
In that still quietness where is space for thought,
Where parting, loss and bloodshed shall not be,
And men may rest themselves and dream of nought:
That in some place a mystic mile away
One whom you loved has drained the bitter cup
Till there is nought to drink; has faced the day
Once more, and now, has raised the standard up.

And think, my son, with eyes grown clear and dry
She lives as though for ever in your sight,
Loving the things *you* loved, with heart aglow
For country, honour, truth, traditions high,
– Proud that you paid their price. (And if some night
Her heart should break – well, lad, you will not know.)

1st published 1917   MAY HERSCHEL-CLARKE

(100) In Hospital

Under the shadow of a hawthorn brake,
  Where bluebells draw the sky down to the wood,
Where, 'mid brown leaves, the primroses awake
  And hidden violets smell of solitude;
Beneath green leaves bright-fluttered by the wing
Of fleeting, beautiful, immortal Spring,
I should have said, 'I love you,' and your eyes
Have said, 'I, too. . . .' The gods saw otherwise.

For this is winter, and the London streets
  Are full of soldiers from that far, fierce fray
Where life knows death, and where poor glory meets
  Full-face with shame, and weeps and turns away.
And in the broken, trampled foreign wood
Is horror, and the terrible scent of blood,
And love shines tremulous, like a drowning star,
Under the shadow of the wings of war.

1st published December 1915   E. NESBIT

(101) April 1918

You, whose forebodings have been all fulfilled,
You who have heard the bell, seen the boy stand
Holding the flimsy message in his hand
While through your heart the fiery question thrilled
'Wounded or killed, which, which?' – and it was 'Killed –'
And in a kind of trance have read it, numb
But conscious that the dreaded hour was come,
No dream this dream wherewith your blood was chilled –

Oh brothers in calamity, unknown
Companions in the order of black loss,
Lift up your hearts, for you are not alone,
And let our sombre hosts together bring
Their sorrows to the shadow of the Cross
And learn the fellowship of suffering.

1st published 1918   H. C. BRADBY

(102)   *Hospital Sanctuary*

When you have lost your all in a world's upheaval,
Suffered and prayed, and found your prayers were vain,
When love is dead, and hope has no renewal –
These need you still; come back to them again.

When the sad days bring you the loss of all ambition,
And pride is gone that gave you strength to bear,
When dreams are shattered, and broken is all decision –
Turn you to these, dependent on your care.

They too have fathomed the depths of human anguish,
Seen all that counted flung like chaff away;
The dim abodes of pain wherein they languish
Offer that peace for which at last you pray.

September 1918   VERA BRITTAIN

(103) Afterwards

Oh, my beloved, shall you and I
Ever be young again, be young again?
The people that were resigned said to me
– Peace will come and you will lie
Under the larches up in Sheer,
Sleeping,
And eating strawberries and cream and cakes –
     O cakes, O cakes, O cakes, from Fuller's!
And quite forgetting there's a train to town,
Plotting in an afternoon the new curves for the world.

And peace came. And lying in Sheer
I look round at the corpses of the larches
Whom they slew to make pit-props
For mining the coal for the great armies.
And think, a pit-prop cannot move in the wind,
Nor have red manes hanging in spring from its branches,
And sap making the warm air sweet.
Though you planted it out on the hill again it would be dead.
And if these years have made you into a pit-prop,
To carry the twisting galleries of the world's reconstruction
(Where you may thank God, I suppose
That they set you the sole stay of a nasty corner)
What use is it to you? What use
To have your body lying here
In Sheer, underneath the larches?

1st published 1918   MARGARET POSTGATE

Part VI: Soldiers

1. Here now is chaos once again

(104) Dead Cow Farm

An ancient saga tells us how
In the beginning the First Cow
(For nothing living yet had birth
But Elemental Cow on earth)
Began to lick cold stones and mud:
Under her warm tongue flesh and blood
Blossomed, a miracle to believe:
And so was Adam born, and Eve.
Here now is chaos once again,
Primeval mud, cold stones and rain.
Here flesh decays and blood drips red,
And the Cow's dead, the old Cow's dead.

1st published 1917   ROBERT GRAVES

(105) Song of the Dark Ages

We digged our trenches on the down
  Beside old barrows, and the wet
White chalk we shovelled from below;
It lay like drifts of thawing snow
  On parados and parapet:

125

Until a pick neither struck flint
  Nor split the yielding chalky soil,
But only calcined human bone:
Poor relic of that Age of Stone
  Whose ossuary was our spoil.

Home we marched singing in the rain,
  And all the while, beneath our song,
I mused how many springs should wane
And still our trenches scar the plain:
  The monument of an old wrong.

But then, I thought, the fair green sod
  Will wholly cover that white stain,
And soften, as it clothes the face
Of those old barrows, every trace
  Of violence to the patient plain.

And careless people, passing by
  Will speak of both in casual tone:
Saying: 'You see the toil they made:
The age of iron, pick and spade,
  Here jostles with the Age of Stone.'

Yet either from that happier race
  Will merit but a passing glance;
And they will leave us both alone:
Poor savages who wrought in stone –
  Poor savages who fought in France.

1st published 1917   FRANCIS BRETT YOUNG

(106) *Futility*

Move him into the sun –
Gently its touch awoke him once,
At home, whispering of fields half-sown.
Always it woke him, even in France,

Until this morning and this snow.
If anything might rouse him now
The kind old sun will know.

Think how it wakes the seeds –
Woke once the clays of a cold star.
Are limbs, so dear achieved, are sides
Full-nerved, still warm, too hard to stir?
Was it for this the clay grew tall?
– O what made fatuous sunbeams toil
To break earth's sleep at all?

written Spring 1918   WILFRED OWEN

(107)   The Face

Out of the smoke of men's wrath,
The red mist of anger,
Suddenly,
As a wraith of sleep,
A boy's face, white and tense,
Convulsed with terror and hate,
The lips trembling. . . .

Then a red smear, falling. . . .
I thrust aside the cloud, as it were tangible,
Blinded with a mist of blood.
The face cometh again
As a wraith of sleep:
A boy's face delicate and blonde,
The very mask of God,
Broken.

1st published 1917   FREDERIC MANNING

(108)   Goliath and David

(For D. C. T., killed at Fricourt, March 1916)

Yet once an earlier David took
Smooth pebbles from the brook:
Out between the lines he went
To that one-sided tournament,
A shepherd boy who stood out fine
And young to fight a Philistine
Clad all in brazen mail. He swears
That he's killed lions, he's killed bears,
And those that scorn the God of Zion
Shall perish so like bear or lion.
But . . . the historian of that fight
Had not the heart to tell it right.

Striding within javelin range,
Goliath marvels at this strange
Goodly-faced boy so proud of strength.
David's clear eye measures the length;
With hand thrust back, he cramps one knee,
Poises a moment thoughtfully,
And hurls with a long vengeful swing.
The pebble, humming from the sling
Like a wild bee, flies a sure line
For the forehead of the Philistine;
Then . . . but there comes a brazen clink,
And quicker than a man can think
Goliath's shield parries each cast.
Clang! clang! and clang! was David's last.
Scorn blazes in the Giant's eye,
Towering unhurt six cubits high.
Says foolish David, 'Damn your shield!
And damn my sling! but I'll not yield.'
He takes his staff of Mamre oak,
A knotted shepherd-staff that's broke
The skull of many a wolf and fox
Come filching lambs from Jesse's flocks.
Loud laughs Goliath, and that laugh
Can scatter chariots like blown chaff
To rout; but David, calm and brave,
Holds his ground, for God will save.

Steel crosses wood, a flash, and oh!
Shame for beauty's overthrow!
(God's eyes are dim, His ears are shut.)
One cruel backhand sabre-cut –
'I'm hit! I'm killed!' young Dàvid cries,
Throws blindly forward, chokes . . . and dies.
And look, spike-helmeted, grey, grim,
Goliath straddles over him.

1st published 1917   ROBERT GRAVES

(109)   *The Target*

I shot him, and it had to be
One of us! 'Twas him or me.
'Couldn't be helped,' and none can blame
Me, for you would do the same.

My mother, she can't sleep for fear
Of what might be a-happening here
To me. Perhaps it might be best
To die, and set her fears at rest.

For worst is worst, and worry's done.
Perhaps he was the only son . . .
Yet God keeps still, and does not say
A word of guidance any way.

Well, if they get me, first I'll find
That boy, and tell him all my mind,
And see who felt the bullet worst,
And ask his pardon, if I durst.

All's a tangle. Here's my job.
A man might rave, or shout, or sob;
And God He takes no sort of heed.
This is a bloody mess indeed.

1st published 1919   IVOR GURNEY

(110)   Break of Day in the Trenches

The darkness crumbles away.
It is the same old druid Time as ever,
Only a live thing leaps my hand,
A queer sardonic rat,
As I pull the parapet's poppy
To stick behind my ear.
Droll rat, they would shoot you if they knew
Your cosmopolitan sympathies.
Now you have touched this English hand
You will do the same to a German
Soon, no doubt, if it be your pleasure
To cross the sleeping green between.
It seems you inwardly grin as you pass
Strong eyes, fine limbs, haughty athletes
Less chanced than you for life,
Bonds to the whims of murder,
Sprawled in the bowels of the earth,
The torn fields of France.
What do you see in our eyes
At the shrieking iron and flame
Hurled through still heavens?
What quaver – what heart aghast?
Poppies whose roots are in man's veins
Drop, and are ever dropping;
But mine in my ear is safe –
Just a little white with the dust.

written June 1916   ISAAC ROSENBERG

(111)   Daughters of War

Space beats the ruddy freedom of their limbs –
Their naked dances with man's spirit naked
By the root side of the tree of life,
(The underside of things
And shut from earth's profoundest eyes).

I saw in prophetic gleams
These mighty daughters in their dances
Beckon each soul aghast from its crimson corpse
To mix in their glittering dances.
I heard the mighty daughters' giant sighs
In sleepless passion for the sons of valour,
And envy of the days of flesh
Barring their love with mortal boughs across –
The mortal boughs – the mortal tree of life.
The old bark burnt with iron wars
They blow to a live flame
To char the young green days
And reach the occult soul; they have no softer lure
No softer lure than the savage ways of death.

We were satisfied of our lords the moon and the sun
To take our wage of sleep and bread and warmth –
These maidens came – these strong ever-living Amazons,
And in an easy might their wrists
Of night's sway and noon's sway the sceptres brake,
Clouding the wild – the soft lustres of our eyes.
Clouding the wild lustres, the clinging tender lights;
Driving the darkness into the flame of day,
With the Amazonian wind of them
Over our corroding faces
That must be broken – broken for evermore
So the soul can leap out
Into their huge embraces.
Though there are human faces
Best sculptures of Deity,
And sinews lusted after
By the Archangels tall,
Even these must leap to the love heat of these maidens
From the flame of terrene days
Leaving grey ashes to the wind – to the wind.

One (whose great lifted face,
Where wisdom's strength and beauty's strength
And the thewed strength of large beasts
Moved and merged, gloomed and lit)
Was speaking, surely, as the earth-men's earth fell away;
Whose new hearing drunk the sound
Where pictures, lutes, and mountains mixed
With the loosed spirit of a thought.
Essenced to language, thus –

'My sisters force their males
From the doomed earth, from the doomed glee
And hankering of hearts.
Frail hands gleam up through the human quagmire and lips of
    ash
Seem to wail, as in sad faded paintings
Far sunken and strange.
My sisters have their males
Clean of the dust of old days
That clings about those white hands
And yearns in those voices sad.

But these shall not see them,
Or think of them in any days or years,
They are my sisters' lovers in other days and years.'

written 1917   ISAAC ROSENBERG

2.   Go on till you die

(112)   from *Denial*

If I should die – chatter only this:
'A bullet flew by that did not miss!'
I did not give life up because of a friend;
That bullet came thro', and that was the end!

. . .

1st published 1919   R. WATSON KERR

(113) *Outposts*

Sentry, sentry, what did you see
At gaze from your post beside Lone Tree?
A star-shell flared like a burning brand
But I saw no movement in No Man's Land.

Sentry, sentry, what did you hear
As the night-wind fluttered the grasses near?
I heard a rifle-shot on the flank,
And my mate slid down to the foot of the bank.

Sentry, sentry, what did you do,
And hadn't your mate a word for you?
I lifted his head and called his name.
His lips moved once, but no sound came.

Sentry, sentry, what did you say
As you watched alone till break of day?
I prayed the Lord that I'd fire straight
If I saw the man that killed my mate.

1st published 1918   F. W. D. BENDALL

(114) *Resolve*

Let me not think of blood to-night –
So doing
It will be harder still to fight:
Peace's wooing
Sucks blood making me white
And tremulous –
Thus, thus
I will harden yet my heart
Gaze into horror's face
Unafraid, without a trace
Of tenderness!

1st published 1919   R. WATSON KERR

(115)   Welcome Death

When you've been dead beat, and had to go on
While others died; when your turn to be gone
Is overdue; when you're pushed ahead
('Go on till you die' is all they said),
Then die – and you're glad to be dead!

written 1916   R. C. G. DARTFORD

(116)   Comrades in Arms

Not ours the zeal that passes with the years,
    The will too faint to battle with desire;
In the dim twilight-time of doubts and fears
    Our lips were singing and our eyes afire.

We have become a glory and a name,
    We who were weak, by this one faith made strong
That somewhere past the powder and the flame
    God is the arbiter of right and wrong.

And if beyond the day's long labour Death
    Stand in our path and shroud us in his pall,
Bartering honour for this wasted breath,
    Ah then! it were the greatest good of all,

Thus, with the last shot fired, the last fight over,
    The golden sunset fading in the sky,
To feel the night around us like a lover,
    And turn our face and smile to her, and die.

written 1917   P. H. B. LYON

(117) from *Midway*

. . . .

The coward cries, 'How long?'
But the brave man bides the hour.
The mills of God grind slow,
From a strange grain strange flour,
Yet the wise shall endure and know,
The strong shall be filled with power.
Forge the chains for the foe.

1st published 1919   GRIFFYTH FAIRFAX

(118) from *Sed Miles*

. . .

It's often said
You're a long time dead,
And the grey worms eat,
Through the nails of your feet,
Through the white of your thighs,
To the whites of your eyes;
You feel pretty cheap
As a drab little heap
Of powder and smell;
For a Fritz gas-shell
Leaves more behind
In the way of rind.

But when West you go,
It's nice to know
You've done your bit
In spite of it;
And Blighty's name
And Blighty's fame
Will find in your
Demise, manure,

To sprout and spread
Till English red
Is the favourite hue
For Bartholomew,

. . .

When West you go,
It's nice to know
You've done your bit
In spite of it.

written December 1916   A. E. TOMLINSON

(119) *Pro Patria Mori*

The shadows softly fall where they are sleeping,
The moonbeams dance
Upon their beds, and they are in God's keeping –
Somewhere in France.

Upon their graves the crimson poppies glory,
And cornflowers too,
White lilies to complete the floral story –
Red, white and blue,

For that they died . . . no clarion calls were blended,
No lifted lance
For each small share, – but just a journey ended –
Somewhere in France.

1st published 1919   RAYMOND HEYWOOD

(120) from *The Glory of War*

. . .

My sergeant-major's dead, killed as we entered the village;
You will not find his body tho' you look for it;
A shell burst on him, leaving his legs, strangely enough,
    untouched.
Happy man, he died for England;
Happy ones are they who die for England.

. . .

February 1918   H. F. CONSTANTINE

(121) *After the 'Offensive'*

This is the end of it, this the cold silence
Succeeding the violence
That rioted here.
This is the end of it – grim and austere.

This is the end of it – where the tide spread,
Runnels of blood
Débris of dead.
This is the end of it: ebb follows flood.

Waves of strong men
That will surge not again,
Scattered and riven
You lie, and you rot;
What have you not given?
And what – have you got?

1st published April 1919   THEO VAN BEEK

(122) Grotesque

These are the damned circles Dante trod,
Terrible in hopelessness,
But even skulls have their humour,
An eyeless and sardonic mockery:
And we,
Sitting with streaming eyes in the acrid smoke,
That murks our foul, damp billet,
Chant bitterly, with raucous voices
As a choir of frogs
In hideous irony, our patriotic songs.

1st published 1917   FREDERIC MANNING

(123) αὐτάρκεια

I am alone: even ranked with multitudes:
And they alone, each man.
                    So are we free.
For some few friends of me, some earth of mine,
Some shrines, some dreams I dream, some hopes that emerge
From the rude stone of life vaguely, and tend
Toward form in me: the progeny of dreams
I father; even this England which is mine
Whereof no man has seen the loveliness
As with mine eyes: and even too, my God
Whom none have known as I: for these I fight,
For mine own self, that thus in giving self
Prodigally, as a mere breath in the air,
I may possess myself, and spend me so
Mingling with earth, and dreams, and God: and being
In them the master of all these in me,
Perfected thus.
                    Fight for your own dreams, you.

1st published 1917   FREDERIC MANNING

3. To the Prussians of England

(124) Does it Matter?

Does it matter? – losing your legs? . . .
For people will always be kind,
And you need not show that you mind
When the others come in after hunting
To gobble their muffins and eggs.

Does it matter? – losing your sight? . . .
There's such splendid work for the blind;
And people will always be kind,
As you sit on the terrace remembering
And turning your face to the light.

Do they matter? – those dreams from the pit? . . .
You can drink and forget and be glad,
And people won't say that you're mad;
For they'll know you've fought for your country
And no one will worry a bit.

written July–October 1917   SIEGFRIED SASSOON

(125) Fight to a Finish

The boys came back. Bands played and flags were flying,
    And Yellow-Pressmen thronged the sunlit street
To cheer the soldiers who'd refrained from dying,
    And hear the music of returning feet.
'Of all the thrills and ardours War has brought,
This moment is the finest.' (So they thought.)

Snapping their bayonets on to charge the mob,
  Grim Fusiliers broke ranks with glint of steel,
At last the boys had found a cushy job.

. . . .

I heard the Yellow-Pressmen grunt and squeal;
And with my trusty bombers turned and went
To clear those Junkers out of Parliament.

written July–October 1917   SIEGFRIED SASSOON

(126)   *Remorse*

Lost in the swamp and welter of the pit,
He flounders off the duck-boards; only he knows
Each flash and spouting crash, – each instant lit
When gloom reveals the streaming rain. He goes
Heavily, blindly on. And, while he blunders,
'Could anything be worse than this?' – he wonders,
Remembering how he saw those Germans run,
Screaming for mercy among the stumps of trees:
Green-faced, they dodged and darted: there was one
Livid with terror, clutching at his knees . . .
Our chaps were sticking 'em like pigs . . . 'O hell!'
He thought – 'there's things in war one dare not tell
Poor father sitting safe at home, who reads
Of dying heroes and their deathless deeds.'

4 February 1918   SIEGFRIED SASSOON

(127)   *Dulce et Decorum Est*

Bent double, like old beggars under sacks,
Knock-kneed, coughing like hags, we cursed through sludge,
Till on the haunting flares we turned our backs
And towards our distant rest began to trudge.
Men marched asleep. Many had lost their boots
But limped on, blood-shod. All went lame; all blind;
Drunk with fatigue; deaf even to the hoots
Of tired, outstripped Five-Nines that dropped behind.

Gas! GAS! Quick, boys! – An ecstasy of fumbling,
Fitting the clumsy helmets just in time;
But someone still was yelling out and stumbling,
And flound'ring like a man in fire or lime . . .
Dim, through the misty panes and thick green light,
As under a green sea, I saw him drowning.

In all my dreams, before my helpless sight,
He plunges at me, guttering, choking, drowning.

If in some smothering dreams you too could pace
Behind the wagon that we flung him in,
And watch the white eyes writhing in his face,
His hanging face, like a devil's sick of sin;
If you could hear, at every jolt, the blood
Come gargling from the froth-corrupted lungs,
Obscene as cancer, bitter as the cud
Of vile, incurable sores on innocent tongues, –
My friend, you would not tell with such high zest
To children ardent for some desperate glory,
The old Lie: Dulce et decorum est
Pro patria mori.

written October 1917   WILFRED OWEN

(128)   War, the Liberator

(To the Authoress of 'Non-Combatants')

Surely War is vile to you, you who can but know of it,
Broken men and broken hearts, and boys too young to die,
You that never knew its joy, never felt the glow of it,
Valour and the pride of men, soaring to the sky.
Death's a fearful thing to you, terrible in suddenness,
Lips that will not laugh again, tongues that will not sing,
You that have not ever seen their sudden life of happiness,
The moment they looked down on death, a cowed and beaten
        thing.

Say what life would theirs have been, that it should make you
        weep for them,
A small grey world imprisoning the wings of their desire?
Happier than they could tell who knew not life would keep for
        them
Fragments of the high Romance, the old Heroic fire.
All they dreamed of childishly, bravery and fame for them,
Charges at the cannon's mouth, enemies they slew,
Bright across the waking world their romances came for them,
Is not life a little price when our dreams come true?

All the terrors of the night, doubts and thoughts tormenting
        us,
Boy-minds painting quiveringly the awful face of fear,
These are gone for ever now, truth is come contenting us,
Night with all its tricks is gone and our eyes are clear.
Now in all the time to come, memory will cover us,
Trenches that we did not lose, charges that we made,
Since a voice, when first we heard shells go shrilling over us,
Said within us, 'This is Death – and I am not afraid!'

Since we felt our spirits tower, smiling and contemptuous,
O'er the little frightened things, running to and fro,
Looked on Death and saw a slave blustering and
        presumptuous,
Daring vainly still to bring Man his master low.

Though we knew that at the last, he would have his lust of us,
Carelessly we braved his might, felt and knew not why
Something stronger than ourselves, moving in the dust of us,
Something in the Soul of Man still too great to die.

written October–November 1917   E. A. MACKINTOSH

(129)   The Modern Abraham

To Siegfried Sassoon

His purple fingers clutch a large cigar –
    Plump, mottled fingers, with a ring or two.
He rests back in his fat armchair. The war
    Has made this change in him. As he looks through
His cheque-book with a tragic look he sighs:
    'Disabled Soldiers' Fund' he reads afresh,
And through his meat-red face peer angry eyes –
    The spirit piercing through its mound of flesh.

They should not ask me to subscribe again!
    Consider me and all that I have done –
I've fought for Britain with my might and main;
    I make explosives – and I gave a son.
My factory, converted for the fight
    (I do not like to boast of what I've spent),
Now manufactures gas and dynamite,
    Which only pays me seventy per cent.
And if I had ten other sons to send
I'd make them serve my country to the end,
So all the neighbours should flock round and say:
    'Oh! look what Mr Abraham has done.
He loves his country in the elder way;
    Poor gentleman, he's lost another son!'

1917   OSBERT SITWELL

(130) The Diners

'It isn't good enough,' you said;
  'They send us out to face the flame
For these whose rotten souls are dead,
  These beasts who've sold themselves to shame.

'And must we fall, as others fell,
  And add our quota to the dust,
To royalise this house of hell,
  To keep ajar the doors of lust?'

You said, 'The powder on that face,
  Those sensual lips, that painted hair,
We fight to save them from disgrace,
  To keep such sacred honour fair.

'Her honour spotless must abide,
  Tho' God should hide his face from earth:
That flabby-finger'd man beside –
  I guess he knows her honour's worth!

'I guess the reptile understands
  What women are, when lights are dim
And men wear diamonds on their hands –
  And so she's sold herself to him!'

You ceased. I look'd around the hall,
  Above the music and the din
I thought I heard dead voices call
  While haunting, tortured eyes looked in.

Hull, September 1917   A. B. NORMAN

(131)   *To the Prussians of England*

When I remember plain heroic strength
And shining virtue shown by Ypres pools,
Then read the blither written by knaves for fools
In praise of English soldiers lying at length,
Who purely dream what England shall be made
Gloriously new, free of the old stains
By us, who pay the price that must be paid,
Will freeze all winter over Ypres plains.
Our silly dreams of peace you put aside
And brotherhood of man, for you will see
An armed mistress, braggart of the tide,
Her children slaves, under your mastery.
We'll have a word there too, and forge a knife,
Will cut the cancer threatens England's life.

written October 1917   IVOR GURNEY

4.   Greater love

(132)   *First Time In*

After the dread tales and red yarns of the Line
Anything might have come to us; but the divine
Afterglow brought us up to a Welsh colony
Hiding in sandbag ditches, whispering consolatory
Soft foreign things. Then we were taken in
To low huts candle-lit, shaded close by slitten
Oilsheets, and there the boys gave us kind welcome,
So that we looked out as from the edge of home,
Sang us Welsh things, and changed all former notions
To human hopeful things. And the next day's guns
Nor any line-pangs ever quite could blot out
That strangely beautiful entry to war's rout;
Candles they gave us, precious and shared over-rations –
Ulysses found little more in his wanderings without doubt.

'David of the White Rock', the 'Slumber Song' so soft, and
  that
Beautiful tune to which roguish words by Welsh pit boys
Are sung – but never more beautiful than there under the
  gun's noise.

written 1919–20   IVOR GURNEY

(133)   *To Sylvia*

Two months ago the skies were blue,
The fields were fresh and green,
And green the willow tree stood up,
With the lazy stream between.

Two months ago we sat and watched
The river drifting by –
And now – you're back at your work again
And here in a ditch I lie.

God knows – my dear – I did not want
To rise and leave you so,
But the dead men's hands were beckoning
And I knew that I must go.

The dead men's eyes were watching, lass,
Their lips were asking too,
We faced it out and payed the price –
Are we betrayed by you?

The days are long between, dear lass,
Before we meet again,
Long days of mud and work for me,
For you long care and pain.

But you'll forgive me yet, my dear,
Because of what you know,
I can look my dead friends in the face
As I couldn't two months ago.

20 October 1917   E. A. MACKINTOSH

(134)   'A man of mine'

A man of mine
                    lies on the wire.
It is death to fetch his soulless corpse.

A man of mine
                    lies on the wire;
And he will rot
And first his lips
The worms will eat.

It is not thus I would have him kiss'd
But with the warm passionate lips
Of his comrade here.

1st published 1919   HERBERT READ

(135)   Two Fusiliers

And have we done with War at last?
Well, we've been lucky devils both,
And there's no need of pledge or oath
To bind our lovely friendship fast,
By firmer stuff
Close bound enough.

By wire and wood and stake we're bound,
By Fricourt and by Festubert,
By whipping rain, by the sun's glare,
By all the misery and loud sound,
By a Spring day,
By Picard clay.

Show me the two so closely bound
As we, by the wet bond of blood,
By friendship, blossoming from mud,
By Death: we faced him, and we found
Beauty in Death,
In dead men breath.

1st published 1917   ROBERT GRAVES

(136) *Apologia Pro Poemate Meo*

I, too, saw God through mud, –
    The mud that cracked on cheeks when wretches smiled.
    War brought more glory to their eyes than blood,
    And gave their laughs more glee than shakes a child.

Merry it was to laugh there –
    Where death becomes absurd and life absurder.
    For power was on us as we slashed bones bare
    Not to feel sickness or remorse of murder.

I, too, have dropped off Fear –
    Behind the barrage, dead as my platoon,
    And sailed my spirit surging light and clear
    Past the entanglement where hopes lay strewn;

And witnessed exultation –
    Faces that used to curse me, scowl for scowl,
    Shine and lift up with passion of oblation,
    Seraphic for an hour; though they were foul.

I have made fellowships –
  Untold of happy lovers in old song.
  For love is not the binding of fair lips
  With the soft silk of eyes that look and long,

By Joy, whose ribbon slips, –
  But wound with war's hard wire whose stakes are strong;
  Bound with the bandage of the arm that drips;
  Knit in the webbing of the rifle-thong.

I have perceived much beauty
  In the hoarse oaths that kept our courage straight;
  Heard music in the silentness of duty;
  Found peace where shell-storms spouted reddest spate.

Nevertheless, except you share
  With them in hell the sorrowful dark of hell,
  Whose world is but the trembling of a flare
  And heaven but as the highway for a shell,

You shall not hear their mirth:
  You shall not come to think them well content
  By any jest of mine. These men are worth
  Your tears. You are not worth their merriment.

written November–December 1917   WILFRED OWEN

(137) *Greater Love*

Red lips are not so red
  As the stained stones kissed by the English dead.
Kindness of wooed and wooer
Seems shame to their love pure.
O Love, your eyes lose lure
  When I behold eyes blinded in my stead!

Your slender attitude
  Trembles not exquisite like limbs knife-skewed,
Rolling and rolling there
Where God seems not to care;
Till the fierce love they bear
  Cramps them in death's extreme decrepitude.

Your voice sings not so soft, –
  Though even as wind murmuring through raftered loft, –
Your dear voice is not dear,
Gentle, and evening clear,
As theirs whom none now hear,
  Now earth has stopped their piteous mouths that coughed.

Heart, you were never hot
  Nor large, nor full like hearts made great with shot;
And though your hand be pale,
Paler are all which trail
Your cross through flame and hail:
  Weep, you may weep, for you may touch them not.

written Winter 1917–18   WILFRED OWEN

(138) Banishment

I am banished from the patient men who fight.
They smote my heart to pity, built my pride.
Shoulder to aching shoulder, side by side,
They trudged away from life's broad wealds of light.
Their wrongs were mine; and ever in my sight
They went arrayed in honour. But they died, –
Not one by one: and mutinous I cried
To those who sent them out into the night.

The darkness tells how vainly I have striven
To free them from the pit where they must dwell
In outcast gloom convulsed and jagged and riven
By grappling guns. Love drove me to rebel.
Love drives me back to grope with them through hell;
And in their tortured eyes I stand forgiven.

written July–November 1917   SIEGFRIED SASSOON

(139)   At Senlis Once

O how comely it was and how reviving,
When with clay and with death no longer striving
     Down firm roads we came to houses
     With women chattering and green grass thriving.

Now though rains in a cataract descended,
We could glow, with our tribulation ended –
     Count not days, the present only
     Was thought of, how could it ever be expended?

Clad so cleanly, this remnant of poor wretches
Picked up life like the hens in orchard ditches,
     Gazed on the mill-sails, heard the church-bell,
     Found an honest glass all manner of riches.

How they crowded the barn with lusty laughter,
Hailed the pierrots and shook each shadowy rafter,
     Even could ridicule their own sufferings,
     Sang as though nothing but joy came after!

1st published 1925   EDMUND BLUNDEN

(140) Concert

These antique prostitutions –
I deplore my own vague cynicism,
Undressing with indifferent eyes each girl,
Seeing them naked on that paltry stage
Stared at by half a thousand lustful eyes.

These antique prostitutions –
Am I dead? Withered? Grown old?
That not the least flush of desire
Tinges my unmoved flesh,
And that instead of women's living bodies
I see dead men – you understand? – dead men
With sullen, dark red gashes
Luminous in a foul trench?

These antique prostitutions.

1st published 1919   RICHARD ALDINGTON

(141) Reserve

Though you desire me I will still feign sleep
And check my eyes from opening to the day,
For as I lie, thrilled by your dark gold flesh,
I think of how the dead, my dead, once lay.

1st published 1919   RICHARD ALDINGTON

(142)   The Secret

Suddenly with a shy, sad grace
She turns to me her lighted face,
And I who hear some idle phrase
  Watch how her wry lips move,
And guess that the poor words they frame
Mean nought, for they would speak the same
Message I read in the dark flame
  Within her eyes, which say,'I love.'
    But I can only turn away. . . .

I, that have heard the deep voice break
Into a sing-song sobbing shake,
Whose flutter made my being quake,
  What ears have I for women's cries?
I, that have seen the turquoise glaze
Fixed in the blue and quivering gaze
Of one whom cocaine cannot daze,
  How can I yield to woman's eyes?
    I, who can only turn away.

I, that have held strong hands which palter,
Borne the full weight of limbs that falter,
Bound live flesh on the surgeon's altar,
  What need have I of woman's hand?
I, that have felt the dead's embrace;
I, whose arms were his resting-place;
I, that have kissed a dead man's face;
  Ah, but how should you understand?
    Now I can only turn away.

Torquay, March 1918   ROBERT NICHOLS

Part VII: Poets and Poetry in Wartime

(143)   The Poets Are Waiting

To what God
Shall we chant
Our songs of Battle?

The professional poets
Are measuring their thoughts
For felicitous sonnets;
They try them and fit them
Like honest tailors
Cutting materials
For fashion-plate suits.

The unprofessional
Little singers,
Most intellectual,
Merry with gossip,
Heavy with cunning,
Whose tedious brains are draped
In sultry palls of hair,
Reclining as usual
On armchairs and sofas,
Are grinning and gossiping,
Cake at their elbows –
They will not write us verses for the time;
Their storms are brewed in teacups and their wars
Are fought in sneers or little blots of ink.

To what God
Shall we chant
Our songs of Battle?

154

Hefty barbarians,
Roaring for war,
Are breaking upon us;
Clouds of their cavalry,
Waves of their infantry,
Mountains of guns.
Winged they are coming,
Plated and mailed,
Snorting their jargon.
Oh, to whom shall a song of battle be chanted?
Not to our lord of the hosts on his ancient throne,
Drowsing the ages out in Heaven alone.
The celestial choirs are mute, the angels have fled:
Word is gone forth abroad that our lord is dead.

To what God
Shall we chant
Our songs of battle?

1st published December 1914   HAROLD MUNRO

(144) *Duty*

Give gladly, you rich – 'tis no more than you owe –
For the weal of your Country, your wealth's overflow!
Even I that am poor am performing my part;
I am giving my brain, I am giving my heart.

1st published August 1914   WILLIAM WATSON

(145) On Being Asked for a War Poem

I think it better that in times like these
A poet's mouth be silent, for in truth
We have no gift to set a statesman right;
He has had enough of meddling who can please
A young girl in the indolence of her youth,
Or an old man upon a winter's night.

written February 1915   W. B. YEATS

(146) 'When you see millions of the mouthless dead'

When you see millions of the mouthless dead
Across your dreams in pale battalions go,
Say not soft things as other men have said,
That you'll remember. For you need not so.
Give them not praise. For, deaf, how should they know
It is not curses heaped on each gashed head?
Nor tears. Their blind eyes see not your tears flow.
Nor honour. It is easy to be dead.
Say only this, 'They are dead.' Then add thereto,
'Yet many a better one has died before.'
Then, scanning all the o'ercrowded mass, should you
Perceive one face that you loved heretofore,
It is a spook. None wears the face you knew.
Great death has made all his for evermore.

written 1915   CHARLES SORLEY

(147)   Our Soldier Poets

Strength for the struggle,
O Muses!
And courage your wooings afford:

He is splendid in conflict
Who chooses
Song for companion to sword.

1st published 1917   EGBERT SANDFORD

(148)   The Soldier–Poets

O men, the doubly armed and dear of name,
Take your promotion in the ranks of Fame!
Splendid with swords you were; but with a rhyme
You dulled Death's razor-edge, and conquered Time.

Hush, mere Menologist, while men rehearse
The living word in Julian Grenfell's verse;
See Mackintosh on metred feet still stride;
Tennant (the Muse's Cavalry) yet ride
A Pegasus shall one day clear the Rhine;
See Hodgson stand, the master of the Line;
Hear Gerald Caldwell, silenced like the rest,
But not the 'immortal birds' within his breast.
These sought the field like Brooke: who died upon it
And yet lives ever in an English sonnet.

Mere bullets take mere bodies – tragic tolls!
Your arrowy words fill armouries for souls.

1st published 1918   WILFRID MEYNELL

(149)   God! How I Hate You, You Young Cheerful Men

On a University Undergraduate moved to verse by the war.

God! How I hate you, you young cheerful men,
Whose pious poetry blossoms on your graves
As soon as you are in them, nurtured up
By the salt of your corruption, and the tears
Of mothers, local vicars, college deans,
And flanked by prefaces and photographs
From all your minor poet friends – the fools –
Who paint their sentimental elegies
Where sure, no angel treads; and, living, share
The dead's brief immortality.
                                        Oh Christ!
To think that one could spread the ductile wax
Of his fluid youth to Oxford's glowing fires
And take her seal so ill! Hark how one chants –
'Oh happy to have lived these epic days' –
'These epic days'! And *he'd* been to France,
And seen the trenches, glimpsed the huddled dead
In the periscope, hung in the rusting wire:
Choked by their sickly fœtor, day and night
Blown down his throat: stumbled through ruined hearths,
Proved all that muddy brown monotony,
Where blood's the only coloured thing. Perhaps
Had seen a man killed, a sentry shot at night,
Hunched as he fell, his feet on the firing-step,
His neck against the back slope of the trench,
And the rest doubled up between, his head
Smashed like an egg-shell, and the warm grey brain
Spattered all bloody on the parados:
Had flashed a torch on his face, and known his friend,
Shot, breathing hardly, in ten minutes – gone!
Yet still God's in His heaven, all is right
In the best possible of worlds. The woe,
Even His scaled eyes *must* see, is partial, only
A seeming woe, we cannot understand.
God loves us, God looks down on this our strife
And smiles in pity, blows a pipe at times
And calls some warriors home. We do not die,
God would not let us, He is too 'intense',

Too 'passionate', a whole day sorrows He
Because a grass-blade dies. How rare life is!
On earth, the love and fellowship of men,
Men sternly banded: banded for what end?
Banded to maim and kill their fellow men –
For even Huns are men. In heaven above
A genial umpire, a good judge of sport,
Won't let us hurt each other! Let's rejoice
God keeps us faithful, pens us still in fold.
Ah, what a faith is ours (almost, it seems,
Large as a mustard-seed) – we trust and trust,
Nothing can shake us! Ah, how good God is
To suffer us be born just now, when youth
That else would rust, can slake his blade in gore,
Where very God Himself does seem to walk
The bloody fields of Flanders He so loves!

written 1916   ARTHUR GRAEME WEST

(150)   The Poet as Hero

You've heard me, scornful, harsh, and discontented,
    Mocking and loathing War: you've asked me why
Of my old, silly sweetness I've repented –
    My ecstasies changed to an ugly cry.

You are aware that once I sought the Grail,
    Riding in armour bright, serene and strong;
And it was told that through my infant wail
    There rose immortal semblances of song.

But now I've said good-bye to Galahad,
    And am no more the knight of dreams and show:
For lust and senseless hatred make me glad,
    And my killed friends are with me where I go.
Wound for red wound I burn to smite their wrongs;
And there is absolution in my songs.

1st published December 1916   SIEGFRIED SASSOON

(151)   from *Rhapsode*

Why should we sing to you of little things –
You who lack all imagination?

. . .

You hope that we shall tell you that they found their happiness
    in fighting,
Or that they died with a song on their lips,
Or that we shall use the old familiar phrases
With which your paid servants please you in the Press:
But we are poets,
And shall tell the truth.

September 1917   OSBERT SITWELL

(152)   *Insensibility*

I

Happy are men who yet before they are killed
Can let their veins run cold.
Whom no compassion fleers
Or makes their feet
Sore on the alleys cobbled with their brothers.
The front line withers.
But they are troops who fade, not flowers,
For poets' tearful fooling:
Men, gaps for filling:
Losses, who might have fought
Longer; but no one bothers.

II

And some cease feeling
Even themselves or for themselves.
Dullness best solves
The tease and doubt of shelling,
And Chance's strange arithmetic
Comes simpler than the reckoning of their shilling.
They keep no check on armies' decimation.

III

Happy are these who lose imagination:
They have enough to carry with ammunition.
Their spirit drags no pack.
Their old wounds, save with cold, can not more ache.
Having seen all things red,
Their eyes are rid
Of the hurt of the colour of blood for ever.
And terror's first constriction over,
Their hearts remain small-drawn.
Their senses in some scorching cautery of battle
Now long since ironed,
Can laugh among the dying, unconcerned.

IV

Happy the soldier home, with not a notion
How somewhere, every dawn, some men attack,
And many sighs are drained.
Happy the lad whose mind was never trained:
His days are worth forgetting more than not.
He sings along the march
Which we march taciturn, because of dusk,
The long, forlorn, relentless trend
From larger day to huger night.

V

We wise, who with a thought besmirch
Blood over all our soul,
How should we see our task
But through his blunt and lashless eyes?

Alive, he is not vital overmuch;
Dying, not mortal overmuch;
Nor sad, nor proud,
Nor curious at all.
He cannot tell
Old men's placidity from his.

VI

But cursed are dullards whom no cannon stuns,
That they should be as stones.
Wretched are they, and mean
With paucity that never was simplicity.
By choice they made themselves immune
To pity and whatever moans in man
Before the last sea and the hapless stars;
Whatever mourns when many leave these shores;
Whatever shares
The eternal reciprocity of tears.

written Winter 1917–18   WILFRED OWEN

(153)   The Romancing Poet

Granted that you write verse,
Much better verse than I,
(Which isn't saying much!)
I wish you would refrain
From making glad romance
Of this most hideous war.
It has no glamour,
    Save man's courage,
    His indomitable spirit,
    His forgetfulness of self!
If you have words –
    Fit words, I mean,

Not your usual stock-in-trade,
  Of tags and *clichés* –
To hymn such greatness,
    Use them.
    But have you?
    Anyone can babble.
If you must wax descriptive,
Do get the background right,
    A little right!
The blood, the filth, the horrors,
Suffering on such a scale,
That you and I, try as we may,
    Can only faintly vision it.
Don't make a pretty song about it!
    It is an insult to the men,
      Doomed to be crucified each day,
      For us at home!
Abstain too, if you can,
From bidding us to plume ourselves
For being of the self-same breed
    As these heroic souls,
With the obvious implication,
We have the right to take the credit,
    Vicarious credit,
    For their immortal deeds!
    What next?
    It is an outrage!
    We are not glory-snatchers!

written April 1918   HELEN HAMILTON

(154)   from *The Other Side*

Being a letter from Major Average of the Royal Field Artillery in Flanders,
acknowledging a presentation copy of a book of war-verse, written by a
former subaltern of his battery – now in England.

The Barn 31/10/17

. . .

Lord, if I'd half *your* brains, I'd write a book:
None of your sentimental platitudes,

But something real, vital; that should strip
The glamour from this outrage we call war,
Shewing it naked, hideous, stupid, vile –
One vast abomination. So that they
Who, coming after, till the ransomed fields
Where our lean corpses rotted in the ooze,
Reading my written words, should understand
This stark stupendous horror, visualize
The unutterable foulness of it all. . . .
I'd shew them, not your glamourous 'glorious game',
Which men play 'jesting' 'for their honour's sake' –
(A kind of Military Tournament,
With just a hint of danger – bound in cloth!) –
But War, – as war is now, and always was:
A dirty, loathsome, servile murder-job: –
Men, lousy, sleepless, ulcerous, afraid,
Toiling their hearts out in the pulling slime
That wrenches gum-boot down from bleeding heel
And cakes in itching arm-pits, navel, ears:
Men stunned to brainlessness, and gibbering:
Men driving men to death and worse than death:
Men maimed and blinded: men against machines –
Flesh versus iron, concrete, flame and wire:
Men choking out their souls in poison-gas:
Men squelched into the slime by trampling feet:
Men, disembowelled by guns five miles away,
Cursing, with their last breath, the living God
Because he made them, in His image, men. . . .
So – were your talent mine – I'd write of war
For those who, coming after, know it not.

And if posterity should ask of me
What high, what base emotions keyed weak flesh
To face such torments, I would answer: '*You!*
Not for themselves, O daughters, grandsons, sons,
Your tortured forebears wrought this miracle;
Not for themselves, *accomplished utterly*
This loathliest task of murderous servitude;

But just because they realized that thus,
And only thus, by sacrifice, might they
Secure a world worth living in – *for you.*' . . .

Good-night, my soldier-poet. *Dormez bien!*

1st published March 1918   GILBERT FRANKAU

(155) Strange Meeting

It seemed that out of battle I escaped
Down some profound dull tunnel, long since scooped
Through granites which titanic wars had groined.

Yet also there encumbered sleepers groaned,
Too fast in thought or death to be bestirred.
Then, as I probed them, one sprang up, and stared
With piteous recognition in fixed eyes,
Lifting distressful hands, as if to bless.
And by his smile, I knew that sullen hall, –
By his dead smile I knew we stood in Hell.

With a thousand pains that vision's face was grained;
Yet no blood reached there from the upper ground,
And no guns thumped, or down the flues made moan.
'Strange friend,' I said, 'here is no cause to mourn.'
'None,' said that other, 'save the undone years,
The hopelessness. Whatever hope is yours,
Was my life also; I went hunting wild
After the wildest beauty in the world,
Which lies not calm in eyes, or braided hair,
But mocks the steady running of the hour,
And if it grieves, grieves richlier than here.
For by my glee might many men have laughed,
And of my weeping something had been left,
Which must die now. I mean the truth untold,
The pity of war, the pity war distilled.
Now men will go content with what we spoiled,
Or, discontent, boil bloody, and be spilled.

They will be swift with swiftness of the tigress.
None will break ranks, though nations trek from progress.
Courage was mine, and I had mystery,
Wisdom was mine, and I had mastery:
To miss the march of this retreating world
Into vain citadels that are not walled.
Then, when much blood had clogged their chariot-wheels,
I would go up and wash them from sweet wells,
Even with truths that lie too deep for taint.
I would have poured my spirit without stint
But not through wounds; not on the cess of war.
Foreheads of men have bled where no wounds were.

I am the enemy you killed, my friend.
I knew you in this dark: for so you frowned
Yesterday through me as you jabbed and killed.
I parried; but my hands were loath and cold.
Let us sleep now. . . .'

written Spring 1918   WILFRED OWEN

(156) *Testament*

For the last time I say – War is not glorious,
Though lads march out superb and fall victorious, –
Scrapping like demons, suffering like slaves,
And crowned by peace, the sunlight on their graves.

You swear we crush The Beast: I say we fight
Because men lost their landmarks in the night,
And met in gloom to grapple, stab, and kill,
Yelling the fetish-names of Good and Ill
That have been shamed in history.
                                   O my heart,
Be still; you have cried your cry; you have played your part.

written May 1918   SIEGFRIED SASSOON

Part VIII: 1918 and After

1.   Morning heroes

(157)   *Gouzeaucourt: The Deceitful Calm*

How unpurposed, how inconsequential
Seemed those southern lines when in the pallor
   Of the dying winter
   First we went there!

Grass thin-waving in the wind approached them,
Red roofs in the near view feigned survival,
   Lovely mockers, when we
   There took over.

There war's holiday seemed, nor though at known times
Gusts of flame and jingling steel descended
   On the bare tracks, would you
   Picture death there.

Snow or rime-frost made a solemn silence,
Bluish darkness wrapped in dangerous safety;
   Old hands thought of tidy
   Living-trenches!

There it was, my dears, that I departed,
Scarce a plainer traitor ever! There too
   Many of you soon paid for
   That false mildness.

1st published 1928   EDMUND BLUNDEN

167

(158)　À Outrance

21 March 1918

The foe has flung his gage,
　His hands clutch at the spoil,
Not ours his wrath to assuage,
　Not ours his sins to assoil.
His challenge must be met,
　His haughtiness brought low.
On guard! The lists are set.
　Stand fast! The trumpets blow.

So stand that none shall flinch
　From the last sacrifice,
A life for every inch,
　For every yard its price.
See – our twin banners dance,
　Linked till the long day's close –
The Fleur-de-lis of France
　Beside the English Rose.

With these to guard her gates
　Against the foeman's power,
Undaunted, Freedom waits
　The issue of the hour.
Her knights are in the field,
　His blade each warrior draws.
Their pride – a stainless shield –
　Their strength – a righteous cause.

1st published 1918　　　　　　　　　　F. W. D. BENDALL

(159)　'The Soul of a Nation'

The little things of which we lately chattered –
　The dearth of taxis or the dawn of spring;
Themes we discussed as though they really mattered,
　Like rationed meat or raiders on the wing; –

How thin it seems to-day, this vacant prattle,
  Drowned by the thunder rolling in the West,
Voice of the great arbitrament of battle
  That puts our temper to the final test.

Thither our eyes are turned, our hearts are straining,
  Where those we love, whose courage laughs at fear,
Amid the storm of steel around them raining,
  Go to their death for all we hold most dear.

New-born of this supremest hour of trial,
  In quiet confidence shall be our strength,
Fixed on a faith that will not take denial
  Nor doubt that we have found our soul at length.

O England, staunch of nerve and strong of sinew,
  Best when you face the odds and stand at bay,
Now show a watching world what stuff is in you!
  Now make your soldiers proud of you to-day!

28 March 1918   OWEN SEAMAN

(160) *In the Gallery Where the Fat Men Go*

('GREAT PICTURES OF THE SOMME OFFENSIVE, DAY BY DAY.
THE ACTUAL FIGHTING.')

See Omnibus and Underground Notices, April 1918

> They are showing how we lie
> With our bodies run dry:
> The attitudes we take
> When impaled upon a stake.
> These and other things they show
> In the gallery where the fat men go.

In the gallery where the fat men go
They're exhibiting our guts
Horse-betrampled in the ruts;
And Private Tommy Spout,
With his eye gouged out;
And Jimmy spitting blood;
And Sergeant lying so
That he's drowning in the mud,
In the gallery where the fat men go.

They adjust their pince-nez
In the gentle urban way,
And they plant their feet tight
For to get a clearer sight.
They stand playing with their thumbs,
With their shaven cheeks aglow,
For the terror never comes,
And the worms and the woe.
For they never hear the drums
Drumming Death dead-slow,
In the gallery where the fat men go.

If the gallery where the fat men go
Were in flames around their feet,
Or were sucking through the mud:
If they heard the guns beat
Like a pulse through the blood:
If the lice were in their hair,
And the scabs were on their tongue,
And the rats were smiling there,
Padding softly through the dung,
Would they fix the pince-nez
In the gentle urban way,
Would the pictures still be hung
In the gallery where the fat men go?

1st published May 1918   LOUIS GOLDING

(161) The Send-Off

Down the close darkening lanes they sang their way
To the siding-shed,
And lined the train with faces grimly gay.

Their breasts were stuck all white with wreath and spray
As men's are, dead.

Dull porters watched them, and a casual tramp
Stood staring hard,
Sorry to miss them from the upland camp.

Then, unmoved, signals nodded, and a lamp
Winked to the guard.

So secretly, like wrongs hushed-up, they went.
They were not ours:
We never heard to which front these were sent;

Nor there if they yet mock what women meant
Who gave them flowers.

Shall they return to beating of great bells
In wild train-loads?
A few, a few, too few for drums and yells,

May creep back, silent, to village wells,
Up half-known roads.

written April–May 1918   WILFRED OWEN

(162)   *Dawn on the Somme*

Last night rain fell over the scarred plateau,
And now from the dark horizon, dazzling, flies
Arrow on fire-plumed arrow to the skies,
Shot from the bright arc of Apollo's bow;
And from the wild and writhen waste below,
From flashing pools and mounds lit one by one,
Oh, is it mist, or are these companies
Of morning heroes who arise, arise
With thrusting arms, with limbs and hair aglow,
Toward the risen god, upon whose brow
Burns the gold laurel of all victories,
Hero and heroes' god, th' invincible Sun?

late Spring 1918   ROBERT NICHOLS

(163)   *Reward*

Months and weeks and days go past,
And my soldiers fall at last.
Months and weeks and days
Their ways must be my ways.
And evermore
Love guards the door.

From their eyes the gift I gain
Of grace that can subdue my pain:
From their eyes I hoard
My reward. . . .
O brothers in my striving, it were best
That I should share your rest.

5 June 1918   SIEGFRIED SASSOON

(164) *Haig is Moving*

August 1918

Haig is moving!
Three plain words are all that matter,
Mid the gossip and the chatter,
Hopes in speeches, fears in papers,
Pessimistic froth and vapours –
Haig is moving!

Haig is moving!
We can turn from German scheming,
From humanitarian dreaming,
From assertions, contradictions,
Twisted facts and solemn fictions –
Haig is moving!

Haig is moving!
All the weary idle phrases,
Empty blamings, empty praises,
Here's an end to their recital,
There is only one thing vital –
Haig is moving!

Haig is moving!
He is moving, he is gaining,
And the whole hushed world is straining,
Straining, yearning, for the vision
Of the doom and the decision –
Haig is moving!

1st published 1919   ARTHUR CONAN DOYLE

(165)   *Spring Offensive*

Halted against the shade of a last hill
They fed, and eased of pack-loads, were at ease;
And leaning on the nearest chest or knees
Carelessly slept.
          But many there stood still
To face the stark blank sky beyond the ridge,
Knowing their feet had come to the end of the world.
Marvelling they stood, and watched the long grass swirled
By the May breeze, murmurous with wasp and midge;
And though the summer oozed into their veins
Like an injected drug for their bodies' pains,
Sharp on their souls hung the imminent ridge of grass,
Fearfully flashed the sky's mysterious glass.

Hour after hour they ponder the warm field
And the far valley behind, where buttercups
Had blessed with gold their slow boots coming up;
When even the little brambles would not yield
But clutched and clung to them like sorrowing arms.
They breathe like trees unstirred.

Till like a cold gust thrills the little word
At which each body and its soul begird
And tighten them for battle. No alarms
Of bugles, no high flags, no clamorous haste, –
Only a lift and flare of eyes that faced
The sun, like a friend with whom their love is done.
O larger shone that smile against the sun, –
Mightier than his whose bounty these have spurned.

So, soon they topped the hill, and raced together
Over an open stretch of herb and heather
Exposed. And instantly the whole sky burned
With fury against them; earth set sudden cups
In thousands for their blood; and the green slope
Chasmed and deepened sheer to infinite space.

Of them who running on that last high place
Breasted the surf of bullets, or went up
On the hot blast and fury of hell's upsurge,
Or plunged and fell away past this world's verge,
Some say God caught them even before they fell.

But what say such as from existence' brink
Ventured but drave too swift to sink,
The few who rushed in the body to enter hell,
And there out-fiending all its fiends and flames
With superhuman inhumanities,
Long-famous glories, immemorial shames –
And crawling slowly back, have by degrees
Regained cool peaceful air in wonder –
Why speak not they of comrades that went under?

written Summer–September 1918   WILFRED OWEN

(166) Justice

October 1918

Across a world where all men grieve
  And grieving strive the more,
The great days range like tides and leave
  Our dead on every shore.
Heavy the load we undergo,
  And our own hands prepare,
If we have parley with the foe,
  The load our sons must bear.

Before we loose the word
  That bids new worlds to birth,
Needs must we loosen first the sword
  Of Justice upon earth;
Or else all else is vain
  Since life on earth began,
And the spent world sinks back again
  Hopeless of God and Man.

A people and their King
  Through ancient sin grown strong,
Because they feared no reckoning
  Would set no bound to wrong;

But now their hour is past,
　　And we who bore it find
Evil Incarnate held at last
　　To answer to mankind.

For agony and spoil
　　Of nations beat to dust,
For poisoned air and tortured soil
　　And cold, commanded lust,
And every secret woe
　　The shuddering waters saw –
Willed and fulfilled by high and low –
　　Let them relearn the Law.

That when the dooms are read,
　　Not high nor low shall say: –
'My haughty or my humble head
　　Has saved me in this day.'
That, till the end of time,
　　Their remnant shall recall
Their fathers' old, confederate crime
　　Availed them not at all.

That neither schools nor priests,
　　Nor Kings may build again
A people with the heart of beasts
　　Made wise concerning men.
Whereby our dead shall sleep
　　In honour, unbetrayed,
And we in faith and honour keep
　　That peace for which they paid.

1st published October 1918　　　　　　**RUDYARD KIPLING**

2.   Peace

(167)   Victory

Finished – this body's agony, soul's strain,
Forced wrong of man to man – can these be finished,
And beauty keep the dying woods again,
And peace at sundown be no more diminished?
Where are those ghastly shapes, hatred and fear,
Cruelty and lust, that even our great-hearted
Have armed as comrades many a dreadful year?
Were they but dreams, thus utterly departed?

Dreams were they, and are gone. And gone youth's glamour,
And gone is questing youth from countless houses.
O you in England, hark to the bells' clamour,
And hear them ask (those dead), if victory rouses
Grief alone, and say: Remembering you
Our love and labour shall make earth anew.

On the march in Belgium,
11 November 1918   GEOFFREY FABER

(168)   Paris, November 11, 1918

For G. A. H.

Down on the boulevards the crowds went by,
The shouting and the singing died away,
And in the quiet we rose to drink the toasts,
Our hearts uplifted to the hour, the Day:
The King – the Army – Navy – the Allies –
England – and Victory. –

And then you turned to me and with low voice
(The tables were abuzz with revelry),
'I have a toast for you and me', you said,
And whispered 'Absent', and we drank
Our unforgotten Dead.
But I saw Love go lonely down the years,
And when I drank, the wine was salt with tears.

1st published 1919   MAY WEDDERBURN CANNAN

(169) Envoie

How shall I say good-bye to you, wonderful, terrible days,
If I should live to live and leave 'neath an alien soil
You, my men, who taught me to walk with a smile in the ways
Of the valley of shadows, taught me to know you and love
        you, and toil
Glad in the glory of fellowship, happy in misery, strong
In the strength that laughs at its weakness, laughs at its
        sorrows and fears,
Facing the world that was not too kind with a jest and a song?
What can the world hold afterwards worthy of laughter or
        tears?

1st published 1919   EDWARD DE STEIN

(170) Everyone Sang

Everyone suddenly burst out singing;
And I was filled with such delight
As prisoned birds must find in freedom,
Winging wildly across the white
Orchards and dark-green fields; on – on – and out of sight.

Everyone's voice was suddenly lifted;
And beauty came like the setting sun:
My heart was shaken with tears; and horror
Drifted away . . . O, but Everyone
Was a bird; and the song was wordless; the singing will never
  be done.

written April 1919   SIEGFRIED SASSOON

(171)   *Ambulance Train 30*

A. T. 30 lies in the siding.
Above her cold grey clouds lie, silver-long as she.
Like a great battleship that never saw defeat
She dreams: while the pale day dies down
Behind the harbour town,
Beautiful, complete
And unimpassioned as the long grey sea.

A. T. 30 lies in the siding.
Gone are her red crosses – the sick that were her own.
Like a great battleship that never saw defeat
She waits, while the pale day dies down
Behind the harbour town,
Beautiful, complete. . . .
And the Occupying Army boards her for Cologne.

1st published May 1919   CAROLA OMAN

3.   Men you've forgotten

(172)   from *Any Soldier to His Son*

What did I do, sonny, in the Great World War? –
Well, I learned to peel potatoes and to scrub the barrack floor.

. . .

So I learned to live and lump-it in the lovely land of war,
Where all the face of nature seems a monstrous septic sore,
Where the bowels of earth hang open, like the guts of
        something slain,
And the rot and wreck of everything are churned and churned
        again;
Where all is done in darkness and where all is still in day,
Where living men are buried and the dead unburied lay;
Where men inhabit holes like rats, and only rats live there
Where cottage stood and castle once in days before La Guerre;
Where endless files of soldiers thread the everlasting way,
By endless miles of duckboards, through endless walls of clay;
Where life is one hard labour, and a soldier gets his rest
When they leave him in the daisies with a puncture in his
        chest;
Where still the lark in summer pours her warble from the
        skies,
And underneath, unheeding, lie the blank, upstaring eyes.

And I read the Blighty papers, where the warriors of the pen
Tell of 'Christmas in the Trenches' and 'The Spirit of our
        Men';
And I saved the choicest morsels and I read them to my chum,
And he muttered, as he cracked a louse and wiped it off his
        thumb:
'May a thousand chats from Belgium crawl their fingers as
        they write;
May they dream they're not exempted till they faint with
        mortal fright;
May the fattest rats in Dickebusch race over them in bed;
May the lies they've written choke them like a gas cloud till
        they're dead;

May the horror and the torture and the things they never tell
(For they only write to order) be reserved for them in Hell!'

You'd like to be a soldier and go to France some day?
By all the dead in Delville Wood, by all the nights I lay
Between our line and Fritz's before they brought me in;
By this old wood-and-leather stump, that once was flesh and
    skin:
By all the lads who crossed with me but never crossed again,
By all the prayers their mothers and their sweethearts prayed
    in vain,
Before the things that were that day should ever more befall
May God in common pity destroy us one and all!

1st published November 1918   GEORGE WILLIS

(173) Memorial Tablet

(Great War)

Squire nagged and bullied till I went to fight,
(Under Lord Derby's Scheme). I died in hell –
(They called it Passchendaele). My wound was slight,
And I was hobbling back; and then a shell
Burst slick upon the duck-boards: so I fell
Into the bottomless mud, and lost the light.

At sermon-time, while Squire is in his pew,
He gives my gilded name a thoughtful stare;
For, though low down upon the list, I'm there;
'*In proud and glorious memory*' . . . that's my due.
Two bleeding years I fought in France, for Squire:
I suffered anguish that he's never guessed.
Once I came home on leave: and then went west . . .
What greater glory could a man desire?

November 1918   SIEGFRIED SASSOON

(174) Haunted

Gulp down your wine, old friends of mine,
Roar through the darkness, stamp and sing
And lay ghost hands on everything,
But leave the noonday's warm sunshine
To living lads for mirth and wine.

I met you suddenly down the street,
Strangers assume your phantom faces,
You grin at me from daylight places,
Dead, long dead, I'm ashamed to greet
Dead men down the morning street.

1st published 1920   ROBERT GRAVES

(175) War and Peace

In sodden trenches I have heard men speak,
Though numb and wretched, wise and witty things;
And loved them for the stubbornness that clings
Longest to laughter when Death's pulleys creak;

And seeing cool nurses move on tireless feet
To do abominable things with grace,
Deemed them sweet sisters in that haunted place
Where, with child's voices, strong men howl or bleat.

Yet now those men lay stubborn courage by,
Riding dull-eyed and silent in the train
To old men's stools; or sell gay-coloured socks
And listen fearfully for Death; so I
Love the low-laughing girls, who now again
Go daintily, in thin and flowery frocks.

1st published 1921   EDGELL RICKWORD

(176)   Mist on Meadows

Mist lies heavy on English meadows
As ever on Ypres, but the friendliness
Here is greater in full field and hedge shadows,
And there is less menace and no dreadfulness
As when the Verey lights went up to show the land stark.
Dreadful green light baring the ruined trees,
Stakes, pools, lostness, better hidden dreadful in dark
And not ever reminding of these other fields
Where tall dock and clover is, and this sweet grass yields
For that poisoned, where the cattle hoof makes mark,
And the river mist drifts slowly along the leas.

But they honour not – and salute not those boys who saw a
    terror
Of waste, endured horror, and were not fearer
Before the barrages like Heaven's anger wanton known –
Feared not and saw great earth spouts in terror thrown,
But could not guess, but could not guess, alas!
How England should take as common their vast endurance
And let them be but boys having served time overseas.

written 1919–22   IVOR GURNEY

(177)   Elegy in a Country Churchyard

The men that worked for England
They have their graves at home:
And bees and birds of England
About the cross can roam.

But they that fought for England,
Following a falling star,
Alas, alas for England
They have their graves afar.

And they that rule in England,
In stately conclave met,
Alas, alas for England
They have no graves as yet.

1st published 1922   G. K. CHESTERTON

(178) 'And There Was a Great Calm'

(On the Signing of the Armistice, 11 Nov. 1918)

There had been years of Passion – scorching, cold,
And much Despair, and Anger heaving high,
Care whitely watching, Sorrows manifold,
Among the young, among the weak and old,
And the pensive Spirit of Pity whispered, 'Why?'

Men had not paused to answer. Foes distraught
Pierced the thinned peoples in a brute-like blindness,
Philosophies that sages long had taught,
And Selflessness, were as an unknown thought,
And 'Hell!' and 'Shell!' were yapped at Lovingkindness.

The feeble folk at home had grown full-used
To 'dug-outs', 'snipers', 'Huns', from the war-adept
In the mornings heard, and at evetides perused;
To day-dreamt men in millions, when they mused –
To nightmare-men in millions when they slept.

Waking to wish existence timeless, null,
Sirius they watched above where armies fell;
He seemed to check his flapping when, in the lull
Of night a boom came thencewise, like the dull
Plunge of a stone dropped into some deep well.

So, when old hopes that earth was bettering slowly
Were dead and damned, there sounded, 'War is done!'
One morrow. Said the bereft, and meek, and lowly,
'Will men some day be given to grace? yea, wholly,
And in good sooth, as our dreams used to run?'

Breathless they paused. Out there men raised their glance
To where had stood those poplars lank and lopped,
As they had raised it through the four years' dance
Of Death in the now familiar flats of France;
And murmured, 'Strange, this! How? All firing stopped?'

Aye; all was hushed. The about-to-fire fired not,
The aimed-at moved away in trance-lipped song.
One checkless regiment slung a clinching shot
And turned. The Spirit of Irony smirked out, 'What?
Spoil peradventures woven of Rage and Wrong?'

Thenceforth no flying fires inflamed the gray,
No hurtlings shook the dewdrop from the thorn,
No moan perplexed the mute bird on the spray;
Worn horses mused: 'We are not whipped to-day;'
No weft-winged engines blurred the moon's thin horn.

Calm fell. From Heaven distilled a clemency;
There was peace on earth, and silence in the sky;
Some could, some could not, shake off misery:
The Sinister Spirit sneered: 'It had to be!'
And again the Spirit of Pity whispered, 'Why?'

1st published 11 November 1920   THOMAS HARDY

(179) *My People*

Because through five red years of war most ruthless,
    Armed in a quarrel they most surely did not seek,
Challenged in their honour and slandered by the truthless
    My people made them strong to help the weak;

Because where still unbroken, perfect in devotion,
    Faithful to the last man, the old first army died,
Thousands after thousands from home and over ocean
    Inherited the spirit of their pride;

Because when their foeman in his fleeting triumph vaunted,
    Prisoned in the pest-camp or frozen where they bled,
Cowed by no disaster, starved but still undaunted,
    My people never flinched nor bowed the head;

Because men rough and simple but great of heart and tender,
    Kindly to each other though rude of speech and free,
Fronted hell well knowing for us was no surrender
    And grimly held their backs towards the sea;

Because the mould that shaped them failed not at the casting,
    And steadfast as their own oaks endured the island-bred;
Love be their portion and their glory everlasting,
    And Britain, keep us worthy of thy dead!

1st published 1923   RENNELL RODD

(180) *Armistice Day, 1921*

The hush begins. Nothing is heard
Save the arrested taxis throbbing
And here and there an ignorant bird
And here a sentimental woman sobbing.

The statesman bares and bows his head
Before the solemn monument:
His lips, paying duty to the dead
In silence, are more than ever eloquent.

But ere the sacred silence breaks
And taxis hurry on again,
A faint and distant voice awakes,
Speaking the mind of a million absent men:

'Mourn not for us. Our better luck
At least has given us peace and rest.
We struggled when our moment struck
But now we understand that death knew best.

'Would we be as our brothers are
Whose barrel-organs charm the town?
Ours was a better dodge by far –
We got *our* pensions in a lump sum down.

'We, out of all, have had our pay,
There is no poverty where we lie:
The graveyard has no quarter-day,
The space is narrow but the rent not high.

'No empty stomach here is found:
Unless some cheated worm complain
You hear no grumbling underground:
Oh, never, never wish us back again!

'Mourn not for us, but rather we
Will meet upon this solemn day
And in our greater liberty
Keep silent for you, a little while, and pray.'

1st published 1925   EDWARD SHANKS

(181)   War Graves

(After the Lacedœmonian)

Tell the Professors, you that pass us by,
They taught Political Economy,
And here, obedient to its laws, we lie.

1st published 1925   GODFREY ELTON

(182) The Survivor

I found him in department C.O. 10.
Three rows of medals, D.S.O., C.B.,
Brown, handsome, fearless, born to handle men:
Brushed, buttoned, spurred. Whom did I wish to see?

'Men you can't send for, General,' I said,
'How great soever your expense of ink;
Men you've forgotten; the unribboned dead
Who fell because you were too brave to think.'

1st published 1925   GODFREY ELTON

(183) War Commemoration

1925

To-day we must recall abysmal follies
That have bequeathed our friends to flies and sour clay,
That bent the air with groaning flights of steel
Or sweetened it with a shell's livid breath,
Turned wholesome plains and gentle lakes to filth,
Tore up our continent in unscavenged belts
Through cross-edged meadows and afforested heights
Where the guns crouched in pits and shouted
Lunatic judgment in dull obedience.
We must remember the weary stand-to
Of millions, pale in corpse-infected mist,
The mad, and those turned monsters, or castrated
In one red, hideous moment; and how, unseen
Dark Mania sat in offices, and designed
New schemes for shambles, learning year by year,
Painfully, secretly, to degrade the world.

1st published 1926   SHERARD VINES

Postscript

(184) War Books

What did they expect of our toil and extreme
Hunger – the perfect drawing of a heart's dream?
Did they look for a book of wrought art's perfection,
Who promised no reading, nor praise, nor publication?
Out of the heart's sickness the spirit wrote
For delight, or to escape hunger, or of war's worst anger,
When the guns died to silence and men would gather sense
Somehow together, and find this was life indeed,
And praise another's nobleness, or to Cotswold get hence.
There we wrote – Corbie Ridge – or in Gonnehem at rest –
Or Fauquissart – our world's death songs, ever the best.
One made sorrows' praise passing the church where silence
Opened for the long quivering strokes of the bell –
Another wrote all soldiers' praise, and of France and night's
    stars,
Served his guns, got immortality, and died well.
But Ypres played another trick with its danger on me,
Kept still the needing and loving-of-action body,
Gave no candles, and nearly killed me twice as well,
And no souvenirs, though I risked my life in the stuck tanks.
Yet there was praise of Ypres, love came sweet in hospital,
And old Flanders went under to long ages of plays' thought in
    my pages.

written 1922–5   IVOR GURNEY

189

Notes on the Poems

The Note on each poem begins with the poem number in bold type (e.g. **12**) and details of first publication as far as we have been able to establish them. Where a poem first appeared in a periodical and was subsequently included in a book by its author, both references are given; thus: *Daily Mail* (18 May 1915); *More War Poems* (1915). Cross-references to other poems are indicated by italicised poem numbers in square brackets (e.g. [*23*]). A poem number followed by *n* refers to a note on the poem.

For outlines of poets' lives and work – including information which may be helpful in understanding their poems in general – and further bibliographical details, see *Biographical Notes* below. Almost all the books of war poems mentioned are listed in more detail in Catherine Reilly's *English Poetry of the First World War: A Bibliography* (1978). The term *Casebook* occasionally used refers to *Poetry of The First World War*, a selection of critical essays in the Casebook series.

Part I: 1914

1   *Daily Chronicle* (31 Aug. 1914), reprinted next day in response to public enthusiasm; *Fighting Lines* (Nov. 1914). Begbie relinquished his copyright in order to make the 'verses' available to anyone who could use them. Sir Frederic Cowen set them to a 'swinging and contagious march melody'. The profits from sales of the song-sheet – published 10 Sept. by the same firm that had issued Kipling's 'The Absent-Minded Beggar' in the Boer War – went to the Prince of Wales's National Relief Fund, a charity set up to help those whose earnings were reduced by the war. The *Chronicle* gave the song repeated publicity, reporting on 20 Nov. that it had been sung at eleven London theatres. Five gramophone recordings were made; there were also posters, cards and a badge (which bore the Union Jack, a sunrise and the last line of the song). 'Sing the Song! Wear the Badge! Play the March!' The War Office distributed copies. *The Times* mildly protested at the song's appeal to shame (3 Oct.). In Jan. 1915, *T.P.'s Weekly* printed a letter from an Australian who described the song as 'balderdash' – whereupon a Scotsman wrote in to say that it had been largely responsible for his own decision to interrupt a successful career in order to enlist. Cp. [*14*], [*94*] and [*14 n*].

2   *Saturday Westminster Gazette* (3 Oct. 1914); '*And They Went to the War*' (1914) – a book consisting of verse portraits of volunteers (miner, poacher, scholar, etc.) and wartime women (including a proud mother who has lost all six of her illegitimate sons).

3 *Westminster Gazette* (11 Dec. 1914); *War Poems* (1917).

4 *Times* (9 Sept. 1914); *Satires of Circumstance* (1914). Originally entitled 'The Song of the Soldiers', this poem was composed on 5 Sept. after the 'well-known men of letters' conference (see Introduction, pp. 8–9 above). Hardy said it was 'meant to appeal to the man in the street'. He waived copyright, so the poem was widely reproduced and became very familiar; it was set to music by at least four composers during the war, and was reprinted by the *Daily Mail* (2 Aug. 1915) as the most typically English of the poems published a year earlier.

Leaving . . . win us: originally 'To hazards whence no tears can win us', quoted by Sassoon in his diary (17 Jan. 1917). *We . . . doing*: 'We know what we are fighting for, and we love what we know' – Cromwell, quoted by Bonar Law at Guildhall (4 Sept. 1914). *Victory crowns the just*: 'the worst line he ever wrote – filched from a leading article in the *Morning Post*' (Sorley, in a 1914 letter).

5 *English Review* (Sept. 1914); *Philip the King* (1914). Written at Lollingdon Farm, near Wallingford, probably in August 1914. The poem contains strong echoes of Gray, Wordsworth, Tennyson and Arnold, making it as much a literary statement as a direct description of the Berkshire downs; Masefield's response to the war is in terms of the great Romantic elegies and nature poems of the past.

6 *New Numbers* (Dec. 1914); *'1914' and Other Poems* (1915). Written soon after the Antwerp retreat in 1914, this is the first of the five sonnets which together form '1914'. See also [*30*].

7 *Refining Fires* (1917). In its contempt for materialism, its assertion of values such as 'Honour' and its welcoming of sacrifice, this poem is typical of an attitude voiced often during the war, especially in the early months.

blood . . . grace: a hint of soldier-Christ imagery.

8 *Poems* (1922). Rosenberg was convalescing in South Africa when war broke out.

9 *Poems* (1931). Probably written in 1914 when Owen was still a tutor in France. The sonnet uses phrasings from Shelley and Shakespeare (*Owen: War Poems and Others*, p. 113).

10 *Nation* (17 Oct. 1914); *Battle* (Autumn 1915). Originally entitled 'Under Fire', this and 'The Messages' were the first of Gibson's war poems to be published. The *Nation* printed ten more on 24 Apr. 1915 and another four on 31 July; these, and sixteen more, were collected in *Battle*, a book reviewed as 'bitterly realistic . . . an extraordinary achievement' (*Herald*, 23 Oct. 1915) and as 'the first considerable attempt . . . to look at the war through . . . the mind of the common Englishman . . . the result, not of direct experience, but of psychological imagination' (*Nation*, 15 Jan. 1916).

11 *Nation* (17 Oct. 1914); *Battle* (Autumn 1915). See [*10 n*].

12 *Labour Leader* (29 Oct. 1914). Refers to H. G. Wells's influential essay, *The War That Will End War*, which was written in August at the suggestion of Lloyd George. Wells, a Fabian socialist, argued that in fighting militarism the Allies were fighting against war itself ('Every sword that is drawn against Germany now is a sword drawn for peace').

13 *Herald* (20 Mar. 1915); *Five Souls and other War-time Verses* (1917). For Hardy's *The Dynasts*, see Introduction, p. 13. Ewer reads the drama as a grim warning of how history repeats itself: under Prime Minister *Pitt* and Foreign Secretary *Castlereagh*, Englishmen fought the *Corsican* (Napoleon); their reward was to see reactionary monarchs restored, the *Bourbons* in France and King '*Bomba*' in Naples, while at home a peaceful demonstration for reform was broken up by the military with many casualties (*Peterloo*, Manchester, 1819).

    March cheerfully away: presumably an ironic allusion to Hardy's recent 'Men Who March Away' [*4*], implying that Hardy had forgotten the message of *The Dynasts*.

14 The final poem in *Fighting Lines* (1914), where it comes as a surprise after recruiting propaganda like 'Fall In' [*1*]. Begbie loathed the facile rhetoric of the right-wing press, which often claimed that 'war exalts'; as a Christian he believed war was evil. Nevertheless, he thought Britain had no choice but to fight for freedom against unprovoked aggression, and he hoped the world might emerge a better place from the conflict; see his *The Vindication of Great Britain* (1916).

15 *Children of Love* (Dec. 1914); 'Soldier' published on its own, *Saturday Westminster Gazette* (7 Nov. 1914). Owen quoted from the first of these four linked poems in 1915 after Monro had 'smiled sadly' at his new uniform (*Owen: Letters*, p. 364).

    David: for a similarly pessimistic use of the David story, cp. [*108*].

Part II: Heroes

16 *October and Other Poems* (1920). Probably written in 1914, for publication in a newspaper. The 'Battle of Gheluvelt' (31 Oct. 1914) was regarded as the turning point in the First Battle of Ypres, when the British Expeditionary Force came close to defeat but managed to drive back a heavy German assault. The date, remembered throughout the war, was commemorated in 1917 by a number of poems – cp. [*86 n*]. Bridges imitates the ancient epitaph by Simonides on Thermopylae: 'Go tell the Spartans, you who pass by, / That here obedient to their laws we lie'; cp. [*17*], [*87*], [*181*].

    Worcesters: the Worcestershire Regiment turned the tide of the battle by filling a break in the line, losing a hundred men as they did so; they were believed to have 'saved the line' and 'saved England'.

17 *Worms and Epitaphs* (1919). From 'Epitaphs (imitated from Simonides)'; cp. [*16 n*]. Neuve Chapelle was a three-day battle in March 1915.

18 Ronald Knox, *Patrick Shaw-Stewart* (1920). This seems to be its author's only complete surviving poem. It was found written on a blank page in his copy of Housman's *A Shropshire Lad*; like many other war poems, it shows Housman's influence in both form and content.

Dardanelles (Hellespont): strait between the coast of Asia Minor (site of *Troy*) and the Gallipoli peninsula (*Chersonese*). The island of *Imbros* was an Allied base in 1915. *Achilles* sailed to Troy across the Aegean from Skyros (where Brooke was buried); for a while, he sulked in wrath in his tents, but then rejoined the battle. *Flame-capped*: Achilles's helmet was made by Hephaestus, god of fire.

19 *Severn and Somme* (1917). Gurney copied the poem into a letter from the front at the end of June 1916, immediately before the Somme offensive. It is a fairly typical example, both of a soldier's attempt to define heroism in Great War terms and of the conventional verse which Gurney published during the war. Its style contrasts sharply with that of his post-war work – (e.g. [52], [76], [132], [176], [184]) – but its attitude is not one he ever rejected. Not included in *Collected Poems* (1982).

song: Gurney recorded on 22 June that his comrades had sung 'O my I don't want to die, I want to go home' while under fire (*War Letters*, p. 75).

20 *Fairies and Fusiliers* (1917). Dated 'Late 1916' in Graves's 1927 collection, this poem expresses his pride in his regiment, the Royal Welch Fusiliers, after the Somme offensives. Owen admired the poem and assumed that Gracchus represented its author (*Owen: Letters*, p. 511). Graves's later poem, 'Sergeant-Major Money', gives a very different view of an old professional.

Three-and-Twentieth: Caesar may have raised a Legio XXIII for his war in Gaul (France) against the rebel chief Vercingetorix; but the reference is also to the RWF, the 23rd regiment of the line in the British Army. *Dead in the first year*: the RWF suffered heavy casualties in 1914–15, and the surviving professionals regarded the new Kitchener recruits as poor replacements. Graves's *Goodbye to All That* (1929) describes the tensions between diehards and recruits, and shows his sense of the war as continuing history.

21 *Poems* (1922).

Titan: The Titans were giants who made war on Zeus; in Greek mythology, this is the first of all wars. *Circe*: the enchantress who turned Odysseus's sailors into swine.

22 *Poems* (1931). The only MS is a rough copy, apparently dating from 1918.

'Orace: originally "Orace Cockles'. Macaulay's heroic poem 'Horatius' (1842) describes how Horatius Cocles and his two comrades held back a Tuscan assault on Rome.

23 *The Young Guard* (1919). Because of the war, the annual Eton *v.* Harrow cricket match at Lord's was not held in 1915.

Caligula: sadistic Roman emperor. *Cassius*: Roman traitor. *gaseous*: poison gas was first used by the Germans in April 1915. *Kultur*: German political and intellectual leaders had been in the habit of making high claims for their culture before the war.

24 *Daily Mail* (18 May 1915); *More War Poems* (1915).

25 *Spindrift* (1918). The incident was at Gallipoli on 20 Oct. 1915, as described in Pinto's autobiography (1969, pp. 167–8): 'A jolly red-haired boy in my platoon called "Ginger" Jenkins . . . peeped over the parapet. . . . I heard the crack of a rifle-shot. . . . As he was being carried away by the stretcher-bearers the platoon sergeant said: "Strong as a little 'orse 'e was. 'E never got no dysentery.' I thought of Rupert Brooke: "If I should die, think only this of me . . ." and Sergeant Cooper's epitaph seemed to me far more to the point than Brooke's highfalutin fancy.' As was sometimes the case when a writer described an event in verse soon afterwards and in prose much later, Pinto's poem is nearer 'highfalutin fancy' than his prose account.

26 *New Witness* (23 Dec. 1915). Originally entitled 'Au Champ d'Honneur', reflecting Scott Moncrieff's taste for French chivalric values; in 1918 he began a translation of *The Song of Roland*, dedicating it to his new friend, Wilfred Owen, in a preface which described modern soldiers as knights. The sonnet was reprinted, with its title in English, in E. B. Osborn's anthology, *The Muse in Arms* (1917).

27 *Daily Mail* (12 July 1916). Refers to the celebrated exploit of Capt. W. P. Nevill on the first day of the Somme.

> *play the game!*: cp. Newbolt's pre-war poem, 'Vitaï Lampada' ('Play up! play up! and play the game!').

28 *Westminster Gazette* (4 June 1917), over the pseudonym 'Tipuca'; *Magpies in Picardy* (1919).

29 *Images of War* (1919). In *Death of a Hero* (1929), Aldington reveals admiration for the bravery shown by public school officers, although he scorns everything else that they seemed to him to represent.

30 *New Numbers* (Dec. 1914); *'1914' and Other Poems* (1915). Originally entitled 'The Recruit', this, the fifth and the most famous of the five '1914' sonnets, was written at Rugby after Brooke had returned from Antwerp. Quoted in a sermon by the Dean of St Paul's on Easter Sunday 1915, and reprinted in *The Times* soon afterwards, it is often alluded to by later wartime poets – e.g. [99], [112]. Two points about the poem are usually overlooked: unlike much civilian verse in 1914, it is not belligerent; and it is a very literary piece, strongly influenced by Dryden – see J. R. Moore, *Modern Languages Review* (April 1959) – and by Belloc – see C. Hassall, *Rupert Brooke*, pp. 482–3.

31 *Collected Poems* (1918). Brooke's last work, written while the troopship was sailing towards Gallipoli. The publication date is worth noting: this haunting poem, which is much more characteristic of Brooke than the five sonnets, was unknown to the public in the years when his fame was at its height.

> *my friends*: these included Shaw-Stewart [18]. *soon to die*: Brooke died on 23 April.

32 *Westminster Gazette* (28 Mar. 1916); *The Old Huntsman* (1917). Sassoon's first poem about the war, composed while he was training in England in 1915. He later said that the poem, 'manifestly influenced by Rupert Brooke's famous sonnet-sequence', expressed the typical 'self-glorifying feelings of a young man about to go to the Front for the first time' (*Siegfried's Journey*, p. 17).

33 *Poetry Review* (spring 1916); *The Undying Splendour* (May 1917). The ninth of a set of thirteen sonnets. Streets, like W. N. Hodgson [34 n], was killed on the first day of the Somme. His poems were collected into a book in 1917 by Galloway Kyle, editor of the *Poetry Review*, who presented Streets as typical of 'the soul of young England', a working-class Kitchener recruit who had seen 'the Vision Splendid' and fought to redeem 'a world grown grey with doubt and timidity'. Streets himself said his poems tried to express how soldiers 'go to meet death grim-lipped, clear-eyed and resolute-hearted'.

34 *New Witness* (29 June 1916); *Verse and Prose in Peace and War* (Nov. 1916). Always published with the date 29 June, which has led critics to imagine Hodgson writing it in the Somme trenches, two days before his death; but the date is that of publication, not composition. Discussed by Paul Fussell, *The Great War and Modern Memory*, p. 61.

35 *Times* (5 May 1917), accompanying a report of Vernède's death; *War Poems* (1917). Written in the trenches before the Somme, Summer 1916 (*Letters to His Wife*, p. viii).

36 *A Subaltern's Musings* (1918).

37 *Last Poems* (1918). Inspired by the morning bugle call, 'Reveille', in training camp at Romford. Thomas's four bugle poems are discussed by Andrew Motion, *The Poetry of Edward Thomas* (1980), pp. 121–5.

38 *Poems* (1917). Inspired by the evening bugle call, 'Lights Out', in barracks at Trowbridge: 'It sums up what I have often thought of that call. I wish it were as brief – two pairs of long notes' (*Collected Poems*, p. 420). By this stage Thomas was expecting to be sent to France.

Part III: The Western Front

39 *Poetry Review* (Mar.–Apr. 1917). Preparing for action, a soldier–poet pities civilians.

40 *Patriotic Poems on the Great War* (1916). The last of three stanzas. The public had long been prepared for a great offensive. Early press reports spoke of thrilling action and success.

frightfulness: refers to the much-publicised German policy of *schrecklichkeit* (subduing a civilian population by means of terror).

41 *War Poems by 'X'* (Oct. 1916). The first and third of five stanzas. The Somme assault commenced on 1 July.

42 *The Old Huntsman* (1917). Sassoon was with the Royal Welch Fusiliers on 3 July, waiting to attack Mametz Wood the following day; there are prose descriptions of the scene in his *Diaries 1915–1918* and *Memoirs of an Infantry Officer*.

43 *Cambridge Magazine* (10 Feb. 1917); *Goliath and David* (1917). Graves saw the dead German in July 1916 (*Goodbye to All That*, ch. xx) and apparently wrote the poem at the time (Seymour-Smith, p. 48).

War's Hell!: an echo of General Sherman's famous comment in 1880, 'There is many a boy here today who looks on war as all glory, but, boys, it is all hell'.

44 *From an Outpost* (1917). Found among Coulson's effects after his death in France on 8 Oct. 1916. Discussed briefly by John H. Johnston, *English*

Poetry of the First World War, pp. 73–5. The maker of 'the Law' is God, not any human authority; in another poem, Coulson says he accepts his fate but after death his soul will 'soar up and summon Thee / To tell me *why*' ('Judgement').

45 *Observer* (17 Dec. 1916); *War Poems* (1917). Vernède began the poem no later than Feb. 1916, fought on the Somme throughout the summer, and finished the poem at Sheppey in Nov. 1916 (*Letters to His Wife*, pp. viii, 76), by which time the failure of the offensive was beyond doubt. So his attitude had formed before the Somme and was confirmed by it. In Dec. 1916 he returned to the trenches.

Peace . . . understanding: Phil. 4:7.

46 *Mudlark: Journal of the 63rd Division* (Sept. 1917); *The Bomber Gipsy* (May 1918). Often anthologised, often misread, it is a poem of pity, but not only of pity. A heroic deed ('fight', 'tale', 'treasure') is celebrated in the metre of Victorian ballads; the last stanza salutes the greatness of the achievement and recognises that it will be forgotten. The attack on Beaucourt by the Royal Naval Division in Nov. 1916 was chaotic and costly, although it captured ground and prisoners; fewer than twenty of over four hundred men answered the roll call afterwards. Herbert and the famous Bernard Freyberg were among the survivors.

Harmsworth: Vere Harmsworth, son of Lord Rothermere, aged twenty-one, killed early in the attack. *William*: William Ker, Herbert's close friend. *James*: apparently James Cook, another close friend. (Information from R. Pound, *A. P. Herbert*, and Brig. B. B. Rackham, who survived the attack and became Herbert's Assistant Adjutant.)

47 *Times* (14 Oct. 1916); *St George's Day* (1918). The official film of the Somme offensive was first shown on 10 Aug. in London; it had very wide publicity and aroused deep enthusiasm among civilian audiences. Newbolt wrote the poem soon after seeing the film, which he found 'moving in a very unexpected way . . . a purification of the emotions . . . especially so when the picture was just of men marching into action – long, long columns . . . the effect was to make me love them passionately and to make me feel that the world would be well lost to die with them. If only I could get that desire of fellowship into a few verses it would be a new poem and an immortal one' (16 Sept., *Later Life and Letters*, pp. 230–1).

48 *Curtains* (1919). A soldier's comment.

munition makers: many scenes in the film were designed to show munition workers that their products were being well used at the front.

49 *The Buried Stream* (1941). Faber added a note that he regarded this poem as too 'colloquial' in style, but he included it as the eighth sonnet in a formal sequence 'as evidence of the state of mind which it expresses. The author's enforced "home leave" came to an end soon afterwards'.

50 *The War Poems* (1983). 'This Christmas night I did a grim, jeering, heart-rending sort of thing about a General. . . . And I remembered old wine-faced Rawlinson at Flixécourt last May, as we swung down the hill with the band playing, two hundred officers and NCOs of his Fourth Army; and how many of them are alive and hale on Christmas Day? About half, I expect; perhaps less. But I'll warrant old Sir Henry made a good dinner in his château

. . . good luck to him and his retinue!' (*Diaries 1915–1918*, pp. 107–8); see also *Memoirs of an Infantry Officer*, VI.3. General Sir Henry Rawlinson was Commander of the Fourth Army in 1916 with a large responsibility for the Somme offensive.

51 *Diary of A Dead Officer* (1919). West described the patrol in a letter of 12 Feb. 1916: 'I had a rather exciting time myself with two other men on a patrol in the "no man's land" between the lines. A dangerous business, and most repulsive on account of the smells and appearance of the heaps of dead men that lie unburied there as they fell, on some attack or other, some four months ago. I found myself much as I had expected . . . more interested than afraid, but more careful for my own life than anxious to approve any new martial ardour.' The poem expresses a similar detachment through its use of narrative and allusion.

Elia: Charles Lamb (1775–1834), who lived in the Temple; the Temple Church contains famous effigies of cross-legged Crusader Knights.

52 *Poems* (1954). Typical of Gurney's retrospective war poems in its evocation of the private's polite avoidance of heroic undertakings.

53 *Masks of Time* (1925). Records an incident of autumn 1917 in the Ypres sector (*Undertones of War*, ch. XXIII).

Worley: Sgt Frank Worley, often mentioned in *Undertones*. *a blighty*: a wound serious enough to require treatment in England (Blighty).

54 *Behind the Eyes* (1921). Quotations from three of John Donne's often licentious love poems ('Song', 'Love's Deity', 'Elegie xix: Going to Bed'); Donne was obsessed with death and putrefaction. Tennyson's *Maud* is the story of a chaste but disastrous love affair, at the end of which the hero seeks redemption by enlisting to fight in the Crimean War.

55 *Poems* (1920). Conceived in Dec. 1917, completed in Sept. 1918, but mostly written c. April 1918 (there is no sure ground for the earlier date suggested at various times by Sassoon, Welland, Silkin and others: see D. Hibberd in *Notes and Queries*, July 1976). Owen vividly described the original experience in a letter of 4 Feb. 1917.

Our brains ache: cp. 'My heart aches . . .', the opening of Keats's 'Ode to a Nightingale'. *east . . . grey*: the German Army wore grey and attacked from the east. *nothing happens . . . doors are closed*: Owen drafted, and rejected, a final ninth stanza which prophesied an event at last: 'we are waiting till the burst earth gulfs for us / And our door opens'. *snow-dazed*: hallucinations can be a symptom of the beginnings of death by exposure. *ghosts*: cp. 'And we should come like ghosts to trouble joy' (sailors dreaming of their 'household hearths'), Tennyson, 'The Lotos-Eaters'.

56 *Poems* (1922). The date of composition is apparently not known.

57 *Poems* (1922). Final version dated 'May 14 1917, BEF, France' (*Collected Works*, 1979, pp. 112, 254–5). Earlier versions contain an additional stanza (between stanzas 7 and 8):

> Maniac Earth! howling and flying, your bowel
> Seared by the jagged fire, the iron love
> The impetuous storm of savage love.
> Dark Earth! dark heaven, swinging in chemic smoke

> What dead are born when you kiss each soundless soul
> With lightning and thunder from your mined heart,
> Which man's self dug, and his blind fingers loosed.

Limbers: gun carriages, here in use by Royal Engineers to transport barbed wire and iron stakes up the line; these regular journeys were made under cover of darkness. *Will they ever come?*: perhaps an ironic allusion to 'Will they *never* come?', a slogan on a 1914 poster calling for recruits.

58 *Eidola* (1917).

59 *Naked Warriors* (1919), a collection of poems composed in the later years of the war. Read described the book in his diary as 'a protest against all the glory camouflage that is written about the war . . . I have to be brutal and even ugly. But the truth should be told . . .' (14 Mar. 1918). 'The Scene of War' was intended both as a protest and as an attempt to capture the cold, hard beauty which the doctrines of Imagism required. Read maintained that the form of a poem should depend on the emotion to be expressed, not on preordained rules, and that strict unity was essential. 'This, then, is the poet's duty and joy: To express the exquisite among his perceptions, achieving so a beauty as definite and indicative as the prints of Hokusai, or the cold grace of immaculate cameos' – 'Definitions towards a modern theory of poetry', *Art and Letters*, I, 3 (Jan. 1918).

H. D.: Hilda Doolittle, the American Imagist poet. *The Happy Warrior*: Wordsworth's 'Character of the Happy Warrior' ends: 'This is the happy Warrior, this is He / That every Man in arms should wish to be'. *Liedholz*: Read described this capture in his diary (1 Aug. 1917) and in his short story, 'The Raid'. *Nietzsche*: German philosopher, much admired by Read at the time. *International*: Socialist organisation founded by Marx in 1864; Read was a convinced Marxist in the war period but, like other supporters of the International, he was disappointed that the workers of the world had failed to unite against war. *Refugees*: escaping from the German advance, Spring 1918 (cp. Read's prose account, 'The Retreat').

Part IV: Christ and Nature

60 *The Times* (27 Dec. 1915); *Three Hills and Other Poems* (1916). Harrow School is on a hill; the Flemish hill is presumably Hill 70, captured and lost in fierce fighting at Loos (Sept. 1915).

61 *Killed in Action* (1916). Also included, with a different ending, in 'W. E.', *Poems for the Bereaved* (undated booklet). Evans recorded that most of his poems were 'written to individuals in my own poor parish, whose faith was sometimes dimmed by the official letter'. He published his verse to reach a wider audience with 'the Master's message that the so-called dead are still marching on'.

King of Might: by implication, not only Satan but also the Kaiser, whose Prussian doctrine was supposed to be 'Might is Right'.

62 *The Unutterable Beauty* (1927). Title: 'Consider the lilies of the field . . . even Solomon in all his glory was not arrayed like one of these' (Matt. 6:28–9).

63 *The Vision Splendid* (Mar. 1917). First stanza originally in 'Christs All' (a typical Oxenham title) in *All's Well!* (1915). Title: a phrase often encountered in wartime writing (cp. *[33 n]*); it originates from Wordsworth's 'Intimations of Immortality', where it describes youth's poetic vision.

64 *Cambridge Magazine* (29 Apr. 1916); *The Old Huntsman* (1917). Composed in Nov. 1915 after commanding working-parties at Festubert in severe weather; rewritten Mar. 1916. Sassoon's first front-line poem. The last two lines were originally 'But in my heart I knew that I had seen / The suffering spirit of a world washed clean', but Sassoon decided that this was 'more than a little pompous' (letter to Edward Marsh, 16 Mar. 1916, Berg Collection, New York).

> *woollen cap*: the Fusiliers were not supplied with steel helmets until February 1916. *freedom*: Sassoon still believed at this stage in the justice of the Allied cause, so he was able to use the soldier-Christ image as a means of explaining suffering.

65 *Siegfried Sassoon: Poet's Pilgrimage*, ed. F. Corrigan (1973). Written at Oxford. *The War Poems* (1983) also gives Sassoon's long note on the poem: 'I never showed this to anyone, realising that it was an ambitious failure. I intended it to be a commentary on the mental condition of most front-line soldiers . . .'.

> *Paraclete*: the Holy Spirit.

66 *A Bunch of Cotswold Grasses* (1919). Title: Advent, the celebration of Christ's coming, occurs in the month before Christmas; by that stage in 1916, the carnage of the Somme was widely known.

67 *Easter at Ypres, 1915* (1916). Poem marked 'Written in trenches by "Glencorse Wood", 19–20th April, 1915'. Other poems in Lyon's book suggest that he was patriotic but looked to a time when nations would no longer waste themselves in war.

68 *Neighbours* (1920). Probably written in the last year of the war. Gibson had experience of Medical Boards, both as a candidate on several occasions and, probably, as a clerk.

69 *Naked Warriors* (1919). The second in a series of four poems entitled 'My Company'; see also *[134]*. In *Collected Poems* (1966), this sequence is printed as part of 'The Scene of War'; see *[59 n]*.

70 *The Years Between* (1919), a book which Kipling originally intended to call *Gethsemane*. He said that the poem referred to 'the horror that overtakes a man when he first ships his gas mask. What makes war most poignant is the presence of women with whom he can talk and make love, only an hour or so behind the line' – C. Carrington, *Rudyard Kipling* (1978), p. 547.

71 *Marlborough and Other Poems* (Jan. 1916). A note in the fourth edition (1919) says there was 'external evidence, though it is not quite conclusive, for dating this poem in August 1914'. 'For Sorley, earth was not hostile to man; it embraced him, as it had Christ. . . . Only through death could Man (as distinct from individual men) flourish. . . . It is perhaps surprising that the poem has been so popular for it embodies a philosophy difficult to comprehend. Sorley stated this philosophy quite succinctly in . . . November 1914: "The earth even more than Christ is the ultimate ideal of what man should strive to be" . . .' – Hilda Spear, Introduction to *Sorley: Poems and Selected Letters* (1978), pp. 22–3.

72 *The Times* (28 May 1915), with the announcement of Grenfell's death.

73 *Goliath and David* (Feb. 1917). Refers to Lieut. David Thomas, Royal Welch Fusiliers, killed 18 Mar. 1916, as described in *Goodbye to All That*, ch. XVIII; see also Sassoon's *Diaries 1915–1918* and *Memoirs of an Infantry Officer* (where Thomas is 'Dick Tiltwood'). Sassoon recorded a similar encounter with the dead man through nature in 'The Last Meeting' and 'A Letter Home' (both 1916). See also [*108*].

74 *Poems* (1917). Written at Hare Hall Camp, Romford. The poem reflects Thomas's decision to apply for a commission and for active service.

 'Have you been out?': the ploughman asks because he sees that the poet is in uniform.

75 *Poems* (1922). Rosenberg was working with the Royal Engineers, taking materials up to the front line at night and returning at dawn – cp. [*57*].

76 *Poems* (1973). Gurney was at Riez Bailleul in 1916.

 Severn: Gurney's poetry is full of references to his beloved Gloucestershire.

77 *Magpies in Picardy* (1919). MS dated June 1916, sent to Harold Monro (Monro MSS, British Library). Wilson wrote on 3 May 1916 that trench experience 'makes one see this Spring's evening beauty through a sort of veil of obscenity, as a madman may see beauty. For mangled bodies are obscene whatever war journalists may say. *War* is an obscenity. Thank God we are fighting this to stop war. Otherwise very few of us could go on. . . . We have *taught* schoolboys "war" as a romantic subject . . . everyone has grown up soaked in the poetry of war – which exists, because there is poetry in everything, but which is only a tiny part of the great dirty tragedy. All those picturesque phrases of war writers . . . are dangerous because they show nothing of the *individual* horror, nothing of the fine personalities smashed suddenly into red beastliness . . .' – quoted in L. Housman (ed.), *War Letters of Fallen Englishmen* (1930), pp. 299–300.

78 *Behind the Eyes* (1921).

79 *Masks of Time* (1925). Originally entitled 'Zero' (zero hour, the start of an attack), later 'Zero 1916'. The poem is similar to Blunden's prose description of a dawn attack at Beaumont Hamel on 3 Sept. 1916 (*Undertones of War*, ch. IX).

 I am clothed . . . mind: Mark 15:5. *Jock*: 'There were Highlanders trailing down the road' (*Undertones*).

80 *Undertones of War* (1928). The date in the title is that of the experience rather than the poem's composition; see *Undertones*, ch. XX. The poem quotes from the description in Keats's 'Ode on a Grecian Urn' of the garlanded heifer, 'lowing at the skies', being led to sacrifice, and of the crowd attending the ceremony ('Who are these coming to the sacrifice?').

81 *Poems* (1930), but not in *Undertones* (1928), so perhaps composed between these two dates.

 Thiepval Wood: a major objective, eventually captured, in the Somme battles of 1916; see *Undertones*, chs XI and XII. *Titania*: Queen of the Fairies.

Part V: Civilians

82 *Daily Mail* (3 Feb. 1915); *More War Poems* (1915). See [*127 n*].

83 *The Times* (21 May 1915); *The Anvil* (1916). Tones as stern as this, and imagery of the war as a forge or crucible, were usually characteristic of less idealistic imperialists than Binyon; but Brooke was dead, the Germans had used poison gas in April, and even to a liberal the war was beginning to look grim.

84 *Poems and Songs* (1915).

Greater Love . . .: John 15:13. This saying of Christ's before the crucifixion was in wide use during the war. *And shed no tears*: cp. [*98*], [*52*].

85 *The Times* (2 Nov. 1916); also published as a 1916 Christmas card; included in *To the Vanguard, and Other Songs of the Seven Divisions* (1917?). Sung, to music by Somervell, at a Choral Commemoration of the First Seven Divisions (the original BEF, Marne-Ypres 1914) at the Albert Hall, 15 Dec. 1917, a ceremony attended by 700 survivors and many famous people. The poem is a period piece, incorporating most of the motifs of civilian patriotic verse: the smallness of the original Army; Britain's *slow awaking* (lack of militarism); Horatius-like heroism; stoical endurance; chivalric imagery (*armour*); religious allusion ('present your bodies a living sacrifice', Rom. 12:1); solder-Christs (*Wounded hands . . . bleeding feet*).

monstrous guns: cp. Owen, 'Anthem for Doomed Youth' ('the monstrous anger of the guns').

86 *The Times* (31 Oct. 1917), under a leader on 'The Anniversary of Ypres'; *Last Poems* (1922). One of a number of poems which appeared in newspapers on 31 Oct. (and on 15 Dec., the day of the Choral Commemoration) to mark the third anniversary of the original BEF's blocking of the German advance at Ypres; cp. [*16*], [*85*].

87 *The Years Between* (1919). Kipling said these epitaphs were 'naked cribs of the Greek Anthology' – C. Carrington, *Rudyard Kipling* (1978), p. 548.

our fathers lied: the politicians and others who, in Kipling's opinion, had turned a blind eye to the danger of war before August 1914. He had supported Lord Roberts's National Service League in its pre-war campaign for conscription.

88 *Along the Years* (1937).

89 Dedicatory verse in *The Survival of the Fittest* (May 1916). W. was William Smith, a close friend of Squire's, killed in April 1917.

90 *Herald* (5 June 1915); *The Survival of the Fittest* (May 1916).

91 *The Survival of the Fittest* (May 1916).

Harmsworth: Alfred Harmsworth, Lord Northcliffe, the great press baron; owner of *The Times*; founder of the *Daily Mail*, which demanded strong government measures to win the war. *Lloyd George*: Minister of Munitions, May 1915; Secretary of State for War, July 1916; Prime Minister, Dec. 1916.

92 *The Survival of the Fittest* (May 1916). After Squire was appointed editor of the *New Statesman* in 1917, his politics seemed to become a little less radical. His 1918 volume (*Poems: First Series*), which included all the poems 'that I do not wish to destroy', omits his 1915-16 satires; his 1926 collection reprints two of them, including this poem.

Moloch: god of blood, fire and war, to whom the Canaanites used to sacrifice their sons.

93 *The Pageant of War* (1916). Title: our blame.

94 *Herald* (10 Nov. 1917).

hard: imprisonment with hard labour, a punishment given to conscientious objectors.

95 *The Questing Heart* (Dec. 1917). The poem echoes Wordsworth (e.g., 'Lines Written in Early Spring').

96 *Sorrow of War* (1919). This seems to describe a conscript rather than a volunteer. Conscription was introduced in Jan. 1916.

97 *Daily Telegraph* (19 Oct. 1916); *Sea Warfare* (1916). 'Jack' is the generic name for a sailor, and Kipling reprinted the poem with other sea pieces. But it was first published on its own, a year after his son was reported missing at Loos. John Kipling's body was never found, and his mother did not give up hope for over a year. So 'My Boy Jack' may be one of the very few personal statements in Kipling's poetry; it seems to contradict the modern belief that he doubted the war's purpose after his son was lost.

98 *The Omega* (1916). Cp. [*84*], [*152*].

99 *Behind the Firing Line* (1917). Since other poems by this writer are patriotic, 'The Mother' should be read as an answer to 'The Soldier' [*30*] but not as a parody of it.

100 *Westminster Gazette* (11 Dec. 1915); *Many Voices* (1922).

101 *Sonnets* (1918). The author's eldest son, Capt. Daniel Bradby, enlisted in Dec. 1914 and was killed at Arras, aged 20, on 9 Apr. 1917.

102 *Poems of the War and After* (1934).

103 *Poems* (1918).

Fuller's: a chain of tea shops.

Part VI: Soldiers

104 *Fairies and Fusiliers* (Nov. 1917).

105 *Five Degrees South* (1917). Young was in training at Salisbury Camp, Jan. 1915–Mar. 1916. His book was much admired by Gurney, who read it at the front and quoted the last two lines of this poem in a letter of 31 Oct. 1917.

parados and parapet: respectively, the back and front walls of a trench (in this case, a practice trench in England).

106 *Nation* (15 June 1918); *Poems* (1920).
clay: according to ancient mythology, life began when the sun warmed wet earth.
107 *Eidola* (1917).
108 *Goliath and David* (Feb. 1917). For David Thomas, see [*73 n*]. For the original story of Goliath, who was killed by the Biblical David, see I Samuel 17; cp. [*15*].
  spike-helmeted, grey: allusions to German uniform.
109 *War's Embers* (1919). Not reprinted in *Collected Poems* (1982).
110 *Poetry*, Chicago (Dec. 1916); *Poems* (1922). Written in June 1916, Rosenberg's first month in the trenches. For discussions of this poem by Paul Fussell, Jon Silkin and others, see *Casebook*.
  sleeping green: cp. Blake, 'The Echoing Green', one of several literary echoes in the poem. The front was comparatively quiet in that June, during the build-up for the Somme attack.
111 *Poems* (1922). Apparently finished behind the lines in May 1917. Rosenberg admitted that the poem was obscure, but believed it to be his best. 'The end is an attempt to imagine the severance of all human relationship and the fading away of human love.' 'It has taken me about a year to write . . . I have . . . striven to get that sense of inexorableness the human (or inhuman) side of this war has. It even penetrates behind human life for the "Amazon" who speaks . . . is imagined to be without her lover yet, while all her sisters have theirs, the released spirits of the slain earth men. . .' – *Collected Works* (1979), pp. 257, 260.
  the sound / . . . thought: 'I have tried to suggest the wonderful sound of her voice, spiritual and voluptuous at the same time.'
112 *War Daubs* (1919). The first of five stanzas. Cp. Brooke [*30*].
113 *Front Line Lyrics* (1918).
114 *War Daubs* (1919).
115 In *Soldier Poets: Second Series* (1917), ed. G. Kyle. Mr Dartford remembers writing the poem during the Somme fighting in 1916.
116 *Songs of Youth and War* (Mar. 1918). Mr Lyon remembers writing the poem in 1917.
  We have become . . . a name: cp. 'I have become a name' (Tennyson, 'Ulysses').
117 *Mesopotamia* (1919). The last of three stanzas.
118 *Candour* (1922). From a 54-line poem; date from author's MSS (Emmanuel College). Title: presumably an allusion to Newbolt's 'Clifton Chapel': 'Qui ante diem periit: / Sed miles, sed pro patria' (Who perished before his day, but as a soldier and for the fatherland).
  Bartholomew: the map publishers. British territories were always shown in red.
119 *The Greater Love: Poems of Remembrance* (1919). Patriotism and consolation were expressed in innumerable poems by soldiers throughout the war and after it.
  Somewhere in France: standard wartime phrase.
120 With this poem, the *English Review* (Sept. 1918) printed Constantine's 'William of Germany', in which blame for the war is put

squarely on the Kaiser and his God ('for he and you together / Have brought these years of misery on the world').

121 *English Review* (Apr. 1919).

122 *Eidola* (1917).

circles: Dante describes Hell as seven subterranean circles.

123 *Eidola* (1917). Title: self-sufficiency. Sassoon quoted from this poem in his May 1917 diary, apparently because it expressed his own state of mind. Manning wrote in a letter to William Rothenstein: 'In every show one undergoes a kind of katharsis (as Aristotle described the function of tragedy); or what St Paul called an "emptying of oneself"; curiously enough it is precisely at such moments that a man becomes most intensely himself' – quoted in J. Marwil, 'Frederic Manning', *St Louis Literary Supplement*, (June–July 1977), pp. 12–14. A similar understanding of tragic action is apparent in Manning's novel, *The Middle Parts of Fortune* (1929).

124 *Cambridge Magazine* (6 Oct. 1917); *Counter-Attack* (1918). Contrast [*82*].

125 *Cambridge Magazine* (27 Oct. 1917); *Counter-Attack* (1918). Title: 'Britain has only begun to fight. . . . The fight must be to a finish – to a knock-out' – Lloyd George (Sept. 1916). The phrase became a newspaper cliché.

Yellow Press: jingoistic newspapers (e.g., *Daily Mail*, *John Bull*). *Fusiliers*: Sassoon was a Captain in the Royal Welch Fusiliers. *Junkers*: members of the Prussian ruling class, regarded as the epitome of militarism.

126 *Counter-Attack* (1918). One of Sassoon's last descriptive trench poems.

127 *Poems* (1920). Title: Owen translated the famous line from Horace as 'It is sweet and meet to die for one's country', adding '*Sweet!* and *decorous!*' (letter of mid-Oct. 1917). The line was frequently quoted during the war, providing titles for many patriotic poems and books – cp. [*119*]. It had been inscribed above the chapel door at Sandhurst in 1913. Two preliminary drafts of the poem are subtitled 'To Jessie Pope, etc.' and 'To a certain Poetess' – cp. [*24*], [*82*].

128 *War, the Liberator* (1918). Date: the book's dustjacket describes this poem as Mackintosh's 'last'; he was killed in Nov. 1917.

'*Non-combatants*': a poem by Evelyn Underhill (*Theophanies*, 1916) which describes women's courage in uncomplainingly letting their men go to face the terrors of war. For a near-opposite pair of viewpoints, cp. Owen, 'Dulce et Decorum Est' [*127*], which was originally addressed to Jessie Pope, and Miss Pope's own verses [*24*], [*82*].

129 *Nation* (2 Feb. 1918); *Argonaut and Juggernaut* (1919), where the poem is dated 1917. Dedicated to his friend Sassoon, on whose war verse Sitwell modelled his own satires.

Abraham: who planned to sacrifice his son, Isaac (cp. Owen, 'The Parable of the Old Man and the Young', 1918). Sitwell was on very bad terms with his own father, who had forced him to join the Army before the war.

130 *Ditchling Beacon* (1918).

131 *Collected Poems* (1982). Gurney's typescript is marked 'Bangour, October 1917'.

Prussians: militarists, particularly civilian journalists and politicians.

132 *Collected Poems* (1982), which includes two versions of this poem. Gurney first went into the trenches in early June 1916, in preparation for the Somme assault. He recorded in several letters how 'C and I crawled into a signallers dugout, and so made the acquaintance of 4 of the nicest people that ever you could meet – and educated. . . . I had no sleep for 36 hours. We talked of books and music. And they sang – Glory be – "David of the White Rock" and the Slumber Song that Somervell has arranged. What an experience!' (*War Letters*, p. 71). The men belonged to a Welsh regiment. Gurney added that soon afterwards he was with 'a much rougher crowd', so his 'first time in' was not typical.

133 The dedicatory poem in *War, the Liberator* (1918). Mackintosh became engaged to Sylvia Marsh while on home duties in 1917, but in Oct. of that year he was sent back to France.

134 *Naked Warriors* (1919). The third in a series of four poems entitled 'My Company'; see also [69] and [59 n].

135 *Fairies and Fusiliers* (Nov. 1917). The two (Royal Welch) Fusiliers must be Graves himself and Sassoon. Both were invalided home in 1917, Graves in February and Sassoon in April. The last stanza of the poem provided imagery for Owen's 'Apologia' [136].

136 *Poems* (1920). Title: A defence of my poem. The defence seems to have been against Graves's criticism of 'Disabled': 'cheer up and write more optimistically . . . a poet should have a spirit above wars' (*Owen: Letters*, p. 596); hence *I, too, have . . . sailed my spirit*. An early draft, entitled 'Apologia lectorem pro Poema Disconsolatia Mea', begins 'If there be a bright side to war, it is a crime to show it'; this is a quotation (from memory) from the last chapter of Henri Barbusse, *Under Fire* (1917), a powerful anti-war novel which Owen had been lent by Sassoon in summer 1917.

wire . . . bound: Owen uses Graves's imagery – [135] – to show that he, too, understood the bond and beauty of comradeship.

137 *Art and Letters* (Spring 1920); *Poems* (1920). Although Owen had thought of soldiers as redeemers as early as 1914, the first drafts of this poem (1917?) are only about comradely and female love, without the religious allusions added in later versions; one is entitled 'To any beautiful [Woman]'. The diction and form are influenced by Swinburne's poem about a girl, 'Before the Mirror'. Title (final version): John 15:13 – cp. [84 n]. In Aug. 1917, Owen said that the notion that soldiers were showing Christ's 'greater love' was 'a distorted view to hold in a general way' (*Letters*, p. 484). He marked the poem 'Doubtful' in his plan for a 1918 book, having become sceptical about the redeemer idea though not about the beauty of comradeship.

blinded in my stead!: cp. a well-known wartime picture by R. Caton Woodville, 'Blinded For You!', showing a soldier clutching his eyes. *God . . . care*: cp. Christ's cry on the cross, 'My God, my God, why hast thou forsaken me?' (Matt. 37:46). *cross*: originally 'Rifles', which can be carried in the 'trail' position, parallel to the ground. *Weep . . . touch them not*: some critics see an echo here of the risen Christ's words to Mary, 'Woman, why weepest thou? . . . Touch me not' (John 21:15–17); the original line was entirely secular: 'O Love yearn for them, kiss them, and touch me not.'

138 *Counter-Attack* (1918), where the poem is entitled 'Exile'. One of several poems recording Sassoon's feelings while a patient at Craiglockhart in 1917. He decided to apply for active service again and was passed fit in Nov. 1917.

mutinous I cried: refers to his 1917 protest (see Introduction, p. 24).

139 *Masks of Time* (1925). Blunden's battalion was sent out of the trenches to Senlis, six or seven miles to the rear, in Oct. 1916. The village and a concert party there are described in *Undertones of War*, ch. XII.

O how . . . reviving: cp. 'Oh how comely it is and how reviving / To the spirits of just men long opprest' (Milton, *Samson Agonistes*, lines 1268–9).

140 *Art and Letters*, II, 1 (Winter 1918–19); *Images of War* (May 1919).

141 *The Egoist* (Mar.–Apr. 1919); *Images of Desire* (May 1919).

142 *Aurelia and Other Poems* (1920). The second in a sequence of four poems (see also [*162*]) entitled 'Yesterday' and dedicated to Sassoon. Writing to Owen's mother after the war, Nichols said that 'The Secret' expressed exactly the same truth as Owen's 'Apologia' [*136*] (letter in the Owen collection, Oxford).

Part VII: Poets and Poetry in Wartime

143 *Children of Love* (Dec. 1914).

professional poets: establishment writers, who were often preoccupied with poetic rules (e.g., William Watson, who wrote a number of very conventional sonnets about the war). *unprofessional . . . singers*: Pound and other Modernist poets were already at work in London.

144 *Westminster Gazette* (26 Aug. 1914); reprinted as the epigraph to *Poems of the Great War* (1914), an anonymously compiled anthology sold in aid of the National Relief Fund: see [*1 n*]. Watson appeals for donations.

145 *The Book of the Homeless*, no. 310 (1916), where the poem was entitled 'A Reason for Keeping Silent' and began 'I think it better that at times like these / We poets keep our mouths shut'; the later version, deprived of this colloquialism, appeared in *The Wild Swans at Coole* (1917) – cp. J. Stallworthy, 'W. B. Yeats and Wilfred Owen', *Critical Quarterly*, 2,3 (Autumn 1969), pp. 199–214. Yeats expanded on his reasons for keeping silent in the Introduction to his *Oxford Book of Modern Verse* in 1936 (*Casebook*, p. 75).

146 *Marlborough and Other Poems* (1916). Found in Sorley's kit after his death in Oct. 1915.

as other men have said: perhaps a reference to Brooke's war sonnets, which Sorley considered 'sentimental' (*Casebook*, p. 39). *many a better*

. . . *before*: 'Die, too, friend, why do you complain? Patroclus also died, and he was a far better man than you are', Achilles to Lycaon (*Iliad*, XXI). Sorley quoted this passage in a letter of Nov. 1914, on hearing of a friend's death: 'no splendider comment on death has been made, especially, as here, where it seemed a cruel waste' (*Letters*, p. 245).

147 *Poetry Review* (Autumn 1917); *Mad Moments* (1919). A characteristic period piece, with its archaisms of *song* and *sword*.

148 *Rhymes with Reasons* (1918). Meynell lists some of the most well-known soldier–poets of the 'officer and gentleman' class: Grenfell, killed 1915 [*72*]; Mackintosh, killed 1917 [*128*], [*133*]; E. W. Tennant, killed 1916; Hodgson, killed 1916 [*34*]; Gerald Caldwell Siordet ('Gerald Caldwell'), killed 1917; Brooke, died 1915 but not in fact on 'the field' [*6*], [*30*], [*31*].

Menologist: one who lists long-dead saints. *immortal birds*: Caldwell's 'To the Dead' imagines walking with the Christ-like dead and hearing them speak 'holy, incommunicable things . . . like immortal birds'.

149 *The Diary of a Dead Officer* (1919); a shorter version appeared as 'War Poets' in the *New Age* (6 Oct. 1916). The full version has a prefatory note referring to H. Rex Freston, *The Quest of Truth* (1916). Freston was killed in Jan. 1916, aged 24, having left Oxford to enlist in 1914. His sonnet, 'O Fortunati', begins:

> O happy to have lived these epic days!
> To have seen unfold, as doth a dream unfold,
> These glorious chivalries, these deeds of gold . . .

all is right . . . cannot understand: echoes Voltaire's satire on eighteenth-century Optimism ('all is for the best in the best of possible worlds', *Candide*). *faith . . . mustard seed*: Matt. 17:20.

150 *Cambridge Magazine* (2 Dec. 1916); *The War Poems* (1983). *My ecstasies*: refers to such poems as 'Absolution' [*32*]. *hatred*: after David Thomas's death in 1916, Sassoon had wanted to kill Germans in revenge.

151 *Nation* (27 Oct. 1917); *Argonaut and Juggernaut* (1919). Extract from an 87-line poem, dedicated (but not addressed) to H. W. Massingham, editor of the *Nation*.

poets . . . truth: Owen probably knew this poem, since he read the *Nation* and met Sitwell in May 1918; he may have remembered it when he wrote in his fragmentary Preface (spring 1918): 'All a poet can do today is warn. That is why the true Poets must be truthful.'

152 *Athenaeum* (16 Jan. 1920); *Poems* (1920). A 'Pindaric' ode, with irregular line and stanza lengths, modelled on Wordsworth's 'Ode on the Intimations of Immortality'; both poems are about imagination being dulled by experience.

Happy the soldier home: Owen repeats the classical 'Beatus ille' (Blessed is he who . . .) construction, used, e.g., by Pope in 'Happy the man whose wish and care / A few paternal acres bound'. The poem alludes repeatedly to Augustan and Romantic poetic attitudes, not in order to satirise them (as critics tend to suggest) but in order to show how war turns civilised values upside down. Pope's peasant could be happy at home without having to be 'insensible'. Wordsworth lamented the adult's loss of imagination; now even a 'lad' is lucky to lose it. *shilling*: the King's shilling, a private's wage. *We wise*: Shelley called poets 'the wise' and maintained that they have a duty to enter imaginatively into all human experience, horror as well as beauty. *dullards*: civilians, insensible by choice rather than as a result of battle. *pity*: 'My subject is War, and the pity of War', Owen's Preface (1918); the word recurs in [*155*].

153 *Napoo! A Book of War Bêtes-Noires* (1918), a collection of satires composed in Apr. 1918 against such wartime targets as 'The Old Man Rampant', 'Our Prussians' (bureaucrats), 'The Savage Optimist', 'The Super-Patriot', etc.

154 *The Judgement of Valhalla* (Mar. 1918). The epigraph and ending of a 170-line poem. The earlier part of the poem comments on the friend's book, which is written in conventional rhetoric, and reminds him of some gruesome front-line experiences. Frankau dismisses the fine sentiments still being expressed in 1917–18, just as West [*149*] had scorned similar writing in 1915–16. However, whereas West had believed that the war was futile, Frankau is sure of its purpose; his certainty is also recorded in his autobiography, *Self-Portrait* (1940), and in other poems.

155 *Wheels* (1919); *Poems* (1920). The Jan.–Mar. 1918 date in *Complete Poems* (1983) is doubtful, since the poem is written on a type of paper which Owen used from Jan. to May or even later. It was not until the March Offensive that he knew he would have to return to the front; the poem may reflect that knowledge. A date of Mar.–May 1918 seems a little more likely. The sources of 'Strange Meeting' are discussed in detail in S. Bäckman, *Tradition Transformed* (1979); the main ones are Dante's *Inferno*, Keats's *The Fall of Hyperion*, and Shelley's *The Revolt of Islam*. The prophecy of post-war chaos and repression seems to owe much to Bertrand Russell's *Justice in War-Time* (1916), which Sassoon may well have lent Owen in 1917. Despite its literary nature, the poem grew from the realities of war, including crowded dugouts and shellshock nightmares.

Foreheads . . . bled: cp. Christ's agony (Luke 22:4).

156 From a hitherto unpublished autograph MS among Sassoon's May 1918 letters to Ottoline Morrell (University of Texas). 'Testament' seems to record a decision to stop writing poems of protest against the war. It was quoted inaccurately by Owen on 31 Aug. 1918 (*Letters*, p. 570); he said Sassoon had written it 'on the boat' (presumably on the way back from Palestine in May). Owen was returning to the front; contrasting himself with his friend, he said on 10 Aug. he was glad to be going out again because 'I shall be better able to cry my outcry, playing my part.'

Part VIII: 1918 and After

157   *Undertones of War* (1928). Blunden's battalion was in trenches south of Gouzeaucourt early in 1918. This proved to be his final tour of duty at the front; he was sent home on a training course a few weeks before the March fighting began, not guessing that the area would soon be devastated (*Undertones*, ch. XXVII).

158   *Front Line Lyrics* (1918). The great German offensive began on 21 Mar. 1918.

159   *Punch* (3 Apr. 1918); *From the Home Front* (1918). Title: perhaps intended to evoke memories of a patriotic sermon of the same title, preached at St Paul's by the Bishop of London, July 1915. The poem is consistent with Seaman's attitude to the war and with the attitude of *Punch* (which he edited). Similar comments on the crisis were made by Herbert, 'The Windmill' (*Punch*, 10 Apr. 1918); Young, 'England – April 1918' (in F. Brereton, ed., *An Anthology of War Poetry*, 1930); Binyon, 'Naked reality and menace, near' (*The Times*, 15 Apr. 1918); and others.

160   *Cambridge Magazine* (18 May 1918); *Sorrow of War* (1919). Originally entitled 'Offensive'. A pacifist, left-wing response to the burst of propaganda during the crisis.

161   *Poems* (1920).

   tramp . . . upland camp: S. Bäckman, *Tradition Transformed* (1979), suggests an interesting parallel with the 'swain' on the 'upland lawn' in Gray's 'Elegy'; this points to the elegiac and ironic nature of Owen's poem. *village wells*: earlier drafts have 'still village wells'.

162   *Aurelia and Other Poems* (1920). The fourth in a sequence of four poems entitled 'Yesterday': see [*142 n*]. The words *flashing* and *morning* were suggested by Sassoon, who expressed liking for the poem when he read it in Aug. 1918 (letter from Sassoon to Nichols, Bodleian Library). The phrase 'morning heroes' was used by Sir Arthur Bliss, himself wounded and gassed on the Somme and at Cambrai, as the title for his war oratorio (1930), in which this poem, Owen's 'Spring Offensive' [*165*], and passages from Homer and Whitman, are sung or recited.

163   *The War Poems* (1983). Sassoon copied this into his diary, 5 June 1918, behind the lines at Habarcq. 'After all, I am nothing but what the Brigadier calls "a potential killer of Germans (Huns)". O God, why must I do it? *I'm not*. I am only here *to look after* some men' (*Diaries 1915–1918*, p. 261).

164   *The Guards Came Through* (1919). Douglas Haig, the British Commander-in-Chief, launched his counter-offensive on 8 Aug. 1918.

   German scheming . . . humanitarian dreaming: German diplomacy and tentative suggestions for peace in 1917, as well as liberal moves at home for peace and reconstruction (e.g., Lord Lansdowne's *Daily Telegraph* letter, 30 Nov. 1917), irritated those like Doyle and Kipling who believed the war had to be resolved by force of arms. *contradictions . . . fictions*: probably refers to an accusation by General Maurice in May 1918 that Lloyd George had lied to parliament about British military strength; a bitter parliamentary debate had ensued.

165 *Poems* (1920). Owen's last poem, completed in late Sept. (or even Oct.) 1918; his views have developed considerably since the simple protests of such 1917 poems as 'Dulce et Decorum Est' [*127*]. The text given here, like those of all the Owen poems in this book, comes from *Complete Poems* (1983); readers familiar with Owen through earlier editions will notice changes. Many of Owen's MSS were either overlooked by earlier editors or were not available to them; the 1983 text is the first to be based on the full range of MS sources. Title: the poem is loosely based on an experience at Savy Wood during the Allied spring offensive, April 1917.

May: traditional month for poetic visions, as in 'Ode to a Nightingale'; the language in these lines is deliberately Keatsian. *a friend*: cp. 'kind old sun' [*106*]. *high place*: common phrase in the Old Testament, sometimes refers to hilltop altars where men sacrificed their sons to Moloch – cp. [*92 n*] – by burning them alive. *Some: 'Some* (civilians) say God rescued them, but . . .'.

166 *The Times* (24 Oct. 1918); *The Years Between* (1919). Said to have been syndicated in 200 Imperial and American newspapers in Oct. 1918; reprinted as a broadsheet, Jan. 1919, with the names of towns and villages destroyed by the Germans. With the war at last drawing to an end, Kipling presses home his often-repeated message that Germany had to be made to recognise and purge her guilt. Similar views were expressed by Frankau (*Daily Mail*, Oct.–Nov.), Seaman (*Punch*, 23 Oct.) and other poets.

sword / Of Justice: 'Take Up the Sword of Justice' was a 1914–15 recruiting slogan. *the Law*: cp. 'lesser breeds without the Law' ('Recessional', 1897) and many other references to 'Law' in Kipling's work. 'The Outlaws' (1914) suggests how Kipling's attitude to Germany did not alter from 1914 to 1918.

167 *The Buried Stream* (1940).

168 *The Splendid Days* (1919). 'The Pension produced some champagne at dinner and we drank the loyal toast. And then across the table G. lifted her glass to me and said "Absent". I did not know her story nor she mine, but I drank to my friends who were dead and to my friends who, wounded, imprisoned, battered, shaken, exhausted, were alive in a new, and a terrible world . . .' (*Grey Ghosts and Voices*, p. 136).

169 Final poem in *The Poets in Picardy* (1919).

170 *Picture Show* (June 1919). Written 'in a few minutes', the poem was 'composed without emotion, and needed no alteration afterwards. Its rather free form was spontaneous, and unlike any other poem I have written . . . it was essentially an expression of release, and signified a thankfulness for liberation from the war years which came to the surface with the advent of spring. . . . The singing that would "never be done" was the Social Revolution which I believed to be at hand' (*Siegfried's Journey*, pp. 140–1).

171 *Westminster Gazette* (6 May 1919); *The Menin Road* (1919).

172 *Nation* (23 Nov. 1918); *Any Soldier to His Son* (1919). The first couplet and closing section of a 90-line poem which appeared anonymously only twelve days after the Armistice. A correspondent to the *Nation*

('Footslogger, BEF', 14 Dec. – evidently soldiers not yet demobbed felt obliged to conceal their identities) praised the poem as vivid and true, a welcome change from 'the unreal and sickly "popular" war poems to which we have so long been subjected'.

chats: soldiers' name for lice.

173 *Nation and Athenaeum* (8 Feb. 1919), with a different ending; *Picture Show* (June 1919). *Lord Derby's Scheme*: recruiting scheme introduced in 1915, in response to public pressure against 'slackers'.

174 *Country Sentiment* (1920). Graves suffered from disordered nerves for years after the war.

175 *Behind the Eyes* (1921).

176 *Poems* (1954).

177 *The Ballad of St Barbara* (1922). Written soon after the war on the assumption that the pre-war political establishment, which Chesterton had always opposed, would be sustained in power. A specific cause for this assumption was that Lord Reading (formerly Rufus Isaacs, a figure in the 1911 Marconi scandal) accompanied Lloyd George to the Paris Peace Conference. To Chesterton, the 1911 scandal had been proof of establishment and Jewish conspiracy; Reading's new appointment seemed to show how ordinary patriotic soldiers were being betrayed by their selfish rulers – see M. Ward, *G. K. Chesterton* (1944), pp. 358–9.

178 *The Times* (11 Nov. 1920); *Late Lyrics and Earlier* (1922). Written at the request of *The Times* for its illustrated supplement on the day of the Unknown Warrior's burial. The editorial on the same day remarked that Hardy had stressed pity, but 'when Mr Hardy makes pity ask why this misery had, and has, to be, the answer is clear. . . . The war had to be because plain duty forbade the free peoples of the earth, and forbade us, above all others, to renounce all justice and all right by cowardly acquiescence in a monstrous crime.' An anonymous poem next day, 'A Reply', repeated the argument, denying that pity should be the central response. Title: Mark 4:20 (Christ's stilling of the tempest).

Spirit of Pity: the Spirit of the Pities, and the Spirits Ironic and Sinister, comment on the Napoleonic Wars in *The Dynasts*. *'Why?'*: Hardy had been more confident in 1914 – 'We well see what we are doing' [*4*].

179 *Trentaremi* (1923).

the old first army: the BEF, 1914 – cp. [*85*]. *backs towards the sea*: echoes Haig's 'backs to the wall' order (April 1918).

180 *The Shadowgraph* (1925). The Cenotaph in Whitehall was unveiled in 1920.

181 *Years of Peace* (1925). Another variation on Simonides – cp. [*16 n*].

182 *Years of Peace* (1925). Possibly influenced by Sassoon's 'The General'. The satirical bitterness in these two Elton poems is not evident in his earlier collection, *Schoolboys and Exiles* (1919). By the 1920s, attacks on generals were more common than they had been during the war.

183 *The Pyramid* (1926).

Postscript

184   *Poems* (1954). Critical opinion turned against wartime literature in the early 1920s, after many articles on what, if anything, had been written that would last (interest revived at the end of the decade).

     to Cotswold get hence: dream of home. *One . . . Another*: Gurney may be referring to two particular poets (Owen and Thomas?). *love . . . in hospital*: he fell in love with a nurse at Bangour, Autumn 1917.

Biographical Notes

The biographical notes include a selection of books by and about individual authors. The following abbreviations are used:

Autob:	autobiography, memoirs	Cr:	criticism
		Dd:	diaries
Bibl:	bibliography	educ:	educated at
Biog:	biography	F:	fiction, fictionalised
Casebook	criticism of or by the poet in *Poetry of the First World War* (*Casebook* series)		memoirs
		Ll:	letters
		Wp:	war poems, or books of or containing war poems by a single author
CP:	*Collected Poems*		

Aldington, Richard (1892–1962); one of the founders of Imagism, 1912, with his future wife (the poetess 'H. D.') and Ezra Pound; literary editor of the *Egoist*, the Imagist magazine. Volunteered in 1914 but was rejected for medical reasons until mid-1916; Pte, later Lieut., Royal Sussex Regt; gassed and shellshocked, 1918. Friend of many literary figures, including D. H. Lawrence. F: *Death of a Hero* (1929), a savagely satirical attack on wartime values. Autob: *Life for Life's Sake* (New York, 1941). Wp: *CP* (1933), etc.

Andrews, George Francis Victor (d. 1963); Birmingham telegraphist; wartime service overseas. Active, pioneer member of the Union of Post Office Workers from before the war; later, editor of the Union's journal. Published three books of poems and a study of industrial democracy. Wp: *Poems and Songs* (1915), *Poems* (1921).

Baker, Olaf (b. 1870s); born in Birmingham but lived in the American wilderness early this century; later lived in Devon and wrote animal stories for children. Biog: note in Kunitz and Haycraft, *A Junior Book of Authors* (2nd edn, New York, 1951). Wp: *The Questing Heart* (1917), *Tramp of Eternity* (1919).

Beek, Theo van (1889–1958); born in S. Africa, where he was known as a promising young poet, but came to Britain *c.* 1909 and never returned; educ: Edinburgh. Lieut., Royal Field Artillery, on the Somme and elsewhere in France. Recited some of his anti-war poems in London during the war, wearing uniform, and was severely reprimanded by his Army superiors. Published poems in journals until the 1930s.

Begbie, Harold (1871–1929); journalist and popular writer on religious and social subjects; his many books include a collection of verse on the Boer War

(1900), a biography of General Booth of the Salvation Army, and *The Vindication of Great Britain* (1916). The *Daily Chronicle* sent him to America in 1914 to report on public opinion and to speak for the Allied cause. Wp: *Fighting Lines* (1914).

Bendall, Frederic William Duffield (1882–1953); educ: Cambridge (Classical scholarship). Professional soldier: Territorials, 1910; Lt.-Col., London Regt, Sept. 1914; O/c British troops, Khartoum, 1915; Malta, Gallipoli, France (wounded); CMG and Colonel, 1918. Later an Inspector of Schools; Director of Army Education, 1940–2. Wp: *Front Line Lyrics* (1918).

Betham-Edwards, Miss Matilda (1836–1919); prolific Victorian author: light fiction, children's stories, books about France (where she travelled widely). Her verses were first published by Dickens. Despite her age, she was moved by the wartime sufferings of France to write her patriotic *War Poems* (1917) and an account of the German occupation of Alsace (1916).

Binyon, Laurence (1869–1943); educ: St Paul's and Oxford; joined staff of British Museum, 1893; in charge of Oriental paintings and prints, 1913–32; CH, 1932. Many poems, several plays; shared with Bridges an interest in developing metre away from set patterns towards natural speech-rhythms. His 'For the Fallen' (*The Times*, 21 Sept. 1914) was probably the most successful of all wartime poems of remembrance; it was set to music by Elgar and quoted on many war memorials. Wp: *The Four Years* (1919), etc.

Blunden, Edmund (1896–1974); educ: Christ's Hospital; awarded an Oxford scholarship in 1914 but enlisted instead of taking it up. Lieut., Royal Sussex Regt; MC, Nov. 1916; Western Front, Spring 1916–early 1918. Oxford after the war; Prof. of English Literature, Tokyo, 1924–7; Prof. of Poetry, Oxford, 1966–8. Many volumes of verse and prose, including editions of Keats, Clare, Owen, Gurney; often wrote about war poetry, rarely if ever mentioning his own. Autob: *Undertones of War* (1928). Wp: although he wrote some war poems before and soon after 1918, Mrs Claire Blunden confirms that most – the best – were composed in the 1920s; some appeared in *Masks of Time* (1925), more in *Undertones of War*, and they were collected in *Poems 1914–1930* (1930). Bibl: B. J. Kirkpatrick (1979). *Casebook*.

Bradby, Henry Christopher (1868–1947); son of a Haileybury headmaster; educ: Rugby and Oxford. Taught at Rugby, 1892–1929; housemaster of School Field, 1910–25, where he succeeded Rupert Brooke's father (and Brooke himself, who was acting housemaster for a term in 1910 after his father's death). Father of Anne Ridler, the poet. Wp: *Sonnets* (1918), *Poems* (n.d.).

Brice-Miller, Beatrix ('Beatrix Brice'); served in some capacity with the BEF during the war. On the strength of her one well-known poem, 'To the Vanguard', she was invited to compile three books on the Ypres battlefields, 1925–9.

Bridges, Robert (1844–1930); Poet Laureate, 1913–30. Declared in a letter to *The Times* (2 Sept. 1914) that the war was a struggle between Good and Evil. *The Times* printed some of his 'official' wartime verses, including 'England Awake' (8 Aug. 1914), 'Lord Kitchener' (13 June 1916), 'The First Seven Divisions' (15 Dec. 1917), and poems thanking the Allies and the Empire in 1918 (14 Oct., 25 and 28 Nov., 20 Dec.). This work is much inferior to his best writing. His anthology, *The Spirit of Man* (1916), was designed to show the lasting values for which literature stands; it included work by his old friend, G. M. Hopkins, who was still unknown to the public. Bibl: G. L. Mackay (1933). Wp: *October and Other Poems* (1920 edn).

Brittain, Vera (1896–1970); went up to Oxford in 1914 but left in 1915 to become a Red Cross nurse; spent four years in London, Malta and France, an experience which turned her from an 'ordinary' patriot into a pacifist. Her fiancé died of wounds in 1915 and her brother was killed in Italy in 1918. Published 29 books. Autob: *Testament of Youth* (1933). Wp: *Poems of the War and After* (1934).

Brooke, Rupert (1887–1915); son of a Rugby housemaster; educ: Rugby and Cambridge; Fellow of King's College. His poetry often shows his scholarly knowledge of Jacobean literature. Leader of the pre-war Georgian poets. Atheist, Fabian socialist, scorner of convention, sometime Decadent – not the typical public-school patriot which modern myth sometimes makes him out to be. Enlisted, without much enthusiasm, Aug. 1914; Sub-Lieut., Royal Naval Division; in the retreat from Antwerp in Oct. 1914. The sight of refugees and burning houses gave him his sudden, intense conviction that the Allied cause was just; his five war sonnets sprang directly from his Antwerp experience. The war now seemed not only noble but also a release from capitalist society (and from private entanglements). Sailed for Gallipoli but died of blood-poisoning, 23 Apr. 1915, before reaching the battle zone. *CP*: (1946). Ll: (1968), both ed. G. Keynes. Biog: C. Hassall (1964), J. Lehmann (1980). Bibl: G. Keynes (2nd edn, 1959). *Casebook.*

Burton, Claude E. C. H.; as 'Touchstone' in the *Daily Mail* and 'C. E. B.' in the *Evening News*, published an average of 300 poems a year for over 40 years (Pound and Harmsworth, *Northcliffe*, 1959). See note on Jessie Pope. Wp: *Fife and Drum* (1915), dedicated to Lord Northcliffe, 'my chief and friend for nearly nineteen years'.

Cannan, May Wedderburn (1893–1973); daughter of the Secretary, Oxford University Press. Became a VAD nurse in 1911, among the general preparations for a possible war; like many Tories, she believed that the pre-war Liberal Government had increased the risk and eventual scale of conflict by dismissing early warnings about Germany as 'militarist' or 'alarmist'. Worked for the Press for part of the war, then as a nurse in France; job in MI5, Paris 1918. In 1918, became engaged to Bevil Quiller-Couch, 'Q''s son, who died of pneumonia in 1919 after having served in the Army throughout the war. Later appointed a librarian at the Athenaeum. Several books of verse. Autob: *Grey Ghosts and Voices* (1976). Wp: *In War Time* (1917), *The Splendid Days* (1919).

Chesterton, Gilbert Keith (1874–1936); essayist, critic, poet, novelist, Catholic apologist. Saw himself as being on the side of the ordinary man against capitalism and socialism; bitterly opposed to the establishment press and international (especially Jewish) finance, but also to Prussia. Attended the 'well-known men of letters' conference in Sept. 1914 and wrote in support of the war effort (*The Barbarism of Berlin*, 1915). Editor of the *New Witness*, 1916, in succession to his brother, who had enlisted. Autob: *Autobiography* (1936). Biog: Maisie Ward (1944). Wp: *The Ballad of St Barbara* (1922); *CP* (1927).

Constantine, H. F.; several poems in the *English Review*, 1918, where he is described as a Major. The Army apparently has no record of anyone of this name and rank. Wrong initials or a pseudonym?

Coulson, Leslie (1889?–1916); journalist before the war. Enlisted in the ranks, Sept. 1914, preferring not to seek a commission; wounded at Gallipoli; in the Somme advance, 1 July 1916; killed, Oct. 1916. On 30 June, he had written, 'If I should fall, do not grieve for me. I shall be one with the wind and the sun and the flowers.' His poems show that his attitude to the war changed between then and his death. Wp: *From an Outpost* (March 1917).

Crosland, Thomas William Hodgson (1868–1924); journalist; books of verse and prose on various subjects, often expressing his strong nationalist, xenophobic views (he regarded one of Sorley's poems about Germany as 'pro-German' 'insidious rottenness'). Published Sassoon's *The Daffodil Murderer* (1913). Biog: W. Sorley Brown (1928). Wp: *War Poems by 'X'* (1916); *CP* (1917).

Dartford, Richard Charles Gordon (b. 1895, in Lisbon); educ: Haileybury and, after the war, Oxford. Capt., 19th London Regt (TF); near-fatal head wound at Loos in 1915. In 1916 'got back to my battalion, going to the Somme, and so came in for the carnage in High Wood, where I saw my colonel, Hamilton, killed just in front of me. It must have been during a rest from this carnage that I wrote the poems' (letter to the editors, Mar. 1984). Awarded MC after months of fighting. From Dec. 1916 until the end of the war, attached as Liaison Officer to Portuguese troops in France; two Portuguese decorations. Major, Intelligence Corps, 1940–5. Wp: three poems in *Soldier Poets: Second Series* (1917).

De Stein, Edward (1887–1965); educ: Eton and Oxford. Major, KRRC, 1914–18. President, Gallaher Ltd; knighted, 1946. Wp: *The Poets in Picardy* (1919).

Dobell, Eva (1867–1963); niece of another wartime poet, Sydney Dobell. Worked as a nurse during the war; her poems show admiration and sympathy for the sufferings of soldiers in hospital. Wp: *A Bunch of Cotswold Grasses* (1919).

Doyle, Arthur Conan (1859–1930); famous as the creator of Sherlock Holmes, although he wrote about many other subjects, including spiritualism. Volunteered as a doctor in 1914, having served in that capacity in the Boer War, but was too old to be accepted. An Imperial idealist, and strongly opposed to Germany. Biog: Hesketh Pearson (1943). Bibl: R. L. Green and J. M. Gibson (1983). Wp: *The Guards Came Through* (1919).

Elton, Godfrey (1892–1973); educ: Rugby (where he heard Brooke lecture) and Oxford. Sec. Lieut., Hants Regt, 1914; Capt., 1918. India, Persian Gulf, Mesopotamia, 1915–16; wounded and captured at Kut; p.o.w., Turkey, 1916–18. Lecturer in Modern History, Oxford, 1919–39. Friendly with Sassoon after the war. Much public service for church and state; Labour candidate, 1924, 1929; 1st Baron Elton, 1934. Autob: *Among Others* (1938). Wp: *Schoolboys and Exiles* (1919), *Years of Peace* (1925).

Evans, William (1871–1939); educ: Lampeter. Ordained priest in the Church of England, 1901; various curacies, including St Mary's, Bryanston

Square, London, 1910–15; Vicar, St Peter's, De Beauvoir Square, in a poor district of the East End, 1915–30. Wp: *Killed in Action* (1916).

Ewer, William Norman (1885–1976); educ: Cambridge. Socialist journalist; foreign editor of the *Herald*, 1919. His satirical poem, 'Five Souls', became well known (its early date – *Nation*, 3 Oct. 1914 – is now often overlooked). Married to Monica Ewer, a romantic novelist. Wp: *Five Souls and Other War-Time Verses* (1917); *Satire and Sentiment* (1918), in which one poem shows that he knew and admired Brooke before the war.

Faber, Geoffrey (1889–1961); educ: Rugby and Oxford. London Regt, 1914–19; Capt., 1916; France and Belgium. Distinguished publisher; founder and first President of Faber and Faber Ltd; knighted, 1954. Despite the conventional style of his poetry, he encouraged many modern writers, including T. S. Eliot, whom he recruited as a Faber director. Wp: *Interflow* (1915), *In the Valley of Vision* (1918), *The Buried Stream* (1941).

Fairfax, James Griffyth (1886–1976); educ: Winchester and Oxford; barrister, 1912. Army, 1914–18; Capt., RASC, Mesopotamia. M.P. for Nantwich, 1924–9. Wp: *The Temple of Janus* (1917); *Mesopotamia* (1919).

Frankau, Gilbert (1884–1952); educ: Eton; worked in the family tobacco business, then travelled round the world in 1912–14. Sec. Lieut., East Surrey Regt, Oct. 1914; transferred to RFA, Mar. 1915; Loos, Ypres, Somme. Propaganda duty, Italy, 1916; Capt.; invalided out with shellshock, Feb. 1918. Served with RAF in Second World War. Novelist in prose and verse, many books; he was said to imitate in real life the dashing, manly heroes of his own fiction. Autob: *Self-Portrait* (1940). Wp: *Poetical Works* (2 vols, 1923).

Garrod, Heathcote William (1878–1960); scholar. Ministry of Munitions, 1915–18. Oxford Professor of Poetry, 1923–8. Many publications, especially on Romantic and Latin poets. Wp: *Worms and Epitaphs* (1919).

Gibson, Wilfrid Wilson (1878–1962); no formal education. Prolific, full-time poet; early poems on conventional subjects, but began writing about the lives of the poor, *c.* 1910; from this it was a short step to the subject of common soldiers, 1914–15. A mainstay in the Georgian group by 1914, friendly with Brooke, Thomas and others; tried to dissuade Brooke from enlisting and was much distressed by his death. Volunteered in 1915, rejected four times for poor eyesight, finally accepted by RASC, 1917; served as 'loader and packer', and probably later as a Medical Officer's Clerk, in Sydenham, 1917–19 (never abroad, despite frequent modern statements to the contrary). Biog: J. Wilson, 'Wilfrid Gibson and the War', *Four Decades*, I,2 (July 1976), pp. 130–40. Wp: *Battle* (1915), see [*10 n*]; *Neighbours* (1920) records his drudgery later in the war; *CP* (1926); etc.

Gilmore, Alfred J.; from Birmingham; apparently a civilian. Wp: *Patriotic Poems on the Great War 1914–15–16* (1916).

Golding, Louis (1895–1958); educ: Manchester G.S. and, after the war, Oxford. Unfit for active service, but worked in the Friends' Ambulance Unit in Salonica and France. Poems in numerous wartime periodicals, often fiercely critical of war and of right-wing civilian values. Many novels, essays, travel books. Biog: J. B. Simons, *Louis Golding: A Memoir* (Mitre Press, n.d.). Wp: *Sorrow of War* (1919), his first book.

Graves, Robert (born 1895); educ: Charterhouse and, after the war, Oxford. Enlisted in Royal Welch Fusiliers, Aug. 1914; Sec. Lieut., later Capt. Severe trench fighting, Apr. 1915–July 1916; a serious wound left him physically and mentally unfit for further active service; home duties until 1919. Autob: *Goodbye to All That* (1929) describes his war experiences, including his close friendship with his fellow Fusilier, Sassoon. Wp: he has not republished most of the war poems in *Over the Brazier* (1916), *Goliath and David* and *Fairies and Fusiliers* (1917), and *Country Sentiment* (1920). Ll: *In Broken Images*, ed. P. O'Prey (1982), includes wartime letters to Sassoon and others. Biog: Martin Seymour-Smith (1982). Bibl: F. H. Higginson (1966).

Grenfell, Hon. Julian (1888–1915); eldest son of the Earl of Desborough, a celebrated amateur athlete; educ: Eton and Oxford. Went through a period of rebellion and self-doubt before the war. Joined Royal Dragoons, 1910, and served in India and South Africa; to France, Oct. 1914; Capt., DSO; wounded, 12 May 1915, and died on the 26th, a month after Brooke. Became second only to Brooke as an idealised poet in the public imagination. Biog: N. Mosley (1976). Wp: no book, his few poems appeared in memoirs and anthologies.

Gurney, Ivor (1890–1937); educ: King's School, Gloucester, and Royal College of Music. Began to write verse, 1912–13. Volunteered, 1914; accepted as Pte, Gloucester Regt, Feb. 1915. Letters express warm admiration for the Georgians, especially Masefield and Gibson. Western Front, May 1916, with no home leave until he was mildly gassed, Sept. 1917; hospital at Bangour, near Edinburgh. Symptoms of mental disturbance were apparent before the war; during a period of illness and training from Nov. 1917 onwards, they became pronounced. Discharged from Army, Oct. 1918. Committed to an asylum with paranoid schizophrenia, 1922, having written much of his best poetry since 1918. Modern medical opinion considers that the war did not cause his madness, though it may have hastened it. Wp: *Severn and Somme* (1917) and *War's Embers* (1919) include conventional poems of comradeship and heroism, mostly omitted from *CP* (1982), ed. P. J. Kavanagh; but the 1982 volume has many newly published post-war poems of high quality. Ll: *War Letters* (1983), ed. R. K. R. Thornton. Biog: M. Hurd (1978).

Halliday, Wilfrid Joseph (1889–1975); educ: Leeds University, MA 1913. Pte, West Yorks Regt, 1914; Sec. Lieut., 1917; severely wounded. The tone of his *Refining Fires* (1917) is nationalist, and hostile alike to trades unions and big business. Published a patriotic anthology, *Pro Patria* (1915). After the war, rejoined the staff of Pudsey G.S.; headmaster, 1940–6. Distinguished for his devoted, scholarly work for the Yorkshire Dialect Society. Biog: note by Stanley Ellis, *Yorkshire Dialect Transactions*, XIII,74 (1974).

Hamilton, Helen; schoolteacher. Several books. Wp: *Napoo! A Book of War Bêtes-Noires* (1918).

Hardy, Thomas (1840–1928); poet and novelist. As author of *The Dynasts* (1903–8), Hardy was a war poet before 1914. Some of the younger generation, including Sassoon, regarded him as the greatest living English poet. *CP* (1976). Biog: R. Gittings (2 vols, 1975 and 1978). Bibl: R. L. Purdy (1954),

J. O. Bailey, *The Poetry of Thomas Hardy: A Handbook and Commentary* (1970).

Herbert, Alan Patrick (1890–1971); educ: Winchester and Oxford. Sub-Lieut., Royal Naval Division, Gallipoli and France; severely wounded, Apr. 1917, and invalided out. Much of his wartime verse in *Punch* was humorous, often satirical of the General Staff, but he also supplied the words for 'The Seamen's Boycott Song' (1918), a strongly anti-German broadsheet. Staff of *Punch* from 1924; Independent MP for Oxford University, 1935–50; famous as a wit and speaker. Many books and plays; knighted, 1945; CH, 1970. Autob: *A. P. H. His Life and Times* (1970). F: *The Secret Battle* (1919). Biog: Reginald Pound (1976). Wp: *Half-Hours at Helles* (1916), *The Bomber Gipsy* (1918).

Herschel-Clarke, May; *Behind the Firing Line and Other Verses of the War* (1917) seems to have been her only publication.

Heywood, Raymond; Lieut., Devonshire Regt; apparently served on the Western Front. Author of two very sentimental books of war verse, *Roses, Pearls and Tears* (1918) and *The Greater Love: Poems of Remembrance* (1919).

Hodgson, William Noel (1893–1916); son of a bishop; educ: Durham School and Oxford (First in Classics, 1913). Volunteered in Aug. 1914; Sec. Lieut., Devonshire Regt; MC, 1915; killed in the Somme advance, 1 July 1916. Wp: *Verse and Prose in Peace and War* (1916).

Hornung, Ernest William (1866–1921); educ: Uppingham; novelist, famous as the creator of Raffles, the gentlemanly cricketing criminal (hero of *The Amateur Cracksman*, 1899, and other books). Keen cricketer. Brother-in-law of Conan Doyle. Lost his only son in the war; despite ill-health, worked for a YMCA library in France and came under fire at Arras. Wp: *The Young Guard* (1919), etc.

Housman, Alfred Edward (1859–1936); Professor of Latin, Cambridge, 1911–36; a brilliant, meticulous scholar. His *A Shropshire Lad* (1896), a collection of brief lyrics marked by skilled simplicity of form and diction and by a pervasive melancholy, was perhaps the single strongest influence on the war poets. *CP* (1939). Biog: R. P. Graves (1979). Bibl: J. Carter and J. Sparrow (1952).

Kennedy, Geoffrey Anketell Studdert (1883–1929); educ: Leeds G.S. and Trinity College, Dublin; ordained as Anglican minister, 1908. Army chaplain, Dec. 1915; three spells in the trenches (Somme 1916, Messines Ridge 1917, final advance 1918), where he risked his life and shared the troops' hardships, but otherwise was posted behind the lines, where he preached powerful, unconventional sermons to large congregations. Known as 'Woodbine Willie' for his ready supply of cigarettes. MC, 1917. In 1916–17, began writing his painfully honest war verse, treating basic Christian issues in plain language and stating both the horror and the heroism of war. Biog: J. K. Mozley (ed.), *G. A. Studdert Kennedy, by his Friends* (1929), W. Purcell, *Woodbine Willie* (1962). Wp: *Rough Rhymes of a Padre* (1918), *The Unutterable Beauty* (1927), etc.

Kerr, R. Watson (b. 1895); educ: Edinburgh; schoolmaster, 1914–15. Sec. Lieut., Tank Corps, 1916–19; severely wounded in the last tank engagement of the war. Later wrote for the *Scotsman*, the *Liverpool Daily Post*, etc. Wp:

War Daubs (1919), in which several poems show a distinct Imagist influence.

Kipling, Rudyard (1865–1936); author of many celebrated poems and stories. His son was reported missing at Loos, Sept. 1915. Although some of his poems attack the way the war was being run (he made similar criticisms of the Boer War), he remained strongly anti-German and continued the support for ordinary Tommies which his pre-war work had often expressed. One of the instigators of the burial of the Unknown Warrior in Westminster Abbey, and responsible for the standard inscriptions used in war cemeteries. Ll: *O Beloved Kids*, ed. E. L. Gilbert (1983). Biog: C. Carrington (1955, revised 1978), A. Wilson (1977), Lord Birkenhead (1978). Bibl: J. McG. Stewart (1959). Wp: *The Years Between* (1919), *CP* (1940), etc.

Kitchin, Clifford Henry Benn (1895–1967); educ: Clifton and Oxford. Enlisted, Sept. 1915; Lieut., Warwickshires; France, 1916–18. Author of crime novels and other works; on the fringes of the Bloomsbury group. Wp: *Curtains* (1919), *Winged Victory* (1921).

Leftwich, Joseph (1892–1983); born at Zutphen of Polish–Jewish parents; came with them to London, aged six. Became one of the 'Whitechapel Boys' with Rosenberg and others, a group of very poor but intellectually very active young artists and thinkers; his 1911 diary (Imperial War Museum) is an important source for Rosenberg biography. A socialist and pacifist, Leftwich would have refused to serve as a soldier, but being a Dutch subject he was exempt. As writer, journalist and translator of Yiddish literature, he later earned high esteem in the Anglo-Jewish community. Biog: *Joseph Leftwich at Eighty-Five*, ed. S. J. Goldsmith (1978). Wp: *Along the Years* (1937), *Years Following After* (1959).

Lyon, Percy Hugh Beverley (born 1893); educ: Rugby and Oxford. Capt., Durham Light Infantry; MC, 1917; wounded and captured, May 1918. Taught at Cheltenham, 1921; Rector, Edinburgh Academy, 1926; headmaster, Rugby, 1931–48. Wp: *Songs of Youth and War* (1918), etc.

Lyon, Walter Scott Stuart (1886–1915); educ: Haileybury and Oxford; advocate, 1912. Joined Royal Scots before the war; Lieut., 1913; mobilised, 4 Aug. 1914; France and Belgium; killed near Ypres, 8 May 1915. Wp: *Easter at Ypres 1915* (1916).

Mackintosh, Ewart Alan (1893–1917); educ: St Paul's and Oxford (classical scholar, 1912). Commissioned in Seaforth Highlanders, Dec. 1914; France, July 1915; MC, May 1916; wounded and gassed, Aug. 1916. Trained cadets in Cambridge, where he became engaged; hoped to enter politics after the war; returned to trenches, Oct. 1917; killed, 21 Nov. Wp: *A Highland Regiment* (1917), *War, the Liberator* (1918).

Mann, Arthur James ('Hamish Mann') (1896–1917); educ: George Watson's Coll. Sec. Lieut., Black Watch, July 1915; Somme, Aug. 1916; killed at Arras, 9 Apr. 1917. Wp: *A Subaltern's Musings* (1918) includes a rhetorical poem to Brooke, and Mann's last poem, 'The Great Dead' (Apr. 1917), in which he still speaks in heroic terms ('how great, how good the sacrifice'), although recognising the suffering war causes.

Manning, Frederic (1887–1935); Australian by birth; a minor literary figure in England before the war. Pte, King's Shropshire Light Infantry, 1915; runner on the Somme; Sec. Lieut., Royal Irish Regt, May 1917, but poor health kept him out of active service and bedevilled his later life. Friendly with Ezra Pound, T. E. Lawrence and others. F: *The Middle Parts of Fortune* (1929), written in a sudden burst and described by Hemingway, T. E. Lawrence, E. M. Forster, Arnold Bennett and others as the finest novel about the war. Wp: *Eidola* (1917).

Masefield, John (1878–1967); his first book of verse came out in 1902; *The Everlasting Mercy* (1911) inaugurated the new Georgian style. Brooke visited him at Lollingdon just before the war. Wartime service with the Red Cross, first in France and then on a hospital ship at Gallipoli; lectured in USA, 1916 and 1918, and wrote several books about the battle fronts, in aid of the Allied cause. Many books of poetry, drama and fiction; Poet Laureate, 1930. Biog: C. Babington Smith (1978). Bibl: C. H. Simmons (1930). Wp: *CP* (1923), etc.

Mercer, Thomas William (1884–1947); began work in a grocer's shop at age of twelve. Socialist journalist and pacifist. Many war verses in the *Labour Leader*, organ of the radical Independent Labour Party. Later worked and wrote for the Co-operative Movement; Labour candidate for Moss Side (Manchester), 1922. Biog: note in *Dictionary of Labour Biography*. Wp: *Harvest* (1918).

Meynell, Wilfrid (1852–1948); journalist and critic; editor of the Roman Catholic *Weekly Register* and *Merry England*. Married to Alice Meynell, the poetess. Wp: *Rhymes With Reasons* (1918).

Monro, Harold (1879–1932); opened the Poetry Bookshop, London, in 1913, whence he published all five volumes of *Georgian Poetry*. Many of the Georgians, including Brooke, were visitors, as were Owen, Sitwell, Thomas, Rosenberg, Leftwich, Elton and many others. Monro was unfit for service abroad but was called up for anti-aircraft duties in June 1916, transferring to the War Office in 1917; Sec. Lieut., Royal Garrison Artillery. *CP* (1970). Biog: Joy Grant, *Harold Monro and the Poetry Bookshop* (1967).

Nesbit, Edith (1858–1924); novelist, poet, children's writer, best known for *The Treasure Seekers* (1899) and other stories of the Bastable children. A Fabian socialist. Wp: *Many Voices* (1922).

Newbolt, Henry (1862–1938); educ: Clifton, where he met Haig, and Oxford. His pre-war poetry celebrating the Imperialist ideal and traditional English values was famous and influential; only Kipling surpassed him in popularity. Poems such as 'Vitaï Lampada' and 'Clifton Chapel' provided language and imagery for many wartime imitators. Knighted, 1915; CH, 1922. Ll: *Later Life and Letters*, ed. M. Newbolt (1942) (contains an interesting paragraph on Sassoon, whom he admired, and Owen). Wp: *St George's Day* (1918), *Poems New and Old* (2nd edn, 1919). *Casebook*.

Nichols, Robert (1893–1944); educ: Winchester and Oxford, which he left after a year. Sec. Lieut., RFA, Oct. 1914; in trenches for a few weeks, Autumn 1915; invalided out with shellshock. Worked for Ministries of Labour and Information later in the war. Friendly with Sassoon, Graves and the Sitwells, 1917–18; Professor of English Literature, Tokyo, 1921–4. Wp: *Invocation* (1915); *Ardours and Endurances* (1917), greatly overpraised at the time; *Aurelia* (1920). *Casebook*.

Nicklin, John Arnold (1871–1917); educ: Shrewsbury and Cambridge

(First in Classics); teacher, then wrote for *Daily Chronicle* and *Tribune*. Apparently no military service. Several books (translations and verse). Wp: '*And They Went to the War*' (1914), and later poems in *Westminster Gazette*.

Norman, Alfred Bathurst; served in Royal Flying Corps. Wp: *Ditchling Beacon* (1918), with an introduction by E. V. Lucas.

Oman, Carola (1897–1978); daughter of Sir Charles Oman, the Oxford historian. Red Cross nurse on the Western Front, 1916–19; worked for the Red Cross again, 1938–58. Distinguished writer of historical novels and biographies; close friend of May W. Cannan. Wp: *The Menin Road* (1919).

Owen, Everard (1860–1949); Anglican clergyman and Classics master at Harrow; edited several classical and English texts, and wrote on religion and classical history. Wp: *Three Hills* (1916).

Owen, Wilfred (1893–1918); educ: Birkenhead Institute and Shrewsbury Technical School; worked briefly as pupil–teacher in Shrewsbury, then as a lay assistant in an Evangelical parish near Reading, 1911–13. Influenced by the Romantics, by 1912 he had formed his ambition to become a poet, losing his religious faith in the process. Language tutor in France, 1913–15. Joined Artists' Rifles, Oct. 1915, persuaded partly by recruiting propaganda and the Gallipoli losses; Sec. Lieut., Manchester Regt, 1916; trenches, Jan. 1917; shellshocked, May 1917. Sent to Craiglockhart War Hospital, Edinburgh, where he met Sassoon in Aug.; Sassoon's encouragement set him writing war poems in earnest; all his best work was done between Sept. 1917 and Oct. 1918, much of it in Yorkshire, where he was posted on light duties. Returned to active service, Sept. 1918; MC, Oct.; killed, 4 Nov. Ll: *Collected Letters*, ed. H. Owen and J. Bell (1967). Biog: Jon Stallworthy (1974). Bibl: W. White (1967). Cr: D. Welland, *Wilfred Owen: A Critical Study* (1960, 1978, S. Bäckman, *Tradition Transformed* (Lund, 1979), D. Hibberd, *Owen the Poet* (1986). Wp: *Poems*, ed. S. Sassoon (1920); *Poems*, ed. E. Blunden (1931); *CP*, ed. C. Day Lewis (1963); *War Poems and Others*, ed. D. Hibberd (1973); *Complete Poems and Fragments*, ed. J. Stallworthy (1983). *Casebook.*

Oxenham, John (1852–1941). Born William Arthur Dunkerley but changed his name to that of a character in Kingsley's *Westward Ho!*. Began as publisher (with J. K. Jerome), but soon found authorship more profitable; prolific writer of verse and fiction for the popular market, basing all his work on a simple non-sectarian Christianity which stressed the value of suffering. Claimed that his little volumes of verse sold over a million copies during the war. Biog: Erica Oxenham (1942).

Pinto, Vivian de Sola (1895–1963); Royal Welch Fusiliers, 1915–19; in 1918, second in command of a company captained by Sassoon, who portrayed him as 'Velmore' in *Sherston's Progress* and tried to persuade him to make his verse less 'pompous' ('and hope I shall have success, as with little Owen', letter to R. Meiklejohn, 7 July 1918). Prof. of English, Nottingham, 1938–61; many publications, particularly on 17th-century poetry. Autobiog: *The City that Shone* (1969). Wp: *Spindrift* (1918).

Pope, Jessie (1868–1941); innumerable poems in magazines, children's books, newspapers, etc.; also wrote light fiction. Her war poems appeared in the *Mail*, where she alternated with 'Touchstone' (see **Burton,** above) as the most regular contributor, and the *Express*. Owen's 'Dulce et Decorum Est'

[*127*] was originally addressed to her. Cr: W. G. Bebbington, 'Jessie Pope and Wilfred Owen', *Ariel*, III,4 (1972), pp. 82–93. Wp: *War Poems* (1915), *More War Poems* (1915), *Simple Rhymes for Stirring Times* (1916).

Postgate, Margaret (1893–1980); educ: Roedean and Cambridge; taught Classics at St Paul's Girls School, 1914–16. Asst. Sec., Labour Research Dept., 1916–25; became well-known as Dame Margaret Postgate Cole, wife of G. D. H. Cole, the Labour historian; served as Secretary and President of the Fabian Society. With her husband, wrote detective stories and many political works. Wp: *Poems* (1918).

Read, Herbert (1893–1968); educ: Leeds University, interrupted by the war. Sec. Lieut., Yorkshire Regt, Jan. 1915; Capt., DSO, MC, Western Front; in the March 1918 retreat. His first poems criticising the war, and the rhetoric which surrounded it, date from 1916; as a left-wing intellectual, he took a detached view earlier than most soldier–poets. Eminent art critic after the war, with many academic posts and honours; knighted, 1953. Autob/Dd: *The Contrary Experience* (1963). Wp: *Naked Warriors* (1919), *The End of a War* (1933), *CP* (1966). *Casebook.*

Rickword, Edgell (1898–1982); joined Artists' Rifles from school, 1916; Lieut., Royal Berkshire Regt; MC; lost an eye and was invalided out. A fine literary critic in the 1920s, on the Symbolists, Eliot, etc.; editor, *Calendar of Modern Letters*, 1925–7; 3 volumes of poems. But after 1930 he devoted himself to political journalism, editing the *Left Review* and *Our Time* and arguing for the humane version of Marxism to which he was always committed. Cr: A. Munton, ed., 'Edgell Rickword: a Celebration', *PN Review*, VI,1 supplement (1978). Wp: *Behind the Eyes* (1921). His war poems were all written after 1918 (information from the poet, 1979).

Rodd, Rennell (1858–1941); educ: Haileybury and Oxford. Friendly with Wilde and the Pre-Raphaelites in the 1880s but chose to become a diplomat. As Ambassador to Italy, 1908–19, played a key role in the events leading to Italy's joining the Allies in 1915; British delegate, League of Nations, 1921, 1923; MP, 1928–32; 1st Baron Rennell of Rodd, 1933. Admired before the war for his poems on English themes. Wp: *Trentaremi* (1923).

Rosenberg, Isaac (1890–1918); son of poor Lithuanian-Jewish parents in the East End (see note on **Leftwich**). Worked as engraver, attending night classes in art; art student, Slade School, 1911–13. Encouraged by Binyon, Edward Marsh, and others. Poor health sent him to S. Africa in 1914. 'I despise war and hate war, and hope that Kaiser William will have his bottom smacked.' Returned home in 1915 but, finding no work, enlisted in Oct. (despite 'the immorality of joining with no patriotic convictions') in a Bantam Battalion; eventually attached as Pte to King's Own Royal Lancasters; endured trench discomforts with courage, determined to expose himself to the experience in the hope that 'it will all refine itself into poetry later on' (1916); killed, 1 Apr. 1918. Biog: J. Cohen, J. Liddiard, J. M. Wilson (all 1975). Wp: *Poems* (1922), *Collected Works* (1937), *Collected Works*, ed. Ian Parsons (1979), includes poems, essays, letters, pictures. *Casebook.*

Sackville, Lady Margaret (1881–1963); daughter of Earl de la Warre; numerous volumes of verse, 1901–60. Active supporter of the Union of Democratic Control; met Sassoon and probably Owen in Edinburgh, 1917;

her consistent pacifism would have won their respect, but Sassoon thought her verse 'fairly rotten' (*Diaries 1915–1918*, p. 187). Wp: *The Pageant of War* (1916), *Poems* (1923).

Sandford, Egbert Thomas (1871–1958?); storekeeper at the victualling yard, Plymouth; transferred to Gosport, 1930. Contributed verse to many periodicals. Wp: *Brookdown* (1915), *Mad Moments* (1919), *Poems* (1927).

Sassoon, Siegfried (1886–1967); educ: Marlborough and Cambridge. Hunting, cricket, verse, 1906–14. Trooper, Sussex Yeomanry, 3 Aug. 1914; Sec. Lieut., later Capt., Royal Welch Fusiliers, May 1915; France, Nov. 1915–Aug. 1916, where he became friendly with Graves. 'In the Pink', the 'first of my "outspoken" war poems', written in Feb. 1916; MC, June 1916, Somme; sick leave in England. Began writing satires against the war, Aug. 1916, soon becoming well known in intellectual circles. France again, Feb. 1917; shoulder wound, April. During convalescence in England, discussed the war with Russell and publicly protested against it in June; sent to Craiglockhart Hospital, where he composed some of his bitterest war poems, showing them to his fellow-patient, Owen. Decided to return to active service; passed fit, Nov. 1917; sent to Ireland, Jan. 1918; Palestine, Feb.–May, then France for the third time. Sent home with head wound, July 1918; convalescence; left the army, Mar. 1919. For some years, socially active in London, friendly with many literary and musical people; literary editor of the *Herald*, involved in Labour politics, etc. But eventually retired to his country house, where he wrote poems and memoirs. Autob: *Siegfried's Journey, 1916–1920* (1945). Dd: *Diaries 1915–1918*, ed. R. Hart-Davis (1983). F: *Memoirs of a Fox-Hunting Man* (1928), *Memoirs of an Infantry Officer* (1930), *Sherston's Progress* (1936). Bibl: G. Keynes (1962). Wp: *The Old Huntsman and Other Poems* (May 1917), *Counter-Attack and Other Poems* (June 1918), *CP 1908–1956* (1961); *The War Poems*, ed. R. Hart-Davis (1983), includes previously unpublished poems. *Casebook*.

Scott Moncrieff, Charles Kenneth (1889–1930); educ: Winchester and Edinburgh (First in English, 1914). Sec. Lieut., KOSB, 6 Aug. 1914; Capt., 1915; MC, 1917. Reviewed Sassoon's war poems as 'a regrettable incident' in 1917; Sassoon describes him unfavourably in *Siegfried's Journey*. Serious leg wound from which he never fully recovered, 1917. Introduced to Owen by Graves, Jan. 1918, and became a close friend, discussing Owen's experiments with rhyme and his own assonantal translation of *The Song of Roland*. Later lived in Italy, where he translated Proust. Biog/Ll: J. M. Scott Moncrieff and L. W. Lunn (1931).

Seaman, Owen (1861–1936); educ: Shrewsbury and Cambridge. Staff of *Punch*, 1897; Editor, 1906–32; knighted, 1914. *Punch* took a strongly anti-liberal line during the war. Biog: J. Adlard (1977). Wp: many poems, light and serious, in *Punch*; collected in *War Time* (1915), *Made in England* (1916), *From the Home Front* (1918).

Shanks, Edward (1892–1953); educ: Merchant Taylors' and Cambridge. Sec. Lieut., South Lancashire Regt, 1914; invalided out before serving abroad, 1915; War Office, 1915–18. One of the leading later Georgians. F: *The Old Indispensables* (1919). Wp: *CP* (1926), etc.

Shaw-Stewart, Patrick (1888–1917); educ: Eton and Oxford, a contemporary of Grenfell; classical scholar. Managing Director, Baring's, at age 24. Sub-Lieut., later Lieut.-Cdr., Royal Naval Division, 1914, in same battalion as Brooke; commanded the firing party at Brooke's funeral. Read Herodotus at Gallipoli; his letters show his extensive knowledge of the area's ancient history; Salonica, 1916; killed in France, 30 Dec. 1917. Biog: Ronald Knox (1920).

Shillito, Edward (1872–1948); Free Church minister in Kent, Hampshire, London. Verse and prose on religious subjects, including many newspaper articles. Wp: *The Omega* (1916), *Jesus of the Scars* (1919).

Sitwell, Osbert (1892–1969); educ: Eton. Grenadier Guards, 1912; Capt., 1915; fought at Loos but blood-poisoning kept him out of further action. He wrote his satires against the war while friendly with Sassoon, 1917 and later. With his brother and sister, Sacheverell and Edith, in the forefront of the literary *avant garde* in a lifelong battle against the Philistines. Succeeded as 5th baronet, 1943; CH, 1958. Autob: 5 vols (1945–50). Bibl: R. Fifoot (1963). Biog: J. Pearson, *Façades* (1978). Wp: *Argonaut and Juggernaut* (1919), etc.

Sorley, Charles Hamilton (1895–1915); educ: Marlborough. Six months in Germany, early 1914. Enlisted in Aug. 1914 rather than taking up his Oxford scholarship; Sec. Lieut., Suffolk Regt; Capt., 1915; to trenches, May 1915; killed at Loos, 13 Oct. 1915. Ll: *Letters* (1919) records his life, literary interests and cool opinions on the war. Biog: T. B. Swann, *The Ungirt Runner* (1965). Wp: *Marlborough and Other Poems* (1916), *Poems and Selected Letters*, ed. H. Spear (1978). *Casebook.*

Squire, John Collings (1884–1958); educ: Blundell's and Cambridge; literary editor, *New Statesman*, 1913; acting editor, 1917–18. Unfit for active service; supported the war effort, with sympathy for the ordinary soldier, but denounced hypocrisy and cant. Editor, *London Mercury*, 1919–34; a Labour candidate in 1918; knighted, 1933. His literary tastes were conservative, and he is remembered for his attack on *The Waste Land*. Biog: P. Howarth (1963). Wp: *The Survival of the Fittest* (1916), *Poems: First Series* (1918), *Poems of Two Wars* (1940), etc.

Stewart, John Ebenezer (d. 1918); from a poor background, he graduated from Glasgow University and became a teacher. Pte, Highland Light Infantry, early in the war; MC, 1916. The records say variously that he became a Capt. or Major in, or attached to, a Staffordshire regt and was killed in Apr. 1918. Wp: *Grapes of Thorns* (1917).

Streets, John William (d. 1916); a Derbyshire miner before the war, he had sent poems to the *Poetry Review* before 1914 and continued to do so from the trenches. Sgt, York and Lancaster Regt; killed, 1 July 1916, the first day of the Somme. Wp: *The Undying Splendour* (1916), with a preface by Galloway Kyle.

Thomas, Edward (1878–1917); educ: St Paul's and Oxford; made his living before the war as reviewer and essayist, often writing about the English countryside; friendly with Gibson, Brooke and other Georgians. Artists' Rifles, 1915; Sec. Lieut., Royal Garrison Artillery, 1916; into trenches, late Jan. 1917; killed at Arras in April. Despite statements to the contrary in anthologies, Thomas wrote all his poems between Nov. 1914 and Jan. 1917; he wrote no poems from the front and is not a 'trench poet', but there was undoubtedly a connection (much discussed by critics) between the war and his sudden flowering as a poet. Ll: to Gordon Bottomley (1968), to Jesse Berridge (1983). Biog: J. Moore (1939), J. Marsh (1978). Cr: W. Cooke, *Edward Thomas: A critical biography* (1970), A. Motion, *The Poetry of Edward Thomas* (1980). Wp: *CP*, ed. R. G. Thomas (1978). *Casebook*.

Tomlinson, Albert Ernest (1892–1968); educ: Middlesborough H.S. and Cambridge (where he heard Brooke lecture). Sec. Lieut., South Staffs. Regt, June 1915; France, Mar.– July 1916 and Aug 1917–Jan. 1918; India until demobilisation, 1918–19. Started writing verse before the war; later wrote many articles and poems about the Suffolk countryside, etc. Wp: *Candour* (1922).

Vernède, Robert Ernest (1875–1917); educ: St Paul's and Oxford, then settled in the country to write novels. Joined the ranks in Sept. 1914 after several attempts; Sec. Lieut., Rifle Brigade, 1915; Somme, Jan.–Sept. 1916; wounded, but insisted on returning to the front in Dec.; killed, 9 Apr. 1917. Partly because of his literary connections, partly because he was a good example of a patriotic older recruit, he became well known as a war poet. He hated war's horrors but excluded such subjects from his verse, believing that Britain's cause was just; several poems in *The Times* in 1914 and later. Ll: *Letters to His Wife* (1917). Wp: *War Poems* (1917).

Vines, Walter Sherard (1890–1974); educ: Rugby and Oxford. Enlisted, 22 Aug. 1914; Lieut., Highland Light Infantry; Capt., Labour Corps; wounded 1915, invalided out 1917 or 1918. One of the early Modernist poets, friendly with the Sitwells; his poems suggest he held Marxist views. Prof. of English, Hull, 1928–52; literary criticism and editing. Wp: *The Two Worlds* (1916), *The Kaleidoscope* (1920), *The Pyramid* (1926).

Watson, William (1858–1935); a highly regarded Edwardian poet; like many other staunch Liberals, he opposed the Boer War but supported Britain's action in 1914. His 1914–18 verse was embarrassingly eulogistic of leading Government figures, especially Lloyd George; knighted, 1917. Cr: Solomon Eagle (J. C. Squire), *Books in General*, pp. 233–6. Biog: J. M. Wilson, *I was an English Poet* (1981). Wp: *The Man Who Saw* (1917), etc.

West, Arthur Graeme (1891–1917); educ: Blundell's and Oxford. Enlisted as Pte, Public Schools Battalion, Feb. 1915, believing the war was in a just cause, but came to hate Army life. Trenches, winter 1915–16; by Summer 1916, when most of his few war poems were written, he had lost his religious faith and learned pacifism from Bertrand Russell's *Justice in War Time* (Russell's *Autobiography* contains two letters from West, Sept. and Dec. 1916); unable to bring himself to desert or protest, went back to France as Sec. Lieut., later Capt., Oxford and Bucks Light Infantry; killed, 3 Apr. 1917. Cr: D. Welland, 'A. G. West: a Messenger to Job', in *Renaissance and Modern Essays*, ed. G. R. Hibbard (1966). Ll/Wp: *The Diary of a Dead Officer* (n.d., probably early 1919), edited anonymously by C. E. M. Joad, who was at that stage a pacifist.

Willis, George; apparently served in the infantry on the Western Front. Several poems published anonymously in the *Nation* soon after the Armistice. Author of *Philosophy of Speech* (1919). Wp: *Any Soldier to His Son* (1919), *A Ballad of Four Brothers* (1921).

Wilson, Theodore Percival Cameron (1889–1918); schoolmaster before the war; lived at Little Eaton, Derbyshire; wrote two sentimental novels and contributed verse to periodicals. Pte, Grenadier Guards, Aug. 1914; Sec. Lieut., Sherwood Foresters, later Staff Captain; killed 23 Mar. 1918. Wp: *Magpies in Picardy* (1919), published and introduced by his friend Harold Monro.

Yeats, William Butler (1865–1939); celebrated Irish poet, playwright and essayist. His refusal to include Owen and other war poets in his *Oxford Book of Modern Verse* (1936) caused controversy. Bibl: A. Wade (3rd edn, 1968). Wp: *Poems* (Variorum edn), 1957. *Casebook.*

Young, Francis Brett (1884–1954); educ: Epsom and Birmingham; novelist and doctor. Major, RAMC in England and Africa; invalided out with malaria. His most famous war poem at the time was a typically patriotic-pantheistic sonnet, 'The Gift' (*The Times,* 31 May 1916). Biog: J. Brett Young (1962). Wp: *Five Degrees South* (1917), *Poems 1916–1918* (1919).

Select Bibliography

For works on individual writers, see *Biographical Notes* above.

Bibliography

Catalogue of the War Poetry Collection (Birmingham Public Library, Reference Department, 1921): this collection has since been much enlarged.

Catherine Reilly, *English Poetry of the First World War: A Bibliography* (London: Prior, 1978).

Criticism

Bernard Bergonzi, *Heroes' Twilight: A Study of the Literature of the Great War* (London: Constable, 1965; 2nd edn, Macmillan, 1980).

Edmund Blunden, *War Poets, 1914–1918* (London: British Council, new edn, 1964).

Maurice Bowra, *Poetry and the First World War* (Oxford University Press, 1961): a lecture on some of the non-British poets of the war.

Paul Fussell, *The Great War and Modern Memory* (Oxford University Press, 1975).

Desmond Graham, *The Truth of War: Owen, Rosenberg and Blunden* (Manchester: Carcanet Press, 1984).

Dominic Hibberd (ed.), *Poetry of the First World War* (London: Macmillan, Casebook Series, 1981).

John H. Johnston, *English Poetry of the First World War: A Study in the Evolution of Lyric and Narrative Form* (Princeton University Press, 1964).

David Perkins, *A History of Modern Poetry* (Cambridge, Mass.: Harvard University Press, 1976), ch. XIII.

John Press, *A Map of Modern Verse* (Oxford University Press, 1969), ch. VIII.

Timothy Rogers (ed.), *Georgian Poetry 1911–1922: The Critical Heritage* (London: Routledge, 1977).

Robert H. Ross, *The Georgian Revolt: Rise and Fall of a Poetic Ideal 1910–1922* (London: Faber, 1967).

Andrew Rutherford, *The Literature of War: Five Studies in Heroic Virtue* (London: Macmillan, 1978), ch. III.

Jon Silkin, *Out of Battle: The Poetry of the Great War* (Oxford University Press, 1972).
C. K. Stead, *The New Poetic: Yeats to Eliot* (London: Hutchinson, 1964), ch. IV.

History

Correlli Barnett, 'A Military Historian's View of the Great War', *Essays by Divers Hands*, XXXVI (1970), pp. 1–18: on 'war books'.
Basil Liddell Hart, *History of the First World War* (London: Cassell, 1970).
A. J. P. Taylor, *English History 1914–1945* (Oxford: Clarendon Press, 1965).
John Terraine, *The Smoke and the Fire: Myths and Anti-Myths of War 1861–1945* (London: Sidgwick & Jackson, 1980).
—— Introduction to Graham H. Greenwell, *An Infant in Arms* (London: Allen Lane, 1972).
Alan Wilkinson, *The Church of England and the First World War* (London: SPCK, 1978).
D. G. Wright, 'The Great War, Propaganda and English "Men of Letters", 1914–16', *Literature and History*, VII (Spring 1978), pp. 70–100.

Miscellaneous

A. St John Adcock, *For Remembrance: Soldier Poets Who Have Fallen in the War* (London: Hodder, rev. edn, n.d. [1920]).
Betty Bennett, *British War Poetry in the Age of Romanticism: 1793–1815* (New York and London: Garland, 1976): an anthology.
Patrick Bridgwater, *The German Poets of the First World War* (London: Croom Helm, 1985).
John Ferguson (ed.), *War and the Creative Arts: An Anthology* (London: Macmillan/Open University, 1972).
Mark Girouard, *The Return to Camelot: Chivalry and the English Gentleman* (New Haven and London: Yale University Press, 1981), ch. XVIII.
Harries, Meirion and Susie, *War Artists* (London: Michael Joseph, 1983).
Laurence Housman (ed.), *War Letters of Fallen Englishmen* (London: Gollancz, 1930): includes letters by Grenfell, Rosenberg, Shaw-Stewart, Sorley, Vernède, West, Wilson.
Peter Jones (ed.), *Imagist Poetry* (Harmondsworth: Penguin Books, 1972): an anthology with an account of Imagism.
E. B. Osborn, *The New Elizabethans: A First Selection of the Lives of Young Men Who Have Fallen in the Great War* (London: Bodley Head, 1919): includes Grenfell, Hodgson, Sorley.
M. van Wyk Smith, *Drummer Hodge: The Poetry of the Anglo-Boer War (1899–1902)* (Oxford: Clarendon Press, 1978).

Notes on the Illustrations

Cover: Based on Paul Nash, *Sunset, Ruin of the Hospice, Wytschaete* (1917–18). Wytschaete, near Ypres, was captured in June 1917 and was behind the British line by the time Nash saw it in November. Human figures appear rarely in his work, even in his war pictures; as a landscape painter, friendly with Edward Thomas and several Georgians, he was appalled by the effects of war on nature. He fought at Ypres in 1917 but was seconded as a War Artist in October. Touring the Passchendaele battlefields in November gave him a new, burning determination to 'rob war of the last shred of glory'. His May 1918 exhibition, which included this picture, won him many admirers, among whom was Herbert Read.

The official War Artists scheme grew from small beginnings in the summer of 1916 into a surprisingly civilised arrangement under which dozens of artists were sent to the many theatres of war, usually for limited periods; they were free to paint how and what they wished in any style they chose, although gruesomeness was discouraged. The best of the works which resulted became national property and now form the basis of the collection in the Imperial War Museum.

Plates 1–14

1. These lines from Binyon's poem were frequently reproduced. They can still be seen on many war memorials and heard in church on Armistice Sunday.
2. R. L. Gales, 'To William II', one of many patriotic poems published as postcards. These cards were often intended to be sold in aid of war charities.
3. Poster by Bernard Partridge, chief political cartoonist of *Punch*. The slogan was used for several posters. Cp. [*166*], lines 11–12. The background shows German 'frightfulness': public opinion was outraged by attacks on merchant shipping, especially the sinking of the *Lusitania* in May 1915.
4. The nation was often represented as an ideal English landscape; cp. [*5*], [*30*]. Here, a Highlander is tactfully added.
5. Cartoon by Leonard Raven-Hill, *Punch*'s second political cartoonist. Later reproduced as a poster. Mr Punch contributes to the late 1914 campaign to recruit players and spectators: 'No doubt you can make money in this field, my friend, but there's only one field to-day where you can get honour.' A footnote adds that Cup matches were to continue 'just as if the country did not need the services of all its athletes for the serious business of war'. Cp. [*23*], [*27*].

230

6. A staged photograph. In his mind's eye, the soldier sees a crowded football stadium. With the slogan, cp. Rosenberg's 'Will they ever come?' [56].

7. The *Graphic*'s free copies of this picture were so popular that the magazine often advertised further copies for sale at a guinea each: 'For Rolls of Honour, memorials in churches or Mission Halls, there is nothing more suitable than a copy of this inspired picture' (August 1917).

8. Cartoon by S. Rowland Pierce. A comment by the leading Labour newspaper on the first week of the Somme. Christ's agony 'confronts the world'; cp. [69] – 'He is despised and rejected of men' (Isaiah 58:3).

9. The Modernist style here emphasises hard surfaces and angles, suggesting medieval figures in armour; it was not only traditional artists who endowed the troops with heroic qualities. Dobson worked as a War Artist in 1918.

10. This cartoon inspired and was reproduced with a poem of the same title in J. S. Arkwright, *The Supreme Sacrifice* (1919): 'Strike and strike hard! – the staggering monster yields – . . . All that men died for on a thousand fields / Is triumphing as last!' Picture and poem probably first appeared in 1918. An ageing, pagan Kaiser gives way before a still youthful Christian 'morning hero'; cp. [*162*]. Raemaekers, a citizen of neutral Holland, was one of the Allies' most valuable propagandists, producing hundreds of anti-German cartoons and earning honours from many countries.

11. One of a series of twelve 'Ideals' illustrated in a series of 66 lithographs by different artists on *Britain's Efforts and Ideals in the Great War*. Commissioned by the Department of Information in 1917, the series was shown in Britain, France and America in 1918 to raise morale at home and British prestige abroad. The ideal of 'war to end war', set out by H. G. Wells and others in 1914, remained influential. Nicholson's daughter, Nancy, married Robert Graves in 1918.

12. Exhibited at the Royal Academy in 1916. Clausen was a well-known establishment artist.

13. Nevinson's early war paintings, based on grim experiences with the French Red Cross, combined Futurism and Cubism, but after a month in France as a War Artist in 1917 he abandoned Modernist styles in favour of an uncompromising realism. His supporters were disappointed, but he did not yield in his new aim of giving civilians 'some insight as to the marvellous endurance of our troops and the real meaning of the hardships they are called upon to face'. (It is interesting to compare Nevinson's remarkable change of style with the fact that few poets made use of Modernism in their war work.) He was forbidden to exhibit *The Paths of Glory*, because by late 1917 War Artists were not supposed to paint corpses (public perceptions having changed since the days when corpses were regarded as evidence of heroic deeds or German brutality). However, he defied the ban in March 1918, after scornfully pasting a strip marked 'Censored' over the canvas.

14. Originally a group portait of politicians and generals in the 'Hall of Peace' at Versailles, assembling for the signing of the Peace Treaty in the

Hall of Mirrors beyond (June 1919). But Orpen, who was there as the official British artist, was so disgusted by the smugness of his subjects that eventually he painted them all out, substituting a soldier's coffin, cherubs, a distant cross, and two versions of his earlier portrait of a shellshock victim, *Blown Up: Mad*. In one of his poems, he wrote of the common soldier: 'No man did more / Before. / No love has been / By this world seen / Like his, since Christ / Ascended'. The painting caused a storm when it was exhibited at the Academy in 1923; despite being voted picture of the year, it was rejected by the Imperial War Museum. In 1928, Orpen gave way, obliterating soldiers and cherubs and presenting the picture to the Museum as a memorial to Haig. He had been one of the first War Artists in 1917 and had spent far longer in France than any of the others. He gave all his war work to the nation.

ACKNOWLEDGEMENTS

The authors and publishers wish to thank the following who have kindly given permission for the use of copyright material:

George Allen & Unwin (Publishers) Ltd., for 'War Graves' and 'The Survivor' by Godfrey Elton in *The Years of Peace* (1925). Edward Arnold (Publishers) Ltd., for 'My People' by Sir Rennell Rodd in *Trentaremi* (1923). Associated Book Publishers (UK) Ltd., for 'The Vision Splendid' by John Oxenham in the book of the same name, Methuen (1919). Theo van Beek for 'After the "Offensive" ' by Theo van Beek (senior) in *The English Review* (1919). Violet Babington Beevor for 'Cricket – 1915' and 'The Beau Ideal' by Jessica Pope in *More War Poems*, Grant Richards (1915). Paul Berry and Geoffrey Handley Taylor for 'Hospital Sanctuary' by Vera Brittain in *Poems of the War and After*, Gollancz (1934). Basil Blackwell Publisher Ltd. for 'Paris, November 11, 1918' by Mary Wedderburn Cannon in *The Splendid Days* (1918). The Bodley Head Ltd. for the extract from 'Denial' and 'Resolve' by R. Watson Kerr in *War Daubs* (1919); and for 'Moonrise over Battlefield', 'French Poets' and 'War and Peace' in *Collected Poems* by Edgell Rickword (1947). Edward Bradby and Anne Ridler for 'April 1918' by H. C. Bradby in *War Poems*, Arrowsmith (1918). Chatto and Windus and the authors' estates for 'The Secret' and 'Dawn on the Somme' by Robert Nichols in *Aurelia and Other Poems*; and '1914', 'Dulce et Decorum Est' and 'Spring Offensive' by Wilfred Owen in *Wilfred Owen: The Complete Poems and Fragments*', ed. Jon Stallworthy; and New Directions Publishing Corporation for '1914', 'Schoolmistress', 'Exposure', 'Futility', 'Dulce et Decorum Est', 'Greater Love', 'Apologia pro Poemate Meo', 'Insensibility', 'Strange Meeting', 'The Send-Off' and 'Spring Offensive' by Wilfred Owen in *Collected Poems of Wilfred Owen*, Chatto and Windus Ltd. (1963). Rosica Colin Ltd., and © Madame Catherine Guillaume for 'Reserve' in *The Egoist* (1919) and 'Machine Guns' and 'Concert' in *Images of War* by Richard Aldington, Allen and Unwin (1919). P. H. M. Dobell for 'Advent 1915' by Eva Dobell in *A Bunch of Cotswold Grasses* (1919). Faber and Faber Ltd. for 'Home Service' and 'Victory' in *The Buried Stream* by Sir Geoffrey Faber (1941). Winifred Halliday for 'Today' by Wilfred J. Halliday from *Refining Fires*, Erskine Macdonald (1917). Robert Harben for 'Joining Up' and 'In the Gallery Where the Fat Men Go' by Louis Golding in *Sorrows of War*, Methuen (1919). David Higham Associates Ltd, for 'Afterwards' by Margaret Postgate in *Poems*, Allen and Unwin (1918); 'Somme Film' by C. H. B. Kitchin in *Curtains*, Blackwell (1919); 'The Modern Abraham' and extract from 'Rhapsode' by Sir Osbert Sitwell in *Argonaut and Juggernaut*, Chatto and Windus (1919); extracts for 'A Man of Mine' and 'The Scene of War' in *Naked Warriors* (1919) by Sir Herbert Read, Faber; and 'Song of the Dark Ages' by Francis Brett Young in Five Degrees South, Martin Secker (1917). Hodder and Stoughton Ltd. for 'Ambulance Train in the Menin Road' by Carola Oman in *The Menin Road and Other Poems* (1919). John Jones for 'Epitaph: Neuve Chapelle' by H. W. Garrod in *Worms and Epitaphs*, Blackwell (1919). Mrs Joseph Leftwich for 'War' by Joseph Leftwich in *Along the Years*, Auscombe & Co. (1937). P. H. B. Lyon for 'Comrade in Arms' in *Songs of Youth and War*, Erskine Macdonald (1918). John Murray (Publishers) Ltd., for 'Envoi' by Sir Edward de Stein in *The Poets in Picardy* (1919); an extract from 'Medway' by James G. Fairfax in *Mesopotamia* (1919);

'Grotesque' and 'Dutolpkeloc' in *Eidola* (1917); 'The Face' and 'Relieved' by Frederick Mauring, 'Duty' by Sir William Watson in *Poems of the Great War* (1917). Peter Newbolt for 'The War Films' by Sir Henry Newbolt in *Selected Poems of Henry Newbolt*, Hodder and Stoughton (1981). Oxford University Press and © Robin Haines for 'Riez Bailleul', 'The Silent One', 'To the Prussians of England', 'Mist on Meadows', 'First Time In' and 'War Books' in *Collected Poems of Ivor Gurney*, ed. P. J. Kavanagh (1982); Robin Haines for 'To England – a note' in *Severn and Somme*; and 'The Target' in *War's Embers*, Sidgwick and Jackson (1919). A. D. Peters & Co. Ltd., for 'Premature Rejoicing' in *Poems 1930*, Cobden Sanderson (1930), 'Vlamertinghe' in *Undertones of War*, Cobden Sanderson (1928), 'Pill-Box' in *Masks of Time*, Beaumont Press (1925), 'Come on, my lucky lads' in *Undertones of War*, 'At Senlis Once' and 'Gouzeaucourt: the Deceitful Calm' in *Poems*, Cobden-Sanderson (1930) by Edward Blunden. V. de Sola Pinto for 'Ginger' in *Spindthrift*, Chapman & Hall by V. de Sola Pinto senior. George Sassoon and Viking Penguin for 'Absolution' in *Westminster Gazette* (1916); 'At Carnoy' and 'The Redeemer' in *Old Huntsmen and Other Poems*, Heinemann (1917); 'The March Past', 'Christ and the Soldier', 'The Poet as Hero' and 'Reward' in *Collected Poems*, Faber (1961); 'Banishment', Does it Matter?', 'Fight to Finish' and 'Remorse' in *Counter Attack and Other Poems*, Heinemann (1918); 'Everyone Sang' and 'Memorial Tablet' in *Picture Show*, Cambridge University Press (1919) and 'Testament' by Siegfried Sassoon. Miriam E. Shillito for 'Hardness of Heart' by Edward Shillito in *The Omega and Other Poems*, Blackwell (1916). Sidgwick and Jackson Ltd. for 'Three Hills' by Rev. Everard Owen in *Three Hills and Other Poems* (1916). The Society of Authors and the estate of John Masefield for 'August 1914' by John Masefield in *Philip the King*, Heinemann (1914) and Mrs Nicolete Gray for 'The Anvil' by Laurence Binyon in the book of the same name, Elkin Mathews (1916); and Holt, Rinehart and Winston, Publishers for 'Epitaph on an Army of Mercenaries' by A. E. Housman in *Last Poems*, Grant Ricards (1922). Raglan Squire for 'The Trinity', 'To 'W. in the Trenches', 'The Higher Life for Clergymen' and 'The Dilemma' by Sir John Squire. Mrs Tomlinson for 'Sad Miles' by A. E. Tomlinson in *Candour*, Elkin Mathews (1922). A. P. Watt, Ltd. and Robert Graves for 'The Legion', 'Dead Cow Farm', 'Not Dead', 'Goliath and David', 'A Dead Boche' and 'Two Fusiliers' in *Fairies and Fusiliers*, Heinemann (1917); 'Haunted' in *Country Sentiment*, Martin Secker (1920) by Robert Graves; Michael Yeats and Macmillan Publishing Co. Inc. for 'On Being Asked for a War Poem' by W. B. Yeats in *Wild Swans at Coole* (1917); Lady Herbert for 'Beaucourt Revisited' by A. P. Herbert in *The Bomber Gypsy*, Methuen (1919); D. E. Collins for 'Elegy in a Country Courtyard' by G. K. Chesterton in *The Ballad of St Barbara*, Palmer (1922) and the National Trust and Doubleday & Co. Inc. for 'Gethsemane', 'My Boy Jack', 'Justice', 'Equality of Sacrifice', 'An Only Son' and 'Common Form' by Rudyard Kipling.

Index of Names

The Biographical Note on each contributing poet is indicated by a page reference in **bold** type. His or her poems are listed in the order in which they appear, each preceded by its italicised *serial number* and followed by the page references to the poem and its corresponding Note.

Index of Titles and First Lines